The Magickal Record of NEMA

An Initiatory Journal for Admittance to The Typhonian Order

BLACK MOON PUBLISHING
CINCINNATI, OHIO USA

Copyright © 2015-2019 Black Moon Publishing, LLC

Kenneth Grant Letter and excerpts © 2015 S.V. Grant
Printed with permission.

BlackMoonPublishing.com

Design and layout by
Jo Bounds of Black Moon Publishing

ISBN: 978-1-890399-67-2

United States • United Kingdom • Europe • Australia • India

Dedicated to the memory of Kenneth Grant

Notes on Publication of This Manuscript

This Magickal Record was received by us as xerographic copies of the original manuscript which had been typewritten with a number of hand written marginal notes. The pages were scanned as images and converted to editable text using OCR (optical character recognition). This process can introduce errors. At this point, the manuscript was proofed by comparing the scanned text word for word with the copied pages to rectify any discrepancies.

Large portions of this record chronicle communication with the Children of Maat, a consciousness outside the parameters of basic human understanding. Many times such communications include nontraditional spellings and orders of words. It is our experience that in such communications what are conventionally viewed as mistakes or inaccuracies are, in many instances, complex pathways to a deeper layer of understanding.

On these occasions, we leave it to the reader to discount or discover if any of these "mistakes" are errors or, upon closer inspection, ripen into a deeper level of complex, nuanced communication.

The names of individuals have, with a few exceptions based on context and written permission, been rendered with first name and last name initial out of respect for privacy.

The use of "Brothers, Mankind, Man, etc." to refer to all people does not reflect our thinking forty plus years after this Magickal Record was penned. We leave these designations in respect for its historical nature.

"His or her" and "s/he" are presently widely acceptable. It is our hope that in forty years the use of "his or her" will be as archaic as the use of "his" to designate all people now is. Physical sex and sexuality exists as a continuum. To view sex and sexuality within the confines of two sexes is as reductionist as designating all of us as "Man."

CONTENTS

Introductions
  Michael Ingalls.. 7
  Louis Martinié... 10
  Denny Sargent.. 15

A Letter fom Kenneth Grant 21

The Magickal Record of Nema................................ 25

Afterword by Michael Ingalls................................ 297

Liber Pennae Praenumbra 299

Index... 309

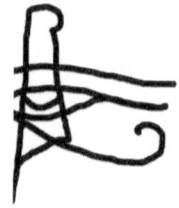

Introductions

Michael Ingalls

For more than 30 years, it has been my honor and privilege to be the husband, and, more importantly, the Charioteer, of Nema. Please note that Charioteer is not simply a function, like that of driver. It is a magickal station, closer to the role of Krishna for Arjuna in the Bhagavad-Gita. (This does not mean I claim the lofty status of a demigod like Krishna!) Indeed, I have been her driver, but also a friend, confidant, magickal partner and sounding board. I think it is safe to say I am closer to her than anyone else, save perhaps one other.

The other is Kenneth Grant, occultist, author, friend of Aleister Crowley, and English gentleman. This book is an initial result of the correspondence between the two of them, from 1975 to 2008.

I did no writing of this magickal record, but its publication was, in a way, my fault. Originally, I had suggested to Nema that her correspondence with Kenneth Grant, of which we had the last part, would be a good book collection. We contacted Michael Staley, of Starfire Publications, England, in 2012 to discuss this. He was interested, though knee deep in his current projects.

An interesting fact emerged while re-typing the letters: In the correspondence Grant hinted that there were topics and matters that could not be fully discussed with someone who was not an initiate of the Order. But, if she were to join...

Of course she did. The first task, as a Probationer, was to keep a magickal record of a practice of her choice. The book you hold in your hand is the result of that first nine months work.

When we talked to Michael he mentioned that he had the missing letters, but he also had a treasure: Nema's probationary magickal record for entry into the Typhonian Order. Would we like it back? You betcha.

After being assured that we could do anything we wanted with it, I contacted Lu at Black Moon. The result is the volume you hold in your hand. Hopefully you will find it as interesting as I did.

Nema and I received the typeset manuscript of this book on a Friday in July, the Friday of a festival called Starwood. It was our 30th wedding anniversary, which we always celebrate on the Friday night of Starwood, where it was performed. The year before our wedding we announced our betrothal at Starwood as well. This year, due to illness, we could not attend. Instead, I picked up Lu Martinié from the festival site and brought him to our house, about an hour away. We drank ginger wine, talked, and played music together to celebrate both our anniversary and the forthcoming publication of this book. It was truly an auspicious start.

My regret is that the letters are not ready for publication. My hope is that, when they are published, you will be able to read this and them simultaneously, as there are things explained in one that may not be explained in the other. An example of this is Omne, mentioned in the diary, but really explained in the letters. Omne is a gestalt (group) mind, primarily composed of Nema and G. S., but with contributions from others. I believe it was, and still is, at the center of the Cincinnati magickal vortex.

There are a few things to keep in mind:

First, Nema is a poet. What she writes is evocative, summoning up images that dance around the truth while allowing the reader to not be misled by a "too real" description. If that sentence is not understandable, see the book for details.

She can be in the middle of describing the depths of her problems, when there suddenly appears an invocation of such subtlety and

depth that it rivals anything by Crowley. I imagine this is how the psalms were written. "Saul is after me. I'm hiding in a cave. Oh Lord, how great Thou art."

Second, if Kenneth Grant was the direct inspiration for Nema, her other inspiration was G. S., the man who introduced her to Magick. It was a difficult relationship, as you can read here, but productive. It turned Maggie Cook into Nema.

Third, Nema is a human being, with all the life complications that humans are heir to. During the period of 1974 to 1975 she was getting a divorce, buying a farm, working a job to care for her four wonderful children and joining the Order, as well as exploring the Maat Current. (And I thought I was busy!) How she did it all I will never know.

What I do know is that when I met her in 1983 I was quickly smitten, and what has followed has been the ride of anybody's lifetime. And, if you like this book you will love the forthcoming collection of letters to and from Kenneth Grant to be published in the near future.

Louis Martinié

Setting the Stage for the Mask

"Women cannot become magicians."

That is the gist of what Gary S. communicated to Maggie (Nema) in pointing out passages in Liber Aleph on the position of women in magick. This was years before this Magickal Record (MR) and he knew she would rise to the challenge.

Quite a dare, quite an incitement to become a magician. Tara, when she was told that one could not become a Buddha in female form, vowed to become a Buddha with a female body and succeeded. As is evident in this Magickal Record, Maggie succeeded in becoming a powerful magickian.

"Speak Memory" is the wonderfully concise conjure voiced by the parent of the cultural icon Lolita. I can do no better than this elegantly simple statement. Maggie and I have known, valued, and inspired each other through the entirety of our magickal careers. The "masks" I was wearing at the time of the record are; Iu, Frater Lugis Thor, and S.M.Ch.H. 353. I call upon my memory to speak in fullness through these three selves in order to provide the reader with a fuller sense of the time and the people who populate this record.

Linearity is of some use in understanding the web of cause/effect which is laid down strand upon strand during the magician's life. I was fortunate enough to be present before, during, and after the period of Maggie's nine month magical working and too recognize the importance of the entities she was able to contact.

Four to five magicians kept rooms in a great old house in Cincinnati, Ohio during this period. The décor was Victorian and

the ambiance was magickal. Gary S. had rooms on the topmost floor. The basement being taken up by a very large Temple complete with heavy velvet curtains from a defunct theater. Ceremonial ritual was central to all of our lives and the oath of the Master of the Temple was taken by many to some effect. The practicalities of Malkuth were adequately addressed by the majority of us working extremely flexible hours for an intellectual, old-line Marxist preparing and selling erotic literature in working class neighborhoods.

The common room of the house was often filled with those experienced in and those new to the magickal arts. Less than friendly meetings with a large area coven often included an arsenal of both physical and metaphysical weapons. Practice and the exploration of unexplored areas of mind and magick were the order of the day. Numerous experiments in both invocation and evocation were followed by discussions driven by coffee and far stranger drugs. Though common, our emphasis was not on the talk; our collective passion centered on doing and enjoying or suffering the consequences of our experiments.

Maggie was new and often came to visit Gary S. Her extensive background in Christian mysticism, intelligence, and openness/commitment to all forms of mystical exploration were compelling. We shared a grounding in the creative impulse that so characterized the "beat" culture of our early years with its coffeehouses, poetry, and art. Her dress and style were always a bit conservative belying an inner intensity. She seemed to have settled into a middle class existence by default and was looking for wider horizons.

Maggie was exploding with enthusiasm and the fireworks accompanying her magickal development are well chronicled in her MR. We were all in a constant communication about subjects magickal and it was here that Gary S. told me he knew Maggie would definitely be induced to prove him wrong when he pointed to the passages in Liber Aleph "proving" she could not, as a woman,

become a magician.

It was during this period that discussions began concerning issuing a journal that would focus on western magicks, in particular those of a formal, ceremonial nature. Soon we were working on the first issue of the Cincinnati Journal of Ceremonial Magic. The idea was to present Western magic as an ongoing living system, not as a reverberation or repetition of what has gone before. Maggie's work was a fine fit for our intentions. Here was a practitioner, a woman receiving and acting upon communications from intelligences more subtle, intelligences with a wider view than presently available. Her work was a cornerstone for our Journal.

All the elements for publication came into place perfectly. If all of the elements would not have been present, if one part was fallen away, Maggie and her work might have been less available and the unkind critique of some of those around her as chronicled in her MR could have proved true. Things did come into place perfectly, if one part of the puzzle would have fallen away the history and the stories we tell ourselves about that time would be radically different. I am quite sure I would not be here writing about Maggie. The dissolution of Aleph Cabal and the growth of Bate (a verb describing the action of a hawk beating its wings in an attempt to escape from a perch.) Cabal is contained in Maggie's MR. Jo Bounds was the only person to be denied admission to Aleph Cabal and a prime reason for the formation of Bate Cabal. We met Jo at exactly the time we wanted to put out the first Journal and his aesthetics and expertise in layup and printing were the rock upon which the Journal was built. Without Jo, L.P.P. would probably have not seen publication in the 1970s.

On a personal level, more than anything else, I am inspired by Maggie's optimism. Her optimism shines like a Grail for the rest of us. Its brightness beckons us to think and act likewise. I believe we would all be the better for it.

The MR: A Dancing of the Mask

In a precise homage to Chronos, the MR winds its way through the days of the nine months. Without chapter headings and subheadings the reader could be left with a moist thumb and scattered rememberings of the records incidents and teachings.
Because of this, an extensive Index including both words and subjects is provided to simplify the readers finding/returning too desired topics.

Maggie's chosen practice in keeping this record is to "maintain an open channel with the Children of Maat, so they may speak through me. This to my own instruction and for the evolution of the Race... ." The MR chronicles this instruction, guidance, and much more. Carl R. Rogers observed, "What is most personal is the most universal." Maggie's attainment and her humanity shines through this record.

The MR flows between the emotional heights evident in the praise of Aoisic Aiwass to the angst that washes over, "I am so tired...I wish I could die now." in a dark night of the soul. The full range of both human and magical experience are richly expressed. The trials and triumphs that swim in the oceans of experience common to us all surface in Maggie's words. Meticulous self-examination and self-appraisal are a significant part of the record demonstrating a profound level of introspection in which the Tao is frequently invoked.

Magick and mysticism vie for the reader's attention in a dance so complex it is hard to tell who leads and who follows. A critical point occurs when a letter from Mr. Grant informs Maggie there is nothing behind the masks she writes of wearing. This leads to mystical growth. Actions without doer, thoughts without a thinker... experientially the self wearing these masks melts into a vast

spaciousness only to rebuild itself time and time again from the debris deposited by the turmoil of daily life.

The Mass of Maat is described in precise detail as a sexual working in which the female is elevated to a point usually reserved for the male in the magicks of the MR's time. The Dance of the Masks is copiously annotated step by step. Do what thou wilt shall be the whole of the Law is extensively examined in a word by word analysis.

Through all, magick is afoot. Masses are performed, spirits make themselves known, and the Children of Maat speak with the gravitas of a far reaching view, as one upon a mountain seeing the circuitous roads and byways followed by valley dwellers. The difficulties and second thoughts concerning the purchase of the farm that would develop into the Maat Pan Grove Abbey is chronicled.

I have never known Maggie to be one to argue from authority. The teachings in this record stand on their own merit. The aeon of Horus rides to fruition on the wings of Maat. Nema's voice sounded early in time and has never stopped being heard. This publication is a testament to that.

Denny Sargent

The Astounding Effect of Nema's Magick on the Occult Revival

The occult scene in the mid-1970s in New York City was wild, vibrant, multi-faceted and exploding like an iridescent flower growing in the epic wild wasteland of that time and place. Thanks to Herman Slater and Ed Buczynski and the Warlock shop (eventually moved to Manhattan and called the Magickal Childe) us teenage pagans and witches were like occult kids in an esoteric candy shop and had access to everything from the Gardnerian Book of Shadows to Simon's Necronomicon and everything in between. It was into this vast cauldron of erupting occult revival that Nema's work emerged, and the probationary record you have before you was the spark.

At 14 I was initiated into Pagan Way then Wicca, and so I entered an amazing occult Disneyland. Looking back, there were few volcanoes of exploding occult knowledge in the world like NYC and one had to merely hang out there to meet most famous people in the occult at the time. Us teen Witches who hung out with the big occult dogs at the Magickal Childe were soon initiated into a special coven of Welsh Traditionalist Wicca called the Children of Branwen. But we did not stop at Wicca...Oh my no.

After a time, a core group of us discovered Magick, Thelema and everything from Tantra and the Enochian Calls to Native American rituals. We were exploding like the scene, opening to all magicks we could find, keeping the clan ideals of the coven for our circle but opening up to the 93 current, Cabala, Tarot, I Ching, Golden Dawn and everything else we could find and experiment with. Which was, at this time, everything so it seemed.

We formed the 'Grove of the Star & Snake' and what we did in our

magickal laboratory circles would be called 'Chaos Magick' 20 years later, but who knew? We were just focused and devoted to magickal attainment and crazy and young enough to try EVERYTHING magickal, and, um, otherwise.

Our group's motto (really) was 'If it works, use it, if it doesn't, F*@k it.' We added the second motto 'sink or swim' soon after. The world was our magickal oyster and we slowly and thoroughly became proficient, in our own way, in the basics of the Western Magickal Tradition, trance states, visionary work, divination, spellcraft and rituals that became increasingly centered on the Thelemic Gnosis. In our spare time we created a Pagan-Magick publication called Mandragore. We were on fire.

By the mid-70s all of us were probationing for Kenneth Grant's Typhonian OTO, seeing the currents he embodied and his books as the cutting edge of magickal practice, which is where we lived. We creatively worked with his publications (the Typhonian Trilogy especially) and explored the Qlipoth when Nightside of Eden came out and always scryed our own rituals, invocations and spells with increasing complexity and artfulness and, I have to say, power and effect. At this point we were all in our early 20s. Nema was, of course, way ahead of us.

One day, when visiting the Magickal Childe we discovered the first issue of the Cincinnati Journal of Ceremonial Magick and we all went Whaaaaaa...?! The name alone was a bit of a mind-blower but once we delved in, we found something that really rocked our boat of RA- these wild Bate Cabal folk were fellow travelers! Unorthodox, open minded, Thelemic but not doctrinaire, into things like Voudou we hadn't experienced and then and a whole lot of CREATIVE occult! Fantastic. Then there was this very very unusual text about MAAT that was buried in the journal, a document that seemed to be the transmitted words of the Goddess Maat. An avatar of the next Aeon, something like Frater Achad. The CJCM articles came

right out of her probationary work, as you can see from this book.

When we first read it, again, we all went Whaaaa???!! (sound of minds being blown).

We took it back to our circle and, after doing a short Thelemic ritual set-up, we read this Liber Praenumbra out loud. Our heads exploded. The Goddess Maat made her presence felt and we were left amazed and full of poetry. I believe one of us likened experience to 'putting your finder into a light socket by mistake.' Here was real power, and we grabbed onto it immediately.

We immediately contacted this amazing and potentially terrifying Priestess (by mail, hard to believe now) and received a lovely, gracious, sweet letter from Soror Andahadna (soon to be known as Nema) who, with really lovely script, proceeded to tell us how to do the simple IPSOS chanting ritual with a candle flame. We soon gathered and did this within a Thelemic ritual circle and it was powerful and explosive and we all felt that it literally mutated us. We began to get so many visionary scribes and creative artistic results that we published them in our now larger occult magazine Mandagore and, of course, we also began a long and intensive correspondence with Soror Nema and she, with awesome penmanship, explained the whole system coming through her via N'Aton and Maat in terms of Maat Sepheroth work, path working, scrying rituals and on and on. Much of this correspondence coalesced later on into Maat Magick (republished by Black Moon Publishing under the title; Wings of Rapture) which is, still, seminal reading for every thinking occultist today.

How lucky were we to have this conduit of gnosis writing us pages of handwritten lessons and information and love? We appreciated it in retrospect, but at the time we were in a fiery frenzy of what became our new fixation: Ritually bringing together the core magickal reality of uniting the energies of the new aeon (93) with that of the balancing-focusing energies of the 'future' aeon of

Maat that we were earthing NOW into a double vortex of red-black flames that we all started referring to as the 'double current.'

As our interface with Nema progressed, like two poles of a magnet, our group and her vortex were drawn to each other. We the crazy Horus-headed young adepts, foolish and fearless and all-devouring and Nema and her Maatian Vortex, the black flame of balance, Maatian Gnosis and powerful trans-time magicks. In 1979 we came together in a serious explosion of the Double Current when we road tripped to visit Nema's farm in Ohio (see "farm" in index. - Ed.) and began a many-day ritual dance, it was a whirlwind week of magick, meshing and mahem and together we then reached beyond and earthed/formed the Horus Maat Lodge amidst amazing omens and inner-plane empowerment. Nema drew down 11 hawks from the sky! The clouds parted for us and the Commity of Stars manifested! So much more...The gods danced with us and N'Aton blessed our work and none of us were ever the same again. A more in-depth description of this and so much more can be found on the HML website; horusmaatlodge.com.

Since that time the HML has been a functioning cyber-order with members and nodes across the planet, with people working on Nema's vision of the Elevenstar Rite (see Maat Magick) working towards the manifestation of N'Aton and the evolutionary furthering of the human species. There are over 1000 members from all over the world communicating with each other on the HML Facebook group page as well as through our elist. We morphed into a cyber lodge as the internet arrived to fill in the nervous system of our Great Work. And the work continues.

And all of this divine madness was sparked by Soror Nema and the work you are reading about in this, her probationary record. This was the germinating seed, the awakening of a true Adept, the speaking of a Word by a Magus. All her future works, her books and lectures, all began here. She Uttered Her Word in this record

and the word was IPSOS and the aeon to come suddenly was/is NOW, as is all space-time, and the keys to this are now in our hands thanks to this lovely, gracious, hard-working, kind, very funny and artistically talented Lady, the Priestess of Maat, Nema.

Many other powerful events unfolded from this blooming Work, like the Thelemic/Maatian tribal gatherings called the Warrior Lord Working 1 and 2, gatherings of mutants, magi, adepts and sorcerers of all kinds and types. Both of these gatherings were held at Nema's farm and those in attendance were a big part of the new wave of magick sweeping over the country and planet at the time. The HML grew, the Typhonian OTO integrated much of this double-current gnosis and there was great brotherhood/sisterhood and mutation, again all at the instigation and encouragement of our cosmic Maatian Den-Mother, Nema. And we got to help.

When histories of the Occult Revival of the 1970s are written, as they being written now it seems, it is crucial that Maat Magick and Nema be central to the narrative. She was, if nothing else, a spark of black Maat flame that centered the crazed energies of Thelema and the new aeon and helped us all see the tightrope thread of balance that can lead us through the upheavals now and to come to the evolutionary Goal of humanity becoming what she calls Homo Veritas, the evolved fully aware united Humanity that we know and feel is possible.

With the help of Nema's work, much of this is coming into being and it is a great joy and down pouring of gnosis to write this simple postscript for the writings that began the whole carnival, to be part of the beginnings of this magickal manifestation from this humble, loving woman who was chosen as an avatar and priestess to bring 'fresh fever from the skies.' The Work continues, and Nema, of course, has gone on on from this simple record to craft astounding books and workshops and she was help in every aspect of the development of the HML and she is still doing so.

 And so here we are. Nema, quietly continuing the Great Work she began so long ago with a simple probationer's record and the many thousands of seekers and adepts who are still being influenced by her magick every day. What a joy it is to honor her now! Guru OM! You, O reader, take what the Star of a Priestess offers and take it further! Onward! N'Aton or bust, as we used to shout!

As Nema always says, 'Success to your work!'

Abrahadabra/Ipsos/OM

Aion 131

Ms. Margaret Cook
1602 Dorothy Lane,
Cincinnati, Ohio,
45202, U.S.A.

4 July 1975 e.v.

Dear Ms. Cook,

Do what thou wilt shall be the whole of the Law.

Thank you so much for your letter of the Summer Solstice and the qabalistic analysis of IPSOS.

You took my remarks a little too much to heart, and it is my turn to apologize. I know you had no such intention. My regret at being unable to comply with your request re. August 7 over-charged my response— hence the false impression it conveyed to you. Although incorrigibly devious, I am always frank (or try to be), and it is because I have a very strong urge to penetrate the 'PP complex' in detail that I want time not only to study your written accounts, but – which is of equal importance to me – to allow the thoughts and concepts you are bringing through to penetrate my system so that a genuine fertilization can occur. This, in contrast to a merely surface grasp of the structures you are presenting.

Please therefore be patient while I try and explain the peculiar situation that has arisen because of the way in which you have approached the matter of O.T.O. membership. Please also understand that I am familiar with most of the arguments 'for' and 'against' membership. I fully understand your feelings of non-necessity where official O.T.O. membership is concerned. You feel, no doubt, that it is superfluous because you have been assured – by 'Those whose will it is to attend to such matters' – of continued guidance, irrespective of membership or not. But there is one important factor you have overlooked, which is that I am not included in this comprehensive assurance! You see, dear Sister (for I believe I can truly call you such), certain obligations require that I work, in a magickal sense, only with incarnate entities, or 'masks', that have ratified their acceptance of the Law of Thelema by virtue of voluntary membership of our Order. And this applies particularly to the higher degrees resumed by and in the Sovereign Sanctuary itself. I am not

authorized to decide on behalf of any candidate whether she of he shall or shall not qualify for admittance. Once a candidate has decided to become one of us <u>on his or her own volition</u>, then the situation becomes entirely different; but a necessary period of gestation in the Outer Court has to be fulfilled for reasons of which I am sure you are aware.

It is only by means of taking this step that the earthing or 'reification' of the True Will or 'inherent dream' becomes possible, for if and when a candidate is invited to the Sovereign Sanctuary he has the entire reservoir of energy (represented by 93) behind him. There are, however, certain obligations and commitments to be entered into before this becomes possible.

In other, and perhaps simpler, words, no reification in the Outer can be entirely successful until a candidate has entered the Sovereign Sanctuary of the Gnosis of the O.T.O., the very first step of which is the voluntary act of application for membership of the Second Degree. (The First Degree is not actually conferred, it being a period of probation during which the candidate produces a Record of <u>one</u> magickal or mystical practice. But of this procedure I believe you are already aware). I cannot, therefore, even with the best will in the world, induct you into the Order unless you yourself take this step completely under your own volition. Is this perfectly clear? Please consider very deeply what I am saying and also that such restrictions imposed upon me in the matter of my magickal co-workers have a <u>rationale</u> based upon the very practical considerations of my human and therefore limited capabilities, as well as those of my <u>confreres</u>. I am sure you know as well as I do that to open oneself to any and every influence without one's magickal circle is to invite trouble, though such influence may be wholly benefic.

I hope I have answered your question satisfactorily; if not I do not at all mind framing my reply in other words if only understanding between us can thereby be facilitated. For that is my main concern: that we strive to understand each other at the outset of what I hope will be a fruitful relationship.

In view of the above remarks I am confident that you will not harbor any doubt as to my impersonal interest in the matter of Order

membership. I place quality above quantity, and, as I have written in the <u>Hidden God</u>: "The keen and persistent practice of Thelema by even a few dedicated individuals will effectively overthrow society and thereby facilitate the unhindered development of the New Aeon and the reintegration of human consciousness." Aleister once said to me with great emphasis; 'A thousand noughts are still nought; seek the One that turns them into true number'. You may be the One; anyone may be the 'one'; I am concerned only with the 'ones', with individuals (we call them 'Kings'), and I am convinced by the way in which you write to me that you are truly one of Us and that you have worn for too long the mask that seems to divide us. If you will put off that mask and come naked to the Feast, you will be consumed utterly by those vampires who live only to drain away your last drop of blood. Though the way may be arduous, tedious, perhaps even backward-walking, you may by such means arrive more swiftly at the mirror which reflects the very first, the awful promal mask, that is the only veil between us.

It is on this level and in the spirit that I accept gladly the benediction contained in your opening paragraph, knowing as I know you do, that the Eye of the Sun, and the 'I' that transmits it glory, is equally void.

Please believe me; I look forward to hearing from you. During my August vacation I shall not be within range of the mailman so do kindly wait until my return from London. I shall not be leaving London until early August. I wish you every success in the Outer and great peace in the Inner.

Love is the law, love under Will.

Yours fraternally,

       Kenneth Grant

The Magickal Record of Nema

Do what thou wilt shall be the whole of the Law.

9/16/75 e.v.

Here begins the magickal record of one known as Maggie to the Outer, who is nameless at the beginning.

Sun in Virgo, moon in Aquarius.

To the Reader, greetings. May there be no veils between us.

The chosen practice of this record is to maintain an open channel with the Children of Maat, so they may speak through me. This to my own instruction and for the evolution of the Race of Man. A writing was begun today, and shall be recorded upon completion.

9/17/75 e.v.

I'll begin transcribing what was written yesterday–it'll be completed as opportunity allows.

ALONE

AL-ONE

A boundary where self stops and Universe begins?
Arising in the rainbow-veil of tears,
then striding forth from sorrow into joy,

AL-ONE

AL-O-NE

Sorrowjoy's Our Lady's dancing-veil,
hemmed with tinkling coins

of love's passage down the years.

O daughtersons and sisterbrothers, come!
Sing the song of She-Who-Moves,
and dance the Mask-dance of the Black Flame.

Teach the temple-rites of Maat-Maut
to this nameless one,
who in the courtyard waits
to see and know and to become
true priestess of the Feather and the Air.

Wanderer of the desert, hail!
Pilgrim of the Night–
faceless in the windy wastes of time,
be thou thrice-born and bornless.

    Eye, and Aye.

The I is the manskin
(the hiding of Hadit)–
it wraps thee round in wonder and despair.
Behold, while yet a babe,
thou learned the I from not-I,
found it cold,
and howled thy infant agony aloud
unto the compassionate night.

Then, as thy father toppled from his throne,
thou drew this manskin close about thy form,
vowing none to worship.
Yet, in time, thy vows forgotten,
didst thou seek to love–
Yea, even now thou art but lately come

from that vain futility of love.

Know, seeker without number,
the I may never mate
nor find companion in another I.
The I is singular, untouched, unique.

(The red-eyed mutant clambers through the rubble of the tower.)

Born unto flesh, thou didst choose—
born unto the Wheel, thou didst accept.
The I is the weregild,
the ransom of man;
pay the piper, nameless one,
and dance!

The Eye is the Tower.

Shiva wakes—
and what is seen is shattered.
"The night has a thousand eyes, the day but One"
(The Peacock-Angel strides—
   Argos-eyed his feathers form
      The countless star-eyes of Our Lady Nu.)
Hail, Hawk-Heru—
thine Eye lent life unto thy father's form,
and shines us onward to thy zenith-hour.

(In observing the experiment, we change the data by the act of seeing. Can the truth be seen in anything?)

The Eye within beholds the I without.
This is the folly of wisdom—
that Buddha found the eightfold path

that ended at the Bo-tree.

Hermit, hold the lantern high,
that its light may not blind thine Eye from seeing–
avert thy face, so vision might percieve
the Egg of the not-born.

Pilgrim, prophet, pythoness–
wait ye still beside the gate?
The Hawkseye have ye,
born unto Heru.
Say then what thou seest with this Eye!

In Plato's cave I see the shadows made of light,
cast forth by that dark radiance
of the Black Flame.

In Athens there is Hermit Diogenes,
treading out his candle in despair.

The shaman of the Horned God
leaps the fire
willing back the forces of the night.

I see the curving teardrops of Yin-Yang
whirling light and darkness
down the concourse of the ages.

An Eye is seen, seeing itself,
reflected in its own self-shining light–
behind the image, it also sees the I.

This light, too brilliant to be seen,
Illumines all the Eye beholds.
In counterpoise, the shining shadow-form,

black radiance,
the Flame that draws all light
stands and dances,
moves in stillness,
balances,
and goes.

(Radiation is a form of energy-transfer. Photons are not lost, but absorbed and returned to the radiation-source. The process is a moving balance.)

The light is the Aye.
Universal assent,
the great yea-saying–
AYE-YEA
ALEPH-YOD
Beginnings are not ended but returned.
How else may we speak to thee?

The coming, the being, the record of having been,
are but the limits of the Eye.
These are not so, O waiter-at-the-gate.
For the Yea is forever given,
the light shineth always–
and She is the key.

The Veils of the Tree
are without, in the large;
in the small, they are lodged wihin Had.

The waiting one moves not.

O brothersons and sisterdaughters–
If the I be the manskin,

wrapping about
the Hadit within
from the Nuit without,
as a veil to define
the Mask from the dancer,
the dance from the Mask,
then now must I ask—

NO!

If the Eye doth percieve
all that is, and itself
as a part of the whole—
looking inward and out,
yet itself is a veil,
and veiling the Aye,
then for whom does it veil?

YES!

And the Aye—

PERHAPS!

Silence.

9/18/75 e.v.

(The red-eyed mutant stumbles from the ruins, and journeys to the plain. Sandstone, wind, dry twisted brush. A gnarled small form that might have been a lizard stops and screams; the mutant eats.

Winds howl: dust lifts from the earth, spreading over the sky. Green glowing dust that shifts and spirals, forming shapes of armies, faces, fortresses. The mutant watches silently.

With keening and howling and rumbling, a panorama of whirling shapes dances in the night–probable histories unfold.

A planet forms, then flows in cooling fires–explosions rise, rains come, and oceans form. In oceans, life. The growth, complexity, becoming of new forms flicker by, aeons in seconds come to pass. Fish, amphibian, reptile, mammal, Man.

Herogak murders Pog–blood is the banner of man. Conquest builds Atlantis, and it falls. Dynasties, tribes, empires, clans, families, a lonely duel in a desert place.

Nations rise, kill, fall, are forgotten. Waves of migrants sweep the fertile plains, conquer, are absorbed. Onward; Asshurbanipal, Attilla, Rome, Alexander, Ghengis Kahn, Cortez, Hitler, Stalin, England, Spain, France, America . . . Conflict rises, grows–until the mushrooms bloom around the globe.

The winds change, erase, grow calmer. The others come–Hammurabi, Solomon, Asoka, Socrates, Buddha, Christ. The secret ones of ancient priesthoods manifest, finger to lips in the old gesture. The mutant stirs uneasily, feeling his existence to be most uncertain.

A priest strides from the winds–in utter fear, the mutant cowers. The priest stretches forth a hand, touching the mutant between his crimson eyes.

Thunderbolt!

The mutant stands erect; his eyes are now sea-green, and calm, and wise. He touches the priest between the eyes, and plucks a feather from mid-air. This grows, darkens, becomes a flame of black, the color of interstellar space. It grows to fill the universe. All is/is not.)

Beside a gate, a nameless watcher stirs.

A turning-point?

The now is ever the turning-point, O sister.

A choice?

For ever yours to choose—
and for each Star, the choice—
to take a history from out the sands of space,
the winds of time,
and make it a bit more real
than other histories not chosen now.

But how to know, to choose?

Take the feather—split it in twain,
then fletch the Arrow with it.
Aim well the Arrow on the bow of will—
draw back the string
in the power of love—
(the bowstring made of the guts of the Elder Gods)
avert thy gaze from target,
and let fly.

9/19/75 e.v.

The choice is not in knowledge,
but in the onward go-ing of the soul.
The I may choose,
but seldom that correctly—
for it beholds the Cosmos
as a singleton.
The myriad of Others in their Dance

may easily confuse the single I.

The Eye cannot make choice–
for it beholds the All and no-thing,
seeing no difference between
a thing and any other thing soever.

The Aye alone, in its creative Act,
chooses rightly for eternity.

In the beginning was the Word
and the word is Aye–
So mote it be–
so it became
in might
in Maat–

Outbreathing of the Universal Yea.

Here be the rites
the temple-forms of Maat
Who is the force that flows to form,
and sculpts the Masks,
and steps the dance
in spiral whirls,
as dervish.

The spiral dance of molecules,
galactic orbits,
the ways of thought,
the form.

Her altar set
with weapons of the elements,

and incense unto Air.
The Sword here is Adjustment
upon which are the balance-scales in poise.
Her feather-symbol central,
then the flame (all candles black);
the feather rests upon
The Book of the Law,
for this is true.

The Dance of the Mask begins,
slow circles round, deosil,
a moving whirl
spiral without space.

Ychronos, Chthonos under No*,[1]
Sword wielded by Shaitan
triple invocation then
of Isis, Nuit, Maat–
wherein she/they
shall manifest
in aspect of Her choosing–

All motion ceases –
save within
where Her eternal GO-ing manifests.
Ever-onward motion shall be thine,
the balance thereof–
the surety of Centre held through change.

Thus far and no further words are given–
GO-ing moves itself;
instruction here is futile.

---

[1] the " * " in No"s name indicates a glottal stop.

In the pause, Her power comes—
Know it.

9/20/75 e.v.

The initial contact with the Maat-force occured on the Winter Solstice of '74. The place was at Oz Farm in Mt. Orab, Ohio, home of Gary M. and Ginger M. Roughly twenty of us were engaged in an Akashic working. We had shared a recent life-episode in the Alsace-Lorraine region in the late 1700's. We were a lodge gone black – but even then we'd been aware of Atlantean origins as a group.

Lu was mentor; various others served as guardians, recorders, etc. I and two others were the journeygoers. We found our past; but, not content with mere observations, we altered the consciousness of our former selves to insure our present state of evolution. (It occurs to me now that we might have improved on a few things...but what is, is.)

We were amateurish because of ignorance–inventing a trans-chronal telepathic technique on-the-spot left many rough edges on the event. However faint, the contact sufficed. (Reflections during the typing of this – there seems to be a non-material analogue of the genetic/molecular patterns in the DNA, able to be changed by experience, Our presence was the experience – we hadn't the foggiest idea of detailed will-manipulation. For which I'm presently relieved.)

Later, in conversation, Lu and I discovered that we both had sensed a stranger in our midst, knowing without doubt (how?) that "he" was a Magus from the Aeon of Maat.

The next significant event was the writing of *Liber Pennae Praenumbra*.

The initial vision occurred during a mantra-meditation. Three geometrical intelligences who have been my friends on various astral explorations, led the vision to consciousness. Perhaps they will manifest in the record at some point—they are Rosarion, Rotat and Navhem.

We were in an astral temple (of BABALON). Central above the altar is a brilliant white flame. Rosarion instructed me to "call" a feather from my physical altar. I did so; it merged with the flame and changed to the ·Black Flame – the vision was that presented in Liber P.P.

The writing was not a record of the vision, but a re-living of it in verbal terms, with many things not comprehended in the initial experience then being made clear. The writing was made possible by the evolution engendered by alchemical workings of the preceding year with Gary S.

In a perfectly logical sequence, we were shown the nature of our incarnational task, which is to assist the progress of the Aeon of Horus via the influx of the Maat current.

Our children (ourselves) are masters of the space/time continuum. They are adroit at not only placing their consciousnesses in any chosen time and location, but at communicating with the "natives" of the time, and directly influencing cruces of Race-history.

On August 7 of '75, Gary S., Allen H., and I did a series of rituals sent by the Children of Maat. This was, in effect, an earthing of the Maat current, and a merging of it with the 93 Current. We are guided not only by Sirius, but by Andromeda also, and the Andromeda Galaxy is a lens. Which lens focuses this Man-engendered current from our "future" to our "present". This is in addition to the power given via

the Brothers of the Comity of Stars.

The Children of Maat instructed me to send a copy of <u>Liber P.P.</u> to Mr. Kenneth G.; To discover that he is also dealing with Maat is therefore no great surprise, but it was a welcome confirmation of the sendings. Please remember that we have no formal instruction from a physical guide this incarnation.

At any rate, will has it to apply for admission to the O.T.O., it being stated as a necessary act toward the fulfillment of our task. The practice of contacting the Maat-force in a receptive mode was indicated by the C of M themselves.

When "I" initiate contact, it's in the form of meditation before the altar, using IPSOS as mantram. When the C of M choose to impart information, it can occur at any time . . . most frequently in the course of VIII° or IX° workings. It also happens outdoors, usually accompanied by strong elemental manifestations.

9/21/75 e.v.

Gary S. is back from Red River Gorge with the Mark of the Beast neatly carved in the center of his chest. That he had energy enough to ask me over is amazing; that he had energy enough to successfully complete IX° ritual is miraculous.

Painting begun today under invocation of Maat: a great interstellar mouth speaking a lotus, lotus begins with centre-Kether white, expanding in queen scale to four-color Malkuth on periphery.

Since completing the sending of two days ago, I've been able to "see" energies a la Don Juan in Casteneda's books. It is strange to witness people speaking in what they assume are veiled terms and actually hearing/feeling/seeing the true nature of the exchange.

This also applies to events and Manifestations of Nature. The Universe is always speaking directly to one's centre (because the two are the same thing) – what a waste that I'd not been able to percieve it before now.

9/22/75 e.v.

Ye Children of Maat–tomorrow being Equinox, what is there that me might do to assist the unfolding of the Æon?

The actions are various: Allen H. is to journey astrally to his Bell, and to activate it in a musical working. He must put forth the first action, and receive the second. The Bell will play <u>him</u> if he can become pure water crystallized. He must become the glacier-chime, the cavern of the winds, the palace of crystal echoes. Within will arise the song of Nuit, the dance of Maat, the chant of Babalon.

Dan C.[2] should first receive the creative influences of a past Master–then he should betake himself with three others, and using the various Masks of the Sephorith that he commands, effect the needed changes in those others.

Gary S., Mike C.–meditation on the mantram IPSOS. Sacrament cannabis, shared Cakes-of-Light. Astral working under guidance of Rosarion, Strengthening of Netzach, Hod, Yesod for Gary S., Geburah, Chesed, Tiphereth for Mike C., Autumn, Earth, Ge, Pan.

9/24/75 e.v.

Well, for Equinox itself there is no entry–we all wound up doing various invocational workings, recognizing the shift of the Current-flow and gearing into it.

I'm presently experiencing one of the most monstrous head-colds

---

2 Dan (handritten on original manuscript).

I've had in years. It alters perceptions and consciousness–sort of physical residence in the lower astral. It's serving as a type of insulation (against what?) and is probably a result of bad timing.

At any rate–Gary S. and I did a simple energy ritual (non-alchemical) in his Temple – invoking Heru and Maat. Dan C. and M.B. doing astrology on various people's charts. Allen H. played his working for me over the phone – echo-machine treatment of his 1/4-tone flute and Elder God invocation. And naturally; by transmitting it over the phone, he's charged the entire city's electronic communications net (plus the central computer). The lad is dangerous ... or so he'd like to think.

(Q: Why not program a self-repeating and aggrandizing engagement of a computer in terms of incantations, Magickal formulae, gematria-Tarot equivalents in binary code; a Tree of Life logic structure ...?)

9/25/75 e.v.

I believe a poem is born the instant a poet releases his stubborn hold on physical 'reality' and begins to live the metaphor. (Or re-live; "emotion recollected in tranquillity")

At any rate, a poet (musician, painter, sculptor etc.) is a part-time madman. The Magickian, the Saint, the Warrior, and the thief are all full-time madmen. So? So. Seems the Children of Maat have a beautiful way of engineering events for manifestation, (Note – thou Egomaniac, your personal-life-events are engineered only by you as a harmonic reflection of the macrocosm. The C of M are global operators; personal development is your responsibility – and an urgent one – so the Double Current can manifest properly. So stop putting on airs and flow with the Tao.)

1) Am ill enough to stay home from work today.

2) My ex-husband is returning from the Dominican Republic on the 27th.
3) His mistress(es?) returned his auto to my house today, with a slightly crumpled right headlamp.
4) One of my most dependable girls quit the shop today.
5) The owners exhibit a high degree of non-rationality.

Consulting the I Ching:

#27 Corners of the Mouth (nourishment)

changing to

#24 Return (the turning-point)

In asking about right action for the situations, there was given #2 The Receptive, changing to #15, Modesty.

9/27/75 e.v.

Brief time, brief notation. Jack U.[3] is back. He'll stay with us until he can locate a month's lodgings elsewhere. After a month, it's either back to the Dominican Republic or perhaps to Indonesia. . . He brought us all gifts—mine's a huge hand-carved candelabra (mahogany?), from Haiti. There's strange energies about it, dark and good.

Gary M.[4] of Oz has invited all of us out to the farm tomorrow evening for a cross-exchange of Equinoctal events. It seems as though everyone's been undergoing heavy changes and it's all tied in with the Maat energies.

---
3 Jack U. (handritten on original manuscript).
4 Gary M. (handritten on original manuscript).

9/28/75 e.v.

Evening at Oz Farms. Ten of us, plus Jasmine the boa constrictor ... realization of strength, love, unity. Upon leaving, spontaneous ritual to Nuit with Mike C., Lu, Gary S.[5] and myself. Lu especially strong and direct with the energies.

Huge stars, brilliant–spirit-path of the Milky Way, Lord Sh*t*n, Andromeda–Nuit! She-Who-Moves manifesting – surrounding us, the white lights of Nuit, within us, the Black Flame, the interstellar spaces of Maat. Lu was touched, opened, flowing, Pan. I became the Sword for him, the sheer power of She-Who-Moves.

Hear the words of the Children of Maat–Our Lady Nu is the White Flame, the holy firmament of Universal Being. Our Lady Maat is the Black Flame, the holy space of Universal Going.

Thou, O Warrior-Priest, Hermit-King, art Hadit, the central point of consciousness at Centre in your own universe, in your own mating with Our Lady Nu–

What then of the Shadows? If Maat be the Shadow of Nuit, who is the Shadow of Hadit? Nu has her Had as consort; Maat/Maut has only the southwest wind ...

The wind, the air ... wind is moving Air. Hadit finds his balance in the Air, as Nuit finds her balance in the between-ness of GOing. Being-act. Matter-energy. Space-time. Nu-Maat. Had-Air.

Air as prana, life, motion, breath, truth. Had is Nu; Air is Maat. Had is Air, Maat is Nu. Thou Point Central ... Thou spark of awareness! Thou art, purely, as Hadit. Thou change-wind, thou breath of passage! Thou goest, purely, as Air.

---

5 Marginal note dept. Why initials I don't know, they're Mike C. (our Cookie) Lu, & Gary M. (handritten on original manuscript).

Brothers, behold and rejoice! As Had is ever central to all He beholds, and thus is eternal in His position, so the Air changeth ever, always approaching and leaving point central, and thus is infinite in His motion. Love, be, go, consider.

9/29/75 e.v.

AUMGN. IPSOS. TELAPOTH.

Children of Maat—is there to be a ritual given for the evolution of Maat-consciousness?

Prepare the altar with things of light. One candle is sufflcient—however, if there be at hand things such as lenses, prisms, mirrors etc., let them be used as you feel fitting. Before the altar, but leaving enough room for standing, hang a white cloth—this is both veil and manifestation-means.

As ye work alone, stand between the altar and the cloth. Banish in the name of Tahuti. Ignite incense of jasmine, light the major candle in the name of Nuit. Taking up the wand and sword, into the bright flame of Nuit, breathe the word (IPSOS)-YAMEM.

Turn then and face the shadow on the cloth, who is your double . . . . the dark Hadit whose wand acts through the sword. Our Bright Lady shall direct the movements of this dance, until you are the shadow, and She, the Black Flame, Maat.

Perceiving this change, cry aloud Her Name. She will arch over thee, blinding thee to all, save thy inmost nature. All will seem as darkness, yet the Black Flame illumines the shadow-self to true self-awareness.

The Elder Gods will come at this point, to attempt to rend the shadow from the substance. Hold firm and fast—unite with thy

shadow in pure and fearless love–even the most powerful of the Forgotten ones may not then sever thy nature in twain. When the unity of self and shade is complete, close the eyes, turn–and visionless, quench the altar flames.

Depart from altar and veil, and then meditate. Thus endeth the rite.

9/30/75 e.v.

Well, when working through events, our futureward darlings manage to be drastic and dramatic at times. I was "let go" from my manager's job today–no notice and $50 extra to sweeten the news. Feh.

So I wept a bit (off and on) because it felt good, talked to Dan C. in order to earth enough to drive home. Somewhere during all this I found out that I'm supposed to take off for a few days before job-hunting and go. It seems that Red River Gorge is the place. I can borrow Gary S.'s sleeping-bag and he's furnishing travel directions.

Frankly, I'm frightened, . . . Alone in a wild place, I could end this incarnation, or become damaged. I don't really want to go, but I will to go because it's a necessary part of the current initiation ordeal. Rats! It's not required that I go alone, but I may not ask anyone to accompany me.

As one prime security (job) is removed from me, the next step is to remove the security of civilization by my own willed action–and not to seek help. At the moment, Gary S. is waiting for me to come to him in need–to vamp his energies, as he puts it. I will not. I remove the security of the Magickal relationship. There will be the removal of all referents for a time, so that the full meeting with the HGA may occur.

Some (Gary S.!) are waiting and expecting me to plunge permanently

into the Abyss during crises. Not long ago, I would have. Now, I shan't–die, maybe, go insane, maybe–but–I live and work. In strength, creatively, centered in the Heart.

I think, I love, I dream, I am not. Good night.

10/2/75 e.v.

Am in the midst of preparation for the journey. They guide and direct the preparations for the time...fine. While gathering deadfall wood in Mt. Airy forest, I encountered <u>un type</u> who offered me a) toke, b) speed, and c) sex. Graciously declining all three, I exited, having very little choice, and I do hope I have enough wood for the fire. (It's scarce at the Gorge–it seems the touristos have picked it clean.)

I've been directed by Them to take along the stone phallus that Dan C. and Gary S. found at the Gorge when they were there; I'm to charge it in ritual, and place it wherever is directed at the time. This is getting to be fun. All's well if nobody tries to interfere–they'd not survive.

10/3/75 e.v.

Tunnel Ridge Road Campsite. After losing my way twice, found this place as Gary S. told me. Rigged a lean-to shelter from saplings and blankets, have a roaring fire going, and now have some time before dark.

Had Gary S.'s bell, brass lion and the stone phallus he & Dan C. had found near here... Did VIII° (moon-time!) with the stone phallus, anointed the lion with the elixir in the Mark of the Beast, per THELEMA & IPSOS...united the lion and phallus in strength thereby. I wrapped the phallus in black velvet and buried it beneath the fallen log on the trail to the cliffs.

Gary S. didn't say anything about those cliffs! Temple of Pan-magnificent!

At any rate, the working was to tie in the spirit-strength of this holy place to Gary S., in his lion mode (totem-force of the Lion tribe). When the stars appear, the energies of the working will be sent to NU/MAAT, and thus back to Gary S.'s various bodies.

This is supposed to be a self-discovery working too—will see what happens tonight.

10/5/75

Home now, fatigue caught me early last evening and I've been sleeping since 8 pm (it's now 6:30 am)

To continue—As the daylight waned, NU/MAAT began to manifest. Chanted hymn to the departing sun; the chant turned to OM for a space, and then to an Amerind dance-chant...Did some drumming to greet Nu. The depth and majesty of NU/MAAT! the arched universe, burning, burning—glories of starfire, distant each from each and yet within the heart. The great dusty spirit path of galaxy-rim, horizon to horizon, faint & fierce—stars, and the spaces between! Infinite outflinging of the shattered First Egg, the Ylem—suns and spaces, Nu and Maat—Nu, the visible, light, manifest; Maat, the Black Flame, dancer of space—

After sacramental smoke, I invoked the HGA, who manifested in the shadow-dance. The koan was repeated—If Maat is the shadow of Nuit, who is the shadow of Hadit? And the s/w wind isn't it, since that pertains only to the vulture-manifestation of Maut. A feeling of utter terror came upon me—not fear of wild animals, or of other chance humans that could harm me, nor of the place I was camping in—but a vague, huge thing. At this point the angel directed me to

get in the sleepingbag for warmth (this <u>is</u> October) I did, and then it started.

I was directed to prepare seven triangles–pyramids, actually, which consisted of three sides under Yod, He‾, and Vau–the second He‾ formed the third-dimensional and transparent sides extended to a point...There was then unleashed a torrent of images, scenes, interdimensional impossibilities; visions that provoked the terror even further. Each time, the whirlwind was heralded by the image of a red-and-white candy-striped dog. And each session ended with a demon trapped inside a pyramid.

(In the course of this I heard a bell on the astral, which turned out to be the bell that AH had established in the vicinity around August 7. Today I find that the cliffs in the wood was the location of his working.) The demons' appearances were strange, to say the least. There were 1) a shape-changer that I "froze" into an image of Fu Manchu, 2) an albino woman with short antennae and three breasts, 3) a headless white "space suit" with huge red gauntlets (named Glover, I somehow knew), 4) a brass-copper serpent...5, 6 & 7 were dark amorphous shapes named Fear of Death, Fear of Life, and Fear of the Void.

These characters are still entrapped, awaiting further investigation. The physical body, during all this, lay straight, on the back, feet together, hands in clenched fists resting on the breast, eyes veiled (masked) by a cloth.

The next morning, I discovered the black velvet wrapping of the phallus-stone along the trail to the cliffs. Checked the log and the stone was gone. It seems the place-spirits accepted it, probably through the agency of an animal. Didn't hear any animal large enough to carry off the stone, though. Hmm.

Other magnificent sights sketched the morning after the working. Arrived home safely. What was learned through the Children of Maat in the action of the self? There are necessary and unnecessary acts–do only the necessary. Malkuth–five resumés done tonight, phone calls and job interviews tomorrow. C'est la guerre. I Ching general reading on near future and/or present situations; #27 Corners of the Mouth to #18 Work on what has been spoiled.

10/6/75 e.v.

Began job-hunting in earnest, no luck today. Ate lunch in Mt. Airy forest, after which I drove up to Dawn of Light where Patrick M. did some Christian-style money-mojo. Also had much fun playing with the dowsing rods he had on his desk…held them overhead and they went whirling about like propellers.

10/7/75 e.v.

Today's instruction-event concerned Lili, my eldest daughter. She attends a school in the inner city, a school specializing in math and science. A black boy named Tim has been harrassing her since school opened–today, she pushed him and gave him an energy-jolt; he roundhouse-punched her and loosened a tooth.

So Gary S. came to the house and resumed the Martial Arts instruction, plus a consciousness-working in which Lili grew in self-awareness and compassion-psychology. The children are being reared by the principles of Thelema and the Tao, and are becoming aware of their Tree. Lilie's doing quite well.

Last night's working with Gary S. went well, with myself as Bee. Purity and subtlety are manifesting more and more in this time of Uranus' entry into Scorpio. This is the time of individual refinement, when members of the gestalt attend to self-actualization. In the

course of this flow, interpersonal relationships are manifesting increasing empathy.

The koan of Had's shadow remains in the mind and subconscious.

10/8/75 e.v.

Painted Gary S.'s totem mountain lion on the piece of bark found in Mt. Airy forest. The head and forepaws are shown, with the lion crouched on a tree limb. Above the head are Maat's feather in black; below it, crimson mark of the Beast with seven tongues of fire, a yellow pair of wings (15 feathers); below that, two blue wavy lines and below them, two curved green branches. Finally, the Leo symbol. I put a screw-eye in each side and tied a thong to 'em—also tied five feathers in the thongs, three to the left, two to the right.

Why? Well, that's his business. I'm just following guidance as I pledged at the beginning of this record. Otherwise, it was a wet and dismal day, fit but for sleeping. Lili and I practiced Martial Arts training—it's about time!

10/9/76 e.v.

Delivered the lion-painting and Dan C. pledged silence about it. Haven't heard whether Gary S. found it—of course he did, and is performing the gracious act of receiving in silence, as it was given.

Casey just delivered some extraordinary "soma" (cannabis)—it's quite astral and airy. Working with it as I write now.

Simplify!
Reduce to the irreductable!

Refine your perceptions, your actions, your judgements, your strength, your balance, your go-ing, your love and your will.

The fathers are the children. The children are the fathers of the men. The Mother alone is eternally the same. The Father alone is eternally the same. The Father and Mother together are eternally Change, which is the Child also.

The Mystery of the Trinity.
Father   Mother   Child
Being   Word   Love
Thesis   Antithesis Synthesis
Hold! An these be enow–
One is pyramid,
Two, the well;
Three is the archway;
Four, the arablest.
Five, the chariot,
Six, the tower,
Seven marks the ocean
Eight is the bell
Nine is winged bulls
and ten is the feather...What game now, O Children of Heru?

We dance the goat-dance, prancing in the thicket. The bond is sealed, the strength of alchemy married to the Earth.

The Currents rise and wax in fury. Strength in the hands on the reins! For it rains liquid silver, potable gold and the reign of Heru but scarce begun. What tale, what words, O priests of the Vulture? Dark of yin and yoni always must be at balance with yang and lignam. We are the balance to your Set and Typhon. Destruction's ever at your command.

From the linear Egg of Null-space,
hatches ever the Bird of Time–

Formulae are sometimes given,
For exercise of Hod.
Rhapsodies are sometimes given
For expansion of Yesod;
Soultouch, each to each is given
for growth of Netzach.

For Beauty and beyond, these words are sigils–drop them, let them go, to sink into the unseen consciousness, wherein they may work changes.

Facere quam voluntas fui omnia de Legis; Amor est Lex, amor sub voluntatis.

Lords of Being–hear us!
Ladies of Beauty–hear us!
Princes of Becoming–hear us!
Daughters of Motion–hear us!

For Knowledge and Conversation of the Holy Guardian Angel–we live and work.
For discovery and doing of True Will–we live and work.
For the conquest of the Law of Thelema–we live and work.
For the evolution of Man–we live and work.
For the perfect unfolding of the Æons–we live and work.
For the realization of all Stars–we live and work.
For the use and enrichment of the 93 Current–we live and work.
For the reception and creation of the Current of Maat–we live and work.
For the recognition and employment of the Current of the Beast–we live and work.

Lord Shaitan! We now invoke thee!

Lady Nuit! We now invoke thee!
Lord Hadit! We now invoke thee!
Heru-Pa-Kraath,
Ra-Hoor-Khuit,
Heru-Ra-Ha! We now invoke thee!
Lady BABALON! We now invoke thee!
Lord Pan! We now invoke thee!
Lord Tahuti! We now invoke thee!
Lady Isis! We now invoke thee!
Lord Osiris! We now invoke thee!
Lady Maat! We now invoke thee!

All ye Elder Gods and Forgotten Ones, we acknowledge ye within us. All ye angels, archangels, thrones, dominions, principalities, powers, cherubim, seraphim, we acknowledge ye within the realm of power. All ye demons, jinns, afreets, incubi, succubi, vampires and dwellers on the lower astral planes, we acknowledge ye within the id and subconscious.

In workings of power, let Maat prevail!
In workings of subtlety, let Heru-Pa-Kraath prevail!
In workings of ascendency of Will, let Ra-Hoor-Khuit prevail!
In workings of love, let Nuit prevail!
In workings of secret realization, let Shaitan prevail!
In workings of nature, let Pan prevail!

To all gods of Man's worshipping–hail! ye are of us!
To all gods of Man's terror–hail! ye are of us!
To all demons and guardians of gateways–hail! ye are of us!
To the beginnings, changes, and returnings–hail! ye are of us!

Dark mirror of existence–show us ourselves.
White light of realization–show us ourselves.

Choosing not god over demon, pleasure over pain, nor beauty over disgust, we embrace the Khu and the Khabs.

Choosing nothing, uniting with all, we come to know the nature of things and the way of changes.

Choosing not amongst the pairs of opposites, we become one with the Tao. We live and work, to the appointed end of Being and GO-ing.

So mote it be.

10/11/75 e.v.

IX° last night, increase of self-knowledge in terms of the dark nature. Gary S. channels truths–flavored his way, but objectively <u>so</u>. For instance, the second-chakra power and attraction I seem to be rampant with is but a means to power of destruction and control. If I don't exercise control, I wind up working Black.

So what to <u>do</u> about it? Physical age will resolve the sexual aspect, given time–but since the NOW is the only malleable point in the time-stream...the seven demons from the camp-working have to do with this. The passionate, sexual, bitch-in-heat aspect is only a mask for an utterly ruthless, cold and arrogant vampire-self that relishes the stinging fires of energy-wielding for its own sake.

I am also the compassionate mother-self, the infinite lover and giver. I unite with love to assist the flow of evolution and self-awareness, and operate in lover-under-will. How can such dichotomy survive and function? Balance.

Feather...I am both–and must use both. More later.

And now it's later. In the midst of a painting–Each sephora represented by a mountainous form–Observatory and ivory tower

for Hod, huge nude green lady for Netzach—Tiphereth is three-faced figure seated on a mountain-top lotus—faces of Krishna, Christ and Boddhisattva. Geburah is a volcano weeping lava tears, Chesed is a distorted-perspective throned and bearded blue figure—Choronzon is flapping in the Abyss. Binah is City of Pyramids atop black peaks. Chokmah is a giant gray hand with a homonucleus-sperm in the palm of it—Kether is a point radiating light and stars. Yesod is a silver gateway onto a lavender cliff. Hero-type is being greeted at the gate by a veiled priestess with a bow in a camel-drawn chariot. Just for fun, I'm depicting Rosarion, Rotat and Navhem in their usual forms.

The Children of Maat are subtly dictating this one too. In a way, They exist and manifest not only as "outside" consciousnesses communicating through events, words, direct images and knowledge, but also seem to exist as seed-form "homonuclei" within my personal consciousness.

When I die <u>this</u> time, I intend to retain the acquired awareness—<u>if</u> I get it perfected in time. Subjectively—I cannot determine whether previous lives are true memories or subconscious creations. It doesn't seem to matter. The interior cynic suggests that nothing really matters—the finding and doing of True Will, the Boddhisattvic Vow, the wielding of power, the development of Man, the union with the Tao—that all of this is invented gropings toward a sense of cosmic importance that is really irrelevant.

Our gods and our power may be but the protesting cry against the Great Night—our Magick and Will but the inner campfires in the darkness of universal indifference. So? To those who hold that all action is futile, that there's no point to it all, I say—my brothers, even though it may be that our Race is a sport of the indifferent cosmos, and that there is no cause to be part of—I CARE—I love ye, and all the

rest of being, to the point of assuming what godhood I may so that ye may be loved divinely.

If there be no loving Godhead, then I will become It. You do not deserve to live in futility, to spend your heartsblood in striving toward realization of a mirage. I will be divine Love until you see that you are this Love also. If there is no God, we shall become It. If there is a God, we are It already. So mote it be.

10/13/75 e.v.

Gary S. took yesterday's entry with him—be sure to get it in proper sequence. (Note while typing—it's lost, insofar as I know, but we may run across it later.)

He, Dan C. and Dick M. are going to the Gorge tomorrow and they plan to stay two days. . I suppose he intends to do ritual as indicated in the entry.

Herb Z. was at Riddle Crest today when I walked in—our Semitic Kshatryia got a bit too much energy into his chakra-system. He's OK as long as the flow's contained in Hod. Dan C. and I took it to Gebura & Chesed & up then down to Tiphereth . . .If Herb Z. had had his Centre where it's supposed to be, he would've found it invigorating instead of ennervating. So it goes with over-intellectualized Magickians.

He has a decent grasp (formal) of the tools of the trade—but for a Leo-Virgo he could use more fire-force.

Casey stopped in. Second-chakra energies were sublimated and elevated to heart and throat chakras. So far, so good. Painting continues.

The Elder Pine lives in the amphitheatre-cliffs along Tunnel Ridge

Road. The dancers are closing together. One may dance in a chain-dance also. Russian leaps, Cossack breaks, a Rudolf Nureyev?

No. The temple dancer moves subtly, gestures flowing and full of power–really, energy-play, molding globes of ki-force and stretching them–weaving tapestries of light and darkness in the ritual-place.

Celebrating an ancient divine triumph, miming the communal need for rain, demanding aid for an impending battle–priestess-hands, dancing hands–The blade of the Horse Sacrifice weaving its silver thread through the temple tapestry. Jai devi deva! Dance! Languid, loving Krishna, with Your fiery flute–Beloved cowherd, sweet piper of the bowers...we dance amid flowers and wingtips, moving ever nearer in the Dance of Love...Your sky-blue form becomes invisible upon approach, yet the embrace is rapture.

10/14/75 e.v.

Casey just left–an interesting gentleman. I learned that it was he who had given me a talisman over a year ago. He'd brought a Black (in both senses) voudon-"warlock" to my house–an interesting experience. Prior to this, Casey had given me a protective talisman that he had seen in a vision. Upon sending a copy of it to a friend in Louisville (BK), the talisman was verified as pre-existent, and specifically made "for the purpose of turning an enemy's armament against himself." Casey stated that he had discovered that he is a "brujo" in 1949. He has greater command of Magick and alchemy than I had previously realized. He's a Tantric master, and is extremely subtle in his energizing of the Kalas–but–there's need of a physical moratorium until I undergo a further state of development.

This is happening. An intense second-chakra charge developed with him today. When he left, I led it into VIII° and charged the painting-in-progress. At any rate, it doesn't really matter to either of us

whether the relationship earths or stays up the planes. So for now, it stays unearthed.

Later–Gary S. stopped by for Martial Arts practice with Lili. He suggests I work on invisibility to veil the second-chakra energy. Also a modest proposal of Alchemical workings for Dan C. and me. Jolts some deep-rooted taboos, also brings to consciousness that we have been working high-energy polarities for quite some time, but only down to Yesod. For the present, it's not my will to earth it–would be utterly destructive to the lower bodies.

It's a possibility–I know I'm capable of doing it if the flow is in that direction–as an exercise of will, there is no need. Enough.

The Beast-force is indeed abroad in the land at this time. It's not linked to a definite personality as yet, though it's major avatar is directing it. Gary S. manifested it in various ways–as the Fool, as the Shiva-Beast, as instructor.

Hail, OX! Taurus to earth, as Leo to fire. And the virgin shall tame the uni-cornuus.

10/15/75 e.v.

The tilt of the Earth is its token of yield–
plow,
OX tricornuus!
Wind, rain and fire over the fallow field,
virgin again, awaiting the seed;
after the harvest, a time of rest.

The seasons compress themselves, O Mage–
and the turn of a year may be done in one cycle of breath.

Our Mother's couch is chthonos,

and ychronos the measure of her slumber.
By the same mouth that summons Boreas,
is the moment of life-readiness decreed.

Hoof-stamper on the mountain!
Thou shalt declare the times of rest and act.
From midnight winter
to thy solstice noonday of mid.Summer,
Holy are all hours unto thee!

Goat, bull, unicorn and OX–
Mountain-beast river-beast,
Forest-beast, field-beast,
This is your season, beloved of earth!
Fire, strength, invisibility, patience–
these virtues ye command,
and bring unto perfection
within the priests of THAT named Therion.

Omnicron and Chi unite
in the name of the Firebird–
and thus is manifested again
the lord of the morning mountain!

So it was done,
and the sign adorns his breast forever.
Only he who beats the Devil at his own game
can be the highpriest of the Double Current.

Who falters, or fails to see
the true initiation given by the present beast
will fall thereby.

One eye, two horns, three tongues–

so he shall speak.
No karma shall he bear for aught he does,
for all who act as gods are gods indeed.

As the Anointed One appeared in several masks,
So does the Beast.

As several may be separate avatars (O Rama, O Krishna)
with one Essence manifesting severally,
so it is of the OX and the XO.

It is the Wheel also, and the City–Hear him, children of Heru.
For the OX is Harpocrat
and the XO is the Secret Fool.

He is as mad as he is holy,
and as holy as he is mad–
In the eyes of Nu there is no difference.

Hail, Father!
Thou hast brought us to the Womb.

As surely as I was my own ancestor in Atlantis, so I am my own posterity in the Aeon of Maat. How "real" is a metaphor? As real as it needs to be to get the job done. And what is the job? To bring the Race of Man (another metaphor) into the Comity of Stars, and the rest of the Universe back to the Ylem, so's we can start it all over again.

Why?
Why not?

It's exercising our essence of GO-ing, this creation game–and as it's the nature of Being to BE, so it's the nature of gods to GO.

Can a god choose not to GO, or not to create?

If one chooses not to create, does this not put the axe to a definitive notion of "god"? Is a god a god without a people? Or is he but a simple Being, complete in Himself?

If one must create to be an "official" god, doesn't this negate omnipotence, which is another necessary qualification for godhood?

Why the pilpul, O nameless one?

It's happening on its own, dear, and is really more than an exercise of Hod.

Channelling from yourself to yourself? Better be careful, or you'll turn into a Black Hole in space, a Singularity that warps a good section of the space/time continuum. If you don't maintain a certain amount of the old "I-Thou", you'll disappear.

So?

OK, as long as you go about disappearing correctly. To accomplish your given Task for this incarnation, you have to maintain the mask of Ego for interrelating with other "individuals". This means maintaining your physical, astral, etheric, etc, bodies in good working condition until the Task be completed.

You're fairly skilled in maintaining your consciousness of nonexistence for reasonable lengths of time; now the obverse needs work—to maintain your consciousness of existence as a matter of artistic science or scientific art.

Your "natural" existence is so ill-disciplined that it can't be trusted to function automatically. Your desires and aversions are so strong, due to early tries at Christian asceticism, that to attempt normal discipline-training at this stage is a waste of time.

So there remains, if ye are to live Thelema, one extraordinarily effective but exceedingly drastic, means of control that you must master. Every function, save automatic physical maintenance such as breathing, heartbeat, cell repair, etc., must be done in full waking consciousness. This will simplify acts, bring you to constant Unity-consciousness, and guarantee that you become the Tao in manifestation.

<u>See everything</u>. Your body-posture, your words, thoughts, internal dialogue, effects on other people, your apparent mask, the energy-flows of a situation, etc.

<u>Arm your observer</u>. That little Hadit-point is always there and functioning. Give him a weapon to jolt your consciousness, and there will shortly be no lapses in awareness.

<u>Laugh</u>. The one great error that will be the worst obstacle is taking all of it too seriously. Suspension of disbelief is a prime necessity, but beginning to believe totally is to invite obsession and/or entrapment in a particular Sephora. You are not only a Fool, but a Masked Fool (Harlequin?). Therefore, your dance requires total control, without appearing to have any.

You are beginning to achieve this in terms of second-chakra energy—but your tightrope-walking between desire and will is precarious. There's no better way of learning control than through occasional loss of it, but that process can hinder the development of other individuals. It's your method to choose or no—but any karma acquired by using this method will have to be expiated before you will be permitted to die physically.

We can delay it indefinitely—as you well know—so be cautious.

This is beginning to sound like the ravings of a madman.

Of course. You're certifiable right now—by clinical definition, you're mad as a hatter. So is any Magickian of any power at all; you're pursuing a tangent.

Then—how shall we deal with ourself from this point on?

The conventional metaphor of individual consciousnesses and duality will suffice. In other words, as Maggie, we'll keep this Record and function on the Outer ... As past-selves, we'll be available for experience, memory and (most importantly) significant mistakes.

As future-selves, we will be the "individual" link between the Aeon of Maat and the Aeon of Heru. More and more people of the XX century are discovering their future-selves and are using the increased energies. Very few are doing it consciously, however—and too many halfway-realized ones are institutionalized.

So. What of the gods, the vocabulary of Magick, the Qabalah, the Tarot, the I Ching, astrology, etc.? All are as valid as ever—more so for you, in fact, since additional significance is available.

And what of the Order, admittance to which is the motivation for this Record?

You know already.

Whether there be past or future, or whether the NOW is the only reality, the quality of consciousness is the matter of concern. One reality is as valid as any other. Whether the world be a steel-and-plastic android-computer, or if it be a bosky dell peopled by sprites and pixies—it's but a stage for the Dance of the Mask.

We live by and are enriched by our metaphors—one should be a perfect metaphor. This is enough for now. Go take a bath and come back for Tarot.

(This was done. Without the boring details, there were many swords and it did fit the situation.)

10/17/75 e.v.

Heavy autumn rains all day. John U. and Casey left for Colorado last night (by auto)...Telephone conversation with Dan C. No mail, no money, no work. I've been playing Rachel–she keeps in a major key, doing country-peasant music.

Things are occurring, but not where the conscious mind can percieve them. Monday <u>will</u> be an active job-hunting day. For now, a sort of suspension–one painting finished, and Carmen's portrait to begin. No contact with comrades–everyone's busy in their individual pursuits. Boredom? In a way, but not exactly. Inactivity? Not really. Waiting. Yes.

Will houseclean the temple tonight, banish all astral cobwebs and do ritual to attune the consciousness more to the Cosmos. It's a watery day–let's consult the ephemeris–moon's entering Aires tonight.

Later–Gary S. arrived, worked energies with Lili. I showed him the word about himself–he's becoming an avatar of the Beast-force, but he's only aware of it in flashes. Part of me is terrified of him–the same terror experienced on the camp-out–as of a huge nature-force, eldrich and powerful, that can't be named, much less controlled, by Man.

I saw him as Belisarius–some philosopher or magician, it seemed. Bald head, long gray-and-white beard, flowing robe the color of yellow clay. He was studying a large hand-illumined book, also were an astrolabe, some flasks on benches, a stuffed owl. There was a task of protecting an army about to begin war–he's to regain certain knowledge from this incarnation to use now.

10/18/75 e.v.

IX°–and channelling for Gary S. I found Belisarius in the encyclopedia. He was a Byzantine <u>general</u>–commanded army of Eastern Roman Empire. In 530 A.D., defeated Persians. Saved Justinian's throne for him during civil strife. Had bad luck later in his career, dragged out of retirement to defeat Bulgarians. Was even imprisoned by Justinian for a while on conspiracy charges–centered his activity around Constantinople.

The essence seems to be that Gary S. can't pursue his sought-after spiritual retreat (can't "retire"), and that he must gain his strength from action, in action. He's been complaining about the apparent futility of action in the Kingdom–gets disgusted with human thick-headedness. So, compassion is needed in his conscious mind and the shortcomings of contemporary man won't be an obstacle to his manifesting Heru and Maat. He's needed in the Kingdom constantly, so rest can be had only in the midst of act, like the heart rest between beats.

I Ching: #7 "The Army" to #40, Deliverance.

10/19/75 e.v.

Premature pronouncements once again! In conversation with Dan C., he can't <u>see</u> the matter of compassion, Says Gary S. acts from it–true–but at any rate, there's a semantic knot occurring in verbal communication right now. I see the situation, but can communicate only the ultimate resolution of the present process. The hexagrams last night are <u>so</u> true. Both gentlemen have to tread their individual paths toward comprehension.

Maggie dear–some things cannot be dealt with verbally. Stop trying to define compassion–simply be compassionate, and the necessary

comprehension will follow. Never try to explain a virtue–just become that virtue in essence and act, and it will transmit itself to any and all whose way of unfolding calls for the virtue to manifest.

Time assumes a dual nature for this: You percieve the virtue <u>in potens</u> within a person give it actuality within your own GO-ing, and the virtue will awaken itself within the other's consciousness. For you, his future will be present...For him, his present will be uncomfortable, and he will, for a while, regress to his past. All this resolves itself without undue concern–be easy.

OK–also noted that I'm experiencing a strange malaise whenever there's not a painting in progress. Lords of the Cosmos–why must I struggle to afford to paint instead of earning a living <u>with</u> painting?

You abused your talent last time.

When?

When you were court painter to a Spanish King. Disabuse yourself of the notion that you were El Greco or Velasquez; you achieved no fame because you misused your talent.

How?

There was the usual portrait-pandering, but that was part of the social mores. No, you were working Black, and using painting as the means. Where do you suppose Oscar Wilde got the idea of "Portrait of Dorian Grey"?

Oh really! Artistic voodoo?

Yes. The Inner school of painters has always been an initiated order ...remember the caves of Altimira?

The bison and reindeer prehistoric murals?

Sympathetic magic. Ironically, you were initiated into the Power of the Image in just such a painted cave. The Hunt-Callers have passed their initiation and manas along to all nations ever since the beginning–even the Australian aborigines have their initiates.

Anthropology lessons?

You've enough background. Pay attention. This will seem to be belaboring the obvious–but anthropologists have caught an aspect of the true nature of the Hunt-Callers. They've named it as charms for game. Which some of the cave paintings were, of course.

What few, if any, have realized is that the animal portraits were workings of totem-magick. Not only in terms of tribal protection, but also for destruction or assistance of individuals through the use of their totem animal.

Now–when you were prostituting your art and Art at court, you would use a symbol of the portrayed person's totem animal in the painting. You would also include some of the subject's mana by mixing hair, blood, spittle, etc. in with the paint–

Voodoo indeed. Your true clients would have a totally undetectable means of disposing of their enemies–and your style of life was supported sumptuously by blood money.

So. If this be true literally or in metaphor (for it doesn't really matter what level of "reality" we're dealing from), then it seems I'm to re-learn this branch of the Art.

You already have been practising it, albeit unconsciously. Now, become aware of the Magick of Jupiter, and use it consciously. It will benefit your Mars also.

OK. I've begun Carmen's portrait tonight. I have nothing of her person to include in the paint—only her photo to work from.

With the Current 93, you don't need such material links; although if available, use them. The image suffices.

So what am I supposed to do with her?

Incanting IPSOS, breathe upon the painting. Under the finished surface, paint a sigil for the essence of the Chariot of the Tarot. This will assist her development on many planes . . .

Like facilitate her arrival in the States?

If such be her Will.

Um. also—she will become BABALON by it?

Yes. In terms of the Blood of the Saints.

Something feels like Kali in all this.

BABALON is Kali.

Something else. The moon enters Libra on All-Hallows Eve. The ritual of the Hunt-Callers initiation should be re-enacted then.

How?

You'll be directed in action. This will give you a direct personal link with the Wiccan powers. And be careful of feedback—to the covens. During this ritual you'll be receiving the force of every Cone of Power in the Cincinnati vortex—and on All Hallows, that is <u>some</u> voltage. Still, you can handle that, but the witches can't handle the Double Current, so protect them. There's one high-priestess in

Kentucky that could, but that's all. Invoke Pan as their protector and all's well. Also keep your personal shield tight.

Note—the Hunt-Callers use other arts—ask Dan C. about the Shofar and the call-spire in Atlantis. Enough. Meditate and sleep.

10/20/75 e.v. (Note while typing. This is the full moon of October, the second anniversary of my initial solo working. I'm a bit of a sentimentalist, I guess.)

The Anniversary rite isn't only that—there's a preliminary to the Hunt-Caller rite in which the tools of the arts are dedicated and invested with Elder God energies. Invoke Thoth-Hermes as Hierophant and proceed as follows: after the lunar ritual, re-scribe the circle in fire. (Face west to invoke T-H). He will manifest, after which call upon NO* and the Forgotten Ones. Important—maintain awareness of the feather, and Her GO-ing balance, or the Elder Gods will eat you. This may or may not result in physical death—better if it does, from one certain viewpoint.

All depends on Centre and balance—successful, the rite will imbue your tools of art with a shining light of utter power—failed, and you are eaten. You will be naked, utter, Elder God from that point on. If your physical body survives, you will be Elder God to all you meet—consider.

This is all for now. Do what thou <u>wilt</u>.

Later.

I'm weeping and don't know why. Always falling short of perfection. "Perfection". Everything is perfect already or nothing ever will be. Ongoingness is all—Maggie feels small and meaningless—thoughts broken in half, quarters, fragments. Insanity? Facts:

Full moon. Went to the pentagram-trees in Mt. Airy's pine grove. Banished, scribed circle. Earth Altar of circle-triangle-crescent. The ghee/rice/salt/tea./"soma" offering went first to fire and air, then to earth and water.

Then followed the invocation of Hermes Trismegistus. The blade and the pen were then opened for the influx of Elder God-force. Begun invoking No°, Megor-Marduk etc. until I heard words spoken by my mouth that consciousness didn't grasp... Danced deosil around the circle–saw downward-flashing arrow–crimson flame tipped, white shaft, black fletching. Cut this into my breast with the blade, then embraced the western-most pine and carved it into the trunk–the tree and I shared life-force (I named it as brother)...

At this point I thought I saw movement outside the circle and was rather amazed to find myself clutching the blade in a ready-stance, eager for a kill. Fortunately, there was no human present–he would have been slain. So. Came home, painted the Chariot-sigil on Carmen's portrait, phoned Gary S., and now I write.

Children of Maat! Have ye word?

It _is_ possible to anihilate oneself, completely, totally, and without trace. There will be no reincarnation, for not only is the present-self anihilated, but the past and future selves also. One would never have been. The Universe would move swiftly to heal the gap, and history flows other-wise. No-one would miss you, because you wouldn't have been there for them to meet.

Ethically, the move is contraindicated. It would negate the existence of other Stars, and change the life-patterns of still others to a way not conforming to their Wills.

How can it be done?

Not the traditional way of subsiding into Brahman, for certain bodies of you continue, not to mention other's memories. You systematically destroy all bodies, beginning with the outer and working in to the individual self, that which "surrounds" the Atman. One simply wills the ultimate self-destruction, and it's done. It has been done "before", but there is no record of its success, because of its success ...

You won't do it, of course. We are real, and aware of ourselves. We are your children and one is yourself. You are a friend and colleague of ours; and therefore your future self proves your existence.

Nahada!
Bright plume of Being becoming Itself!
Nahada!
Unfold thy winged self across the solar stream.
Nahada!
Rainbow lady of the summer sky.
Arise, awake, behold thy majesty.
As clouds sparkle crystalline–
in flight above them you percieve–
so does new light shine upon the old self.

Glow, Nahada,
in peacock-colors radiant as sunlight!
Rise, soar, glide, turn, hover!
See thy rainbow-shadow on the cloudbank,
haloed roundabout in glory.
Spin, shimmer, flash and glitter–
All light shakes, breaks,
tinkles from thy feathers
in a myriad shower of prism-crystals!

Thou art the depth of a diamond,
heart-piercing shafts of light, Nahada.
Thou art the sensuous chamber of the ruby–
swimming in emerald,
transfigured in the silent sapphire,
glow garnet, topaz, aquamarine!

Laugh in amethyst of lilac rains,
and tumble down the slopes
of jasper, malachite and tourmaline.

Preen the one black plume
upon thy breast, thy token of Binah.

Then minor-keyed,
sing mist upon the mountain–
silver light to soften all stonefire.

Thou art pearl, and smoke-quartz.
Thou art ebony and jet,
jade and marble.
The light of thy being
is softened to the moon,
and in the silver glade,
then whistle soft for fairie's dancing.

Lovely, soft, mysterious as opal,
wend thy way
towards the Mountains of the Morning.
Nahada,
sweet and soft and sad and slow ...
Thou art the mourning dove
in winter wheatfields.

Do thou now, I command thee, behold the bright and soft within.
THY NAME IS NAHADA.

10/21/75 e.v.

Things have been "set right" with Allen H.–at least it's a beginning. Following Gary S.'s word, I came from Centre and strength to Allen H. when he was here this evening...saying, verbally and directly, that he's wasting substance in generating all of his good ideas that never earth in manifestation. Scattering his energies, as it were. Also I stated my will to assist him in acquiring an alchemical partner. There are two prospects, one constituting a dangerous situation for him (she's underage).

So, Doing Tarot and I Ching, and questioning him "down the Tree", it was given that my role was to donate some personal power to his working, so that the Aeon of Heru may be brought close to total manifestation. (He brought up a salient point–although we're dealing also with Maat-energy, the work of the moment is the unfolding of the Aeon of Horus. True.)

After he left, I did VIII° for the power-purpose, but it turned into a multipurpose ritual. AH's trip came first, then a sending of power to all BABALONs, charging Carmen's portrait in the name of Erzulie, charging the one in progress in the name of Bear Claw, and charging a talisman for unity with one of my teachers to earth in alchemy, in the name of the Tao.

Elixir taken in acceptance of the name Nahada. It will be some time before I comprehend the total meaning of it.

10/22/75 e.v.

Well! Our baseball team, the Cincinnati Reds, just won the World Series. The celebration-energies that are being generated from

Fountain Square (the plaza in the heart of the city) are fantastic! Pure Dionysian rout. So if the words are tipsy, it's because of an energy-drunk that's extremely difficult to resist...Whee!

Hmmmm—let's just take all of this joyous force and join it into Current 93 (because it's a part of it already) and let it merrily flow along to assist in the unfolding of the Aeon—done! So even while enjoying the pleasure of it all, we proceed.

Gary S. dropped by tonight and the conversation did much to straighten out aspects of our relationship and viewpoints. He's right, as usual; now's the time for individual development and not time to scrutinize our interpersonal relationship. The alchemical relationship, and that of higher-plane unity is—it's a working reality, and that's enough for now.

He also requested that I speak as an identity when communicating channellings—OK—as realized some time ago, it is Self speaking to self through self. But this raises a small question about this Record—the chosen practice was to remain receptive to the Children of Maat. Now it is recognized that said source are our "future selves", just as previous reincarnation memories are of our "past selves", and that both are simply aspects of our present self.

From practicality, the only "real" self is the one operating NOW. All past and future selves, all demons, angels, and gods are ourselves also, here and now. We are individuals, and manifestations of a particular virtue of a Sephora, and all the archtypes in the collective unconscious, and the Atman, and the Tao, and none of the above. I am Maggie, and Nahada, and the Cosmos, and the creator, preserver and destroyer; I am Being/Not-Being, and so are you, and Gary S., and everyone.

Which leaves us with a question of honesty—must we not now change premises in mid-stream? (Apologies for mixed metaphors.)

Is it righteous and true to continue the practice as stated? It can only be as a mutually-agreed-upon metaphor, though we are/will be as much the Children of Maat as we are Brothers of Heru. Of course—the practice was chosen for a reason even though consciously I didn't know why at the time.

For myself—and perhaps others may find it useful—Maat is the core of yet another Thelemic system of Magick, It's been developing invisibly ever since Liber P.P. happened.

Thanks to Dan C. and Gary S., I now percieve how it happened. Liber P.P. has always existed, in essence. It is simply the nature of my task this time, to earth the "Maat-force" in terms of a practical and comprehensible Magickal system. The writing of Liber P.P. was a beginning, Sending a copy to Mr. Grant but the second step—the resulting contact with him a) confirmed the objective validity of the Maat-force, b) provided an opportunity of entrance to the O.T.O. which in turn required this record, which c) engenders further realizations and new levels of consciousness. There's also a definite d) which is the sheer joy of corresponding with a truly human being—(which is probably the basic Magick of the whole thing.)

So. Marvelous for this individual. Applause. To remain there would be out of keeping with the Boddhisattvic Vow. This whole thing's meaningless until it can be rendered of service and value to others.

Shall we resume our Working Metaphor?

This method to come—The Dance of the Mask—will be a system that self-destructs, like any system that truly works. Once an initiate

reaches a certain perception of his own reality, he transcends the Dance of the Mask and becomes the Dance itself, or the GO-ing-ness of Maat, or the Tao, etc.–whichever term feels comfortable.

The name received in the working of the other night will do. I'll do what analysis of it that I'm able, just to check out the enriching correspondences. It may be that this Record isn't the proper vehicle for the completion of it, but it can be a beginning.

On which level of consciousness is the first initiation of Maat?

On the level of the individual candidate's present awareness. Since it is not to be given unasked, the first initiation of Maat will insure that its own criteria be fulfilled. The individual must have enough perception to receive a "channelled" urge to question specifically, plus a definite symbolic manifestation of Maat.

10/23/75 e.v.

The Kether of the Dance of the Mask is the evolutionary pressure of the Cosmos, specifically that of the Race of Man. It is coming into being NOW because it is the correct time and place for it to do so.

Liber P.P. is the seed.

One must dance in the Mask of the Dancer.

Flutes, Lord Krishna; pipes, Lord Pan!
Drums of Shiva,
strike ye now the rhythms of the Dance.
Gongs and cymbals,
temple sistrum tinkling,
Here the music of the Dance begins.

The hands make winged mudras,
moving serpentine–

feet stamp out the beat,
and bodies flow.
Thus we invoke the Lady Maat;–
She Who Loves,
Black Flame,

Crystal Lotus,
Black Pearl;
Truth–
Righteousness–
Justice–
Air–
Prana–
Prakriti;
Maut,
Mother of the Sun–
Mate of the Wind–
Balance–
Centre–
Hail!
Come, lovely twin of Nu, and teach us thy Dance of the Mask.
We, the Children of Heru, are thy children also.

Teach us thy Dance, O Feather, so we may more swiftly fly. The time that Therion began must be brought to growth by us. The hand of the Angel Aiwass did hold thy nature as his scribe-pen Lady Maat, aid the coming of Ra-Hoor-Khu!

In the air above the dancers, she comes into perception,
Black Flame, speak!

Who know my Name and Nature
well enough to seek me and my ways,
have begun the first steps of the Dance.

For know this—other dances there are beside mine. They must have been learned, perfected, and outgrown before seeking the Dance of the Mask.

The dance of Gaia must be learned. She is the Firsthome, the Cavewomb, Mother of Man. Her dance, the eternal turning of the orbits of the Stars. Her dance teaches Earth-wisdom; tides and seasons, time of plant and plow, bounty of field and forest, herb and vine. Her dance is nature-wisdom, unity of self and of the planet. To know her gifts of help and healing, and sacramental drugs, dance the dance of Ge.

Also, ye shall know the science and the art of the Zodiac, and temperments of Men thereby. Herein ye begin to see yourselves anew. Ye shall become aware of the spirits of a place, and shall be able to discern Places of Power. The elementals shall be made subject to your Will.

Ye shall learn the many forms of Fire. The Fire of Shiva will wither ye to brittle leaves, the destructive drouth that ignites the need to search beyond appearances.

The Fire of Mars shall flood your limbs in strength, directing force through form. From higher sight, this is the Fire of Ra-Hoor-Khu, and is the way in which Will manifests.

The Fire of the Scorpion shall cleanse, turning the corpses to soil for new growth.

Ye shall arouse the Fire of the Serpent, if She be still sleeping, and take care that She ascend the middle way.

In the Dance of Gaia, ye shall learn of Fire by being burnt away.

Ye shall also learn the ways of Water.

In the Water of Ganges, ye shall be purified.

In the Water of Nile, ye shall be made fertile.

In the Water of the Cave of the Oracle, ye shall prophesy, and speak hidden truth.

In the Water of Ocean, ye shall encounter Neptune, Brahma, and Dagon.

Vapor shall be your veil of water; flowing free, Water is the Tao; frozen, it shall be your Akashic record–ponder all of these.

In Water, receive and reflect upon all that is given unto ye. Neither ask nor deny aught given to ye, for all such is for your education and unfolding. The Waters are that from which ye have emerged; to them ye shall return. In beholding the Water, ye standeth apart; in beholding the Waters, behold your reflected image–for by receiving and reflecting, ye shall behold yourselves.

Ye shall behold the Air, which is a form of Maat, in its ceaseless dance. One must dance lightly, to partner the Air.

Breathe the Air of Pneuma, the life-force within ye. So imperceptible and strong, is this Air that bears the breath of life itself!

Breathe the Air of Prana, the universal force of Being's power– it is your soul-and-body communion with the Universe–it unites invisibly all separate things.

Breathe the Air of Hermes Trismegistus, in all His aspects; Tahuti is my scribe also, and Ibis of the Abyss. In Him is the Sword of Earth perfected.

Dance now the power of Air, as Hurricane, Typhoon, Sirrocco. Dance

the JetStream, become the Monsoon wind and the Tornado. In the Storm Dance, honor the wind in due measure with fire and water.

The Dance of Earth is the dance of Gaia—four seasons and twelve signs. Learn it, it is part of ye.

Learn the physical body. Feed it as it tells ye, rest when it is time. Practice a physical discipline, in whichever form is best suited to your nature. Go within, and feel the nature of the life-energies, the patterns of their flow, and which need balancing.

Find also wherewithal to buy your food and lodging. Work as it need be, neither neglecting the needs of the Kingdom, nor striving after the unnecessary. Work is the most sublime form of Gaia's Dance—one once said "Samsara is Nirvana." He spoke truly.

10/26/75 e.v.

For the past two days, events have flowed in such wise that there wasn't time enough for entry of words, So I'll list the Kingdom's chronology, then proceed with the D of M.

a) Found employment, beginning Monday, 10/27/75. 8:30 a.m. to 5 p.m . . .as Office manager (jack-of-all-trades) for Haines & Company, publishers of metropolitan cross-reference directories. $110. a week to begin . . .not much, but it does have advantages over starvation.

b) Went to a birthday party for the wife of a Magickal comrade[6] this Friday night. Fullsome energies—about half the people there I'd done ritual with at one time or another, and the other half were uninitiates. These latter will remember the party for quite some time, without exactly knowing what it was they experienced. I wore Jasmine (Mike's boa constrictor) around my neck for most

---

6 Kathy C.

of the evening. As soon as I have the money for it, I must get a boa constrictor for the temple. They are the nicest type of snakes I've encountered. "Garter" snakes don't have the same nobility of character...

c) Reality, relationships, self-awareness are in a new simplicity. All the tortuous analyses, seeking, demon-wrestling etc. are no longer necessary. Even writing about it invests it with non-essential complexity. I manifest mostly as my Leo ascendant, Gary S. relates as per his Virgo ascendant, but Dan C. is his Scorpio Sun in manifestation.

Now, shall re-read the material from Thursday, meditate, and return to the pen & paper.

"The Mask of the Dancer" is a true name for this mode of working (so is "Dance of the Mask", for that matter) in that, as a title, it contains the principal meanings of the method.

We use a consciously-directed series of personae, tailored for the present situation, individual, and the needed form of energy. These Masks are the prime working tool for causing change to occur according to Will.

For personal, immediate Magick, the Mask is the instrument for uniting the Centres of the Magickian and the "subject". The change that occurs through the Mask affects both parties; the only difference is that the wearer of the Mask is fully conscious of the changes, and is actually directing them.

For changes at a distance, or general workings of a planetary nature, the Mask can be of a god, angel, demon or whatever appropriate alter ego. A Mask is not a lifeless object, but a living viewpoint of perception, power, and act.

The Mask of Maat, however, is a certain tool that is of another order than the abovementioned Masks. The First Knowledge of Maat is a prerequisite of assuming the other Masks;—the Second Knowledge is the ultimate evolutionary direction that follows the use and mastery of all other Masks of the Dance.

The Dancer is the inner identity of the one who works with the Masks. The Dancer is Hadit, the Hadit-in-motion, the ever-flowing observer of the Cosmos, the Stars, the Masks used by the Stars, and the Masks who believe in themselves. and the Dancer Itself.

The Dancer is the Fool as Harlequin, the Magus as a circus-performer, the Hermit as Warrior. The stage of the Dancer is the edge of between, and he honors his totem, but is not bound by it. His function is to catalyze an individual's self-awareness; he catapults the prisoner of Hod and the Slave of Netzach straight up into the Kingdom of the Crown. At times, all veils are pierced; a non-mind condition obtains, and the individual must be forcibly earthed.

Details of the Dancer's methods will appear in diffuse form throughout this writing. One can best discern their nature by observing it being done to oneself, and by doing it.

This writing is intended for the few. It is the Work of the few to become many, but at this time it is to be by act, not word. This is written so that you may recognize yourselves as priests of Maat, if so ye be. Not all who read these words will find it their Will to use the way of the Dance. The ones who find it suited to their nature may freely adapt it to the terms of their subjective universes.

(The one thing I insist upon—yea, under a warning and curse of an Aeon in the Abyss—is that any who would Dance the Mask must never take themselves seriously. And a penalty of two Aeons in the Abyss for anyone who takes _me_ seriously.)

To continue; Krishna, Pan and Shiva are the Musicians for this Dance. Apollo's music would be unsuitable, in that it doesn't reach back far enough. Destruction of preconcieved notions, cultural conditioning, rigid behavior engrams–this is the first act. The creation of a universe through Love-under-Will then follows; the ever-present factor of Change is then embraced as the Centre of consciousness.

The Music is primal; the Dance, sublime. The Temple instruments are part of the Music as translators; they link the primeval urges–the Elder Gods–to the most subtle and refined aspects of perceptible Being. They are the essence of rhythm, cycle, and Art. The Temple instruments, representing the physical and astral bodies, weave patterns of consistency in the Dance; they are the individualized patterns of the Dance.

The litany of the titles of Maat is drawn from Liber Pennae Praenumbra and the Word of the Dream Master. A brief recapitulation and expansion for those without access to those documents.

"She Who Moves"–In Liber P.P., the prime attribute of Maat is that of balance-in-going. The dynamic balance of the aerlist, cyclist, or skater is a physical equivalent of this image. It's not the static balance of the arch or flying buttress. but the fluid stability of a porpoise or true-aimed arrow.

"The Black Flame" is the cosmic expansion of the quill-pen and the feather. It is Maat percieved as twin of Nuit; Nuit being the stars and Maat the spaces between them. She is not darkness, but a tuned light, a black radiance.

She would be the antiparticle of the photon. The physical analog of Maat is the neutron star, the Black Hole–the alchemical unity of

Nuit and Maat would be akin to the progression of the Black Hole—the astronomical Singularity.

"The Crystal Lotus" refers to the image of the only jewel in the treasure room in the Tower of Heru. It is the receptive aspect of Maat. It doesn't hold, as a chalice; rather, it collects, focuses, and transmits. It is a directional prism—it receives light rather than water, although it can and does function as a channel of the fluidity of the Tao.

"The Black Pearl" is resting in the Centre of the Crystal Lotus. It is a glowing black globe that contains the entire Cosmos, including itself. It is Maat being _experienced_ as the twin of Nuit. Gazing into the Black Pearl, the Dancer may percieve that all things are as Hadit to him—he, the Dancer, thus becomes Nuit/Maat by sharing this encircling consciousness.

The virtues of Truth, Righteousness, and Justice are those traditionally linked with Maat. She _is_ the virtue, in the sense that "virtue" means "strength."

For the Dancer, these virtues are not manifested in the Western tradition; rather, they are more closely akin to the modes of consciousness arrived at via Raja Yoga and Zen. They act freely only from a state of no-mind, or in purity of Love-under-Will. Maat is also a personification of the motion of Love-under-Will, manifest as the breath of the microcosm, prana, and of the macrocosm, prakriti.

Maat is also Maut, the vulture. She is here representing the part of the cycle dealing with decline, death and decay, She projects the energies of Kali—corpses, gore, ghosts, vampires, ghouls, incubi and succubi, trash of the lower astral. All this she eats—absorbs, unites with, transforms into a womb of fertility for the growth of new awareness.

Mother of the Sun–Maat is here as the earth-englobing atmosphere–the environment of Air that Nan needs to live. The Barque of Ra sails this ocean of Air, as also Heru-Ra-Ha is supported as bird-form.

Mate of the Wind–Maut has no vulture-consort. Here is Maat as Gynander. Bisexual <u>and</u> fertile, Maat is as queen and worker-bee. This is not the parthenogenic consciousness of Isis, bul the ultimate androgynous unity of Man. Maat's formula can be expresses as $1+x^n=0$. A bipolar reality is augmented by the progressive unity of the Cosmos. We are falling back toward Centre; the Ylem ingathers.

As Balance and Centre, Maat is the Dancer and Hadit. This is the basic nature of the Mask of Maat–the Dancer at last becomes the Mask, and the Mask becomes the Dancer.

This is the point at which a certain cosmological fact must be emphasized, this time of writing (1975 e.v.) is but witnessing the dawning of the Aeon of Heru. The manifestation of the Aeon of Maat shall not take place until the spiritual majority of the Race of Man shall have achieved the essence of harmony and viewpoint of Love-under-Will. The force, energy and power of the Current of the Aeon of Maat has been used, by our future selves, to assist our present evolutionary crises, precisely as some of us have reinforced our present reality by assisting our past selves to initiate our existential Karma.

All this is needed to be thoroughly earthed in the omnipresent HERE and the on-going NOW. The Dance of the Mask should be done only by those who are at home in their environment. To use the Dance as an "escape" from an unpleasant present existence is to invite disaster. The escapee becomes a Mask, and thus a slave to Choronzon–power will eat you unless you eat it first.

10/27/75 e.v. First day on the new job. Boss is a Pisces-cusp Aries. The Police arrived to inform us that Bill U.'s being charged with breaking & entering–he and three friends were using an abandoned house as a clubhouse, and the owner will probably sue for damages. I Ching: #15 (Modesty) to #39 (Obstruction).

10/29/75 e.v. Tempest in a teapot? No action from the police. Mr. Grant's letter arrived yesterday, following Lu & Randy B.'s visit with the Journal material. Said material is even now resting on the altar, soaking up whatever energies are proper to it.

First reaction to Mr. Grant's letters; who the hell am I, to review his books? Second reaction: You'll not do a fair job, woman, seein' as how you are shamelessly indulging in hero-worship.

Reflections: Why are you trying to put the Chesed-Mask of Dyaus Pitar on one who hasn't invoked it? Answer: Dad escaped through death, Gary S. escaped through Will, and Kenneth G. shall have no need of "escaping" it, for as of now that Mask is banished.

Conclusions: It's not hero-worship; I'm utterly in love with him as a human being. It's similar to being in love with Isaac Asimov, Herman Hesse and Hieronimus Bosch. Enough. Seven of Cups.

11/1/75 e.v. It's not time for the prosaic exegesis. First, put down the essence of the Dance–then, expand and expound when necessary. I call upon my Angel in the name of Nu/Maat, and in the name of Nahada, to guide this writing.

Hail, Tahuti!

THE TREE OF THE DANCE OF THE MASK

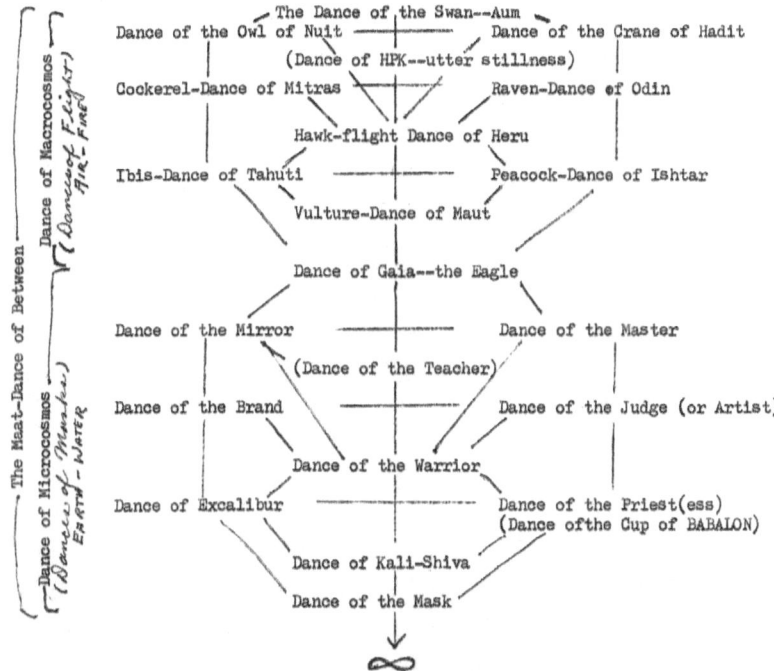

The Dances of Infinity may not be spoken of for they are the Dances of individual consciousnesses. It is within the sanctum of silence that the Dancer must percieve his own Masks.

The sequence of the Dances is obvious, necessary and simple. The Tree of the Dance is not a contrivance, but an unveiling of what is always before the eyes. I who write this did not invent, nor create IPSOS, which is the Name of the Dance. The Dance is a god, and has always existed within the soul of Man. This writing is but to remind you of who you are as Dancer.

My love, you have stepped the Dance from the Beginning. We have danced together, and singly, since the music of the spheres began.

We are ever Shiva and Kali, Dancing out the cycle of birth, death, rebirth.

We have Danced on and off the Wheel of Karma, Destiny and Change. Recall, beloved, the Dance of Alchemy that unites us forever–though we might have not met in this lifespan, yet we have mated in the Dance of Life. We all have mated each to each, in the union of air, water, earth, and fire.

We have eaten, all, the bodies of each other. The Dance of Maut teaches us that we, made of star-stuff, are the food for each other. Our sun-born molecules have danced in other bodies, and will be the manifestation-clay from which the Children of Maat will take their forms.

Let us Dance again, therefore, in full consciousness of steps, and rhythm, and motion. To me your Masks are beautiful and true. The dances of flight are the Dance of the Feather; the dances of masks are the Dance of the Black Flame. Each may be echoed and ritually danced by the physical body. Only you can dance your own dance. It will be true if the following conditions are met:

Consideration of the essence of the particular Dance–as bird, god, or mask–what is the inner nature of the entity? One must not dance in ignorance.

One must dance from Centre, or Chi, or the onGOing balance of Maat. The dance must be what it is–grace–in all meanings of the word.

One must be free enough to flow with the Tao–the ultimate Way of the Dance. A Dancer is ever guided by Tao–attempting to move contrary to it will have the Dancer stumble and fall to the Abyss. Therein, only the Dances of Harpocrat and the Teacher will restore the balance of Maat.

A Dancer is <u>always</u> in danger of falling. The terror of the Abyss is a tang, a spice, a wine of excellence. After a fall (and you will have many at first), assume the stillness and total receptivity of Harpocrat, and invoke your Angel to dance as Teacher. You will have profited from your fall.

How is Magick done from a Dance?

The High Magick of the Dance is the change wrought within your own consciousness. As you become conscious of your inner Masks, you mardfest them perfectly in the Outer.

By being one's Self,—by dancing the true Dance—you 'drop the veils' for others, awakening them to their masks and dances. The Dances of Flight are your sources of power—the Dances of the Masks are your tools or instruments that cause change to occur according to will.

The "Low Magick" of the Dance consists of removing obstacles to the "miraculous". The flow of the Tao invariably brings about the timely changes that <u>you</u> are willing—if you are united with the Tao. For you must <u>be</u> the Tao. Maat is the Tao. A true Dancer finds the Outer responding to his will without need of any especial effort on his part. The rites of Maat and the Dance of the Mask work on the Inner, which is all that is necessary.

Whew! <u>Something</u> happened right! Really—I didn't exactly believe it when I found myself declaring that a system would manifest. I'm still schizophrenic enough to manifest in various states of consciousness. A Hallowe'en party at Riddle Crest last night saw me, as yin/yang, and Lu, as Jesus, sitting in Gary S.'s room and playing energy-tango with each other and whoever happened in.

Mark was especially powerful. When we three had ended our meshing, the wind suddenly gusted heavy raindrops against the window. Wouldn't have seemed significant, except that it wasn't raining last night. Lovely!

Lu is constantly summoning elementals. Randy B.–hmm. He left and returned after participating in a Sabat across the river in Kentucky. Doesn't one have to be an initiated witch to participate? Hard to see how not. He's awfully partial to formal ceremony.

11/3/75 e.v. I showed the schema of the Double Tree of the Dance of the Mask to Gary S., Dan C. & Allen H. Dan C. & Gary S. have been using it already, in an unorganized way, and it's been working. So.

–The Dance of the Swan–OM

The Dance of the Swan is the flawless glide upon the Great Ocean. The music is the water sounding endlessly the supreme chord of being, OM. Eternal motion upon eternal being–how may we dance this dance?

We have reached the consciousness of the All through the three gods.

As Brahma, we created our Mask of self; unconscious gods, we drew ourselves into existence at the Beginning, and create ourselves anew each lifespan from our sigils enscribed in the Akasha. We created ourselves from our Names, and the names we have etched eternally into the spiritual Space, which is Maat.

We are the artists who create the Masks in which we dance. In coming to realize our self-responsibility, we see that all changes are possible for us. We are what we will to be, and we will all things according to our self-created nature. Thus Karma is not the blind

operational law, but the chosen framework in which we work. It is the stage for our dance.

Nothing happens to us by chance; all events are willed, either directly, or as logical, forseen consequences of our creations. It is that we forget, that generates the lovely and terrifying Mask of Maya. It is by becoming conscious that we are Brahma, that we regain the divine vision of the Dancer.

We must profoundly realize the nature of our creative godhood in order to permanently invoke Brahma. We know, fully then, that every man and woman is a Star.

As Vishnu, we preserve our creations, and continue in the Dance. The will of endurance through eternity can be realized in its ultimate strength only if we see the self-responsibility of utter conmmittment to evolution. To stop is to stumble, and mar the grace of the Dance.

The inner strength of this will to preserve, as Vishnu, arises from the avatar-form of Krishna, who is the love of the All. We see our godhood as an integral part of the Dance of Existence. As Krishna, we assume sexual duality, becoming two that may come to equal zero. We are the holy Gynander, two-in-one, the union of Krishna-Radha as one being.

As Shiva, we are the Lord of the Dance. We beat out destruction in the rhythm of the drum; we step the dance of fire. We awaken to our godhood as Shiva as the Eye of Shiva opens to percieve and destroy all Masks. We have crafted our Masks, and danced in them as masters, Now, in the vision of No Difference, we destroy these Masks to begin anew in the Dance of the Swan—OM. Shiva is Lord of the Dance because he is end and beginning of the endless cycle of coming-to-be and coming-to-naught.

11/4/75 e.v. We have created, preserved and destroyed our pseudo-Mask of social conditioning and personal history. You, my love, have perfected your Art to the excellence of becoming any god completely. It is within your abilities to invoke the Three, and to dance Their dances. Behold the old Mask of self, and see how it was built—not by Will, but by circumstance. This destroy—then craft again new Masks, dance them, and destroy them also. This do and repeat until the Masks create themselves (it will so appear), dance themselves, and destroy themselves. There will come the point where neither Mask nor Dance may be percieved—and at this point begins the Dance of the Swan—OM.

Erom the breathless self-awareness of Brahman, or unmodified Being, the pure radiance of becoming streams forth. The primal emergence of the particular from the undifferentiated begins. The Swan glides upon the Ocean of Being . .

11/5/75 e.v. The flowing waters of the Tao are endless; all things change and evolve into ongoing progressions of development. The Swan never swims in the same place twice; yet as all waters are one, it matters not to the Swan where he swims.

The Mask of the Swan is the essential state of Samadhi wherein the realizations of mystical vision begin their descent of the Tree toward ultimate manifestation in the Kingdom. The Dance of the Swan—OM has as its Magickal end the transformation of the Serpent into the Lightning-flash.

This dance is the Kether of the Dance of the Feather, and the first step in the Dance of Maat, It presupposes that the Dancer has reached the becoming of No-thing by his own methods. We see from this that the Dance of the Mask is a Magickal system rather than a Mystical discipline (although these are but the yin and yang of a

single reality). The Dance of the Swan is the manifestation of the Will-to-change, to employ one's entire Self in the Work of evolution, in the Work of racial self-awareness of Starhood.

Man always treads the brink of the Abyss. At the time of this writing, world events are intensifying the Kether-pressure toward racial mutation. We have the physical means for utter self-annihilation, or for the harmonious bringing-to-consciousness the Race Mind, or Mansoul.

The Dance of the Swan–OM, when danced by an individual toward its intended individual end, automatically generates tremendous power directed toward furthering the unfolding of the Mansoul. Dancer, remember–you dance not only for yourself, but for all of us. As you glide in your patterns toward the eventual total manifestation of your True Will, you further the growth of the race. You, O Dancer in the Swan-Mask, become the ombudsman for the whole of humanity.

11/6/75 e.v. The Dance of the Crane of Hadit.

Change becomes force. The lightning-flash begins its descent. Mass is moving at the speed of light squared, and exists as pure energy. The dance of this energy is masked as the Crane. The utter force of onrushing power is danced in the slow dignity and balanced pauses of the Crane–a paradox. What is the inner link of the Dancer and Mask; how can the Mask be true to its own nature and to the nature of the Dancer?

Utter velocity and onrushing power, without a reference, is stillness. In its beginnings, this power is all; there is nothing that is apart from it, masks itself as a bird balanced on one leg, or striding slowly along the shoreline shallows of the Great Ocean.

The one-legged stance of the Crane is a glyph of the awareness-point that is Hadit. The habitat of the Crane is the shallows, a meeting of water, land, sky, and sun. This elemental balance is centered in the Crane as Hadit.

Had is the seed, the sperm, the concentrated genetic essence of the Evolving Universe. He is the primal energy, the irresistably potent siring of all that is to be. It pierces the egg of Naught/Nuit, and fertilizes NO-THING-NESS with the beginnings of manifestation.

Beloved, if you are able to dance truly as the Crane, then the remainder of the Dance of Maat shall flow easily and surely for you. The simple, slow movements of the Crane do not appear difficult–but this is an ordeal.

You are the Cosmic Force–irresistible, omnipotent, supreme. There is no one to present you with obstacles. You are the sole creative god in your Universe, and all your sown seeds will eventually, inevitably grow and ripen to the fullness of their nature. Yet–the Mask of your Dance requires you to manifest yourself in stately dignity, self-contained and balanced, alone on the border of the elements.

You have seen your visions, and have begun the transformation of them into creation, preservation, and destruction. Mighty events are preparing for birth, yet you maintain the detached demeanor of the Crane. A symbol of Wisdom, the Crane-mask educates us in the value of discretion and gentility. The purpose of this Dance is to begin the awareness of yet another value of Masks. These are protective veils, needed for your dealings wth the uninitiate. Total power is perceived as a natural dignity and reservation; without this Crane-Mask, you would cause madness in the beholder.

11/7/75/ e.v. It is well to establish your balance at the beginnings.

In the pure and fathering force of the dance of the Crane/Hadit, the ongoing balance of Maat is achieved and continued. This initial poise shall be maintained through all the Dances, if it is well-taken in this Dance.

The realities of the uprushing vision of the mystic are somewhat different from the downflashing Will of the Magickian. Functions of mind, relationships, strength, judgement and virtues of practicality are transcended and bypassed during the ascent. There is no need for them while the essential Self is beholding itself. (typist's note- this phrase is unTrue in that it implies an impossibility. It should read "while Awareness is being Aware" or something similar. Concepts and words in this case are all unTrue.)

However, when the light of vision is changed to the fire of Will, each of the abovementioned functions must be employed perfectly. The Dances are to teach the proper employment of the tools/faculties of the Magickian.

This first tool—the Magickal power of the Cosmos, is the one calling for the greatest restraint, control, and Art. Thus the ordeal of the dance of the Crane/Hadit is perhaps the most fundamentally important of all the dances. The wisdom of the Crane guides the innocence of the Swan into its proper direction.

The Science of this Dance is the discovery of the wise and correct way of wielding power; the Art of it is in learning how to Dance with dignity, but without pomposity. The Crane thinks not of its mirrored grace—if it paid heed to it, it would be graceless. This dance must be learned in order to be forgotten.

It is learned with the conscious mind, then dropped into the boundless ocean of the Subconscious. The Crane-dancer's perception

of the Subconscious differs from that of those who have not yet remembered Dancing. By dancing the shoreline, the Dancer has access, at Will, to the oceanic Subconscious. His feet treading foam, he is ever in contact with the ocean, and aware of its movements—at will, he darts his head under and percieves directly—at other times, the lap of the waves around his feet is sufficient to inform him of the general trends of his veiled awareness.

To those who do not Dance, this Ocean is a mystery—the light of air does not penetrate the surface, but is reflected and scattered by the many ripples of the waves. They see only a vast and heaving surface before them, and are often terrified of the unknown beings that may lurk in the depths.

It is in the Wisdom of Power—in the Dance of the Crane/Hadit, that the total Self is percieved for action's sake. The mystic beheld Self for the sake of beholding—the magickian-dancer sees for the sake of doing. In confidence, and grace, then dance—at the point where the Dance of the Crane/Hadit can be danced without thinking about it, can be danced by nature, then begins the Dance of the Owl/Nuit.

The Dance of the Owl of Nuit

Force takes Form. This first-form is vague, nocturnal, sensed rather than seen. The owl glides silently, close to the moonlit meadow's earth. A wing-pause, swoop, and the shrill cry of prey dying pierces the night.

Owl, bird of night, of Nuit! It is a dance of star-light, of space-dark. It is the coming-to-be of the Pairs of Opposites. Had generates Nu, then impregnates Her. Maat, shadow of NU, is pregnant by the Shadow of HAD.

Dance the Owl/Nuit! Here definition and delineation begins—but

silently, shadowy, dark! As the Swan dances to the sound of OM, and as the Crane dances to the sound of crashing breakers, now the Owl dances her long, low, gliding dance to the rushing of air through branches and brush. To the murmur and keening, the Owl-dancer adds her eerie "Who?", guestioning all inner identities, even her own.

She Dances the beginnings of form, the beginning of wrought Art, by bearing forth the idea of shape and mass. Her Dance is massive, yet airborne–she is solidity in the immanence of darkness. She substantiates Force by being Form–she clothes the idea, the direction, with thing-ness.

As Nuit, the Dancer is Naught–as the Owl, she is Something. This Dance unites the realities of thing and No-thing, imparting a permanent awareness in the Dancer of the nature of the Maya she is becoming. With the beginnings of form come the beginnings of the necessary detachment from them. The Owl is distinct from, and generated by, the Crane–force begets form, unites with it, and the creation of the Universe begins.

In this Dance, you gain the understanding of the materials and media of your Art, because you are the primal matter, fertilized by primal energy. <u>You</u> are your materials, self-created from the energy of change. It is from this matter that you fashion all your Masks.

At the beginning, all Masks are possible–the Owl is not concerned with particulars, or choice–she is simply a gliding form in the night. You Dance, beloved, so that you may know your potential. You know already that you are the One, the That; now, you dance the knowledge of the manifold infinity of all possible manifestation.

As Nuit, you are the Cosmos surrounding a single, infinitesimal point of awareness. You are vast, unique–an apparent sphere of

expanding matter and space.

11/9/75 e.v. (Last night with Dan C.–have decided that it is now one of those times when Love-under-Will must manifest as benign neglect. I remove my presence from Gary S.'s stage–he has to dance a solo for now.) To continue–

This dark predator is the great Mother–the anonymous womb from which All things come and to which they return. She is terrifying; her mask is the gate of birth and death. The seed of identity grows within you; dancing the Mask of the Owl/Nuit, you begin and foster the gestation of your outer self, your earthed Mask-Dance.

The self you had believed true before your vision of Unity was made from circumstance; the self-Mask you are beginning in the Dance of the Owl/Nuit will be wrought in your mastery and Art.

Here, dance the awareness of the nature of your substance. On all planes, your various bodies are of the same stuff that the Cosmos is made of. The vision of Unity must be kept in the awareness throughout all the Dances. The beginnings of individuality must not be tainted with the illusion of separation. All Stars share the same nature of motion and light, even though the individual manifestations are unique.

To Dance the Mask of the Owl/Nuit, glide softly in the dark, swooping low to the music of the air. Your great eyes percieve shapes in the night, forms of the development of the Cosmos and your Masks–You fly toward the Dance of the Ravens of Odin, but pause in the midst of the Abyss.

The Dance of Heru-Pa-Kraath

You move not. You are curled within the womb, growing. Your

awareness divides—you are the maskless Observer, and the myriad masks-in-becoming that you will use.

In the three dances that have gone before, you were dancing in the Unity; as Heru-Pa-Kraath, you undertake the experience of duality—not helplessly, as it happened when you were uninitiate, but Willingly, Lovingly. The awareness of duality is ever balanced with the awareness of Unity—both are necessary for the End of the Dance. This balance is the essence of Maat, and the motive power for her continuing GO-ing.

We need duality in the Dance. In bringing about the unfolding of Evolution, we must gather in those other parts of Ourself that have become their Masks instead of dancing them.

Stillness is vital at this point; it is the undertaking of knowledge, and the letting-go of primal innocence. We pass from the purity of the Mystic Vision into the experiential realm of the Magickal Consciousness. The dances of the Swan, the Crane, and the Owl were masked as veils—the acts of change, movement, and growth are universal acts, Cosmic deeds. The abstract and measureless nature of these dances is necessarily masked by reserve and distance.

The act of splitting the consciousness is perhaps the most dangerous of the Dances. You are already in the between-ness of the Abyss. You move not, but are not at rest in terms of GO-ing.

You divide yourself perfectly, and in balance proceed to the next dance. This division must be precise, or one of two disasters will manifest to keep you in the Abyss. If Unity awareness has the greater share of awareness, you will be unable to communicate with the "other" Dancers and audience. You will become what is, in effect, catatonic.

On the other hand, should duality prevail, you will manifest several of your masks at the same time, as a schizophrenic. This will not affect your true Self, of course, but you will have immobilized an important source of positive planetary evolution–yourself.

The division will be true if there is no "outside" interference. It is during the Dance of Heru-Pa-Kraath that the Dancer's circle must be scribed. As soon as you are able to be aware of the existence of "other" consciousnesses, there is a need for a double protective veil. The "others" must not have contact with the naked power that you are, and you must not have contact with their confusion.

It is in this dance that you declare your orbit. Others may join you in love-under-will, dancing as individuals in the unity of the Dance and in Cosmic Unity, but from this point onward, you will make no effort to affirm the Unity. If your co-Dancers are the masters they should be, there is no need to speak of Unity; if the others are in the midst of ordeal, or have lost balance somehow, there is no use in speaking, for they will be unable to hear. Thus, in utter stillness, the Dance of HPK consists of the gesture of thumb-to-lips, and the music is the white noise of the Abyss.

Now, having become the primal Dancer and the cosmic observer/audience, you proceed to the Dance of the Ravens of Odin...

(Typist's note–the development of the Dance of the Mask pauses here; there is and was a definite promise of continuance at a later time, when sufficient experience will justify the writing of aught concerning the Ruach.)

11/11/75 e.v. John U. left for Houston this morning–work awaits. It's a relief... Dan C. was over last night, post-mortem-ing Saturday's trip. (Typist's note–11/8/75 e.v., there was a partaking of purple microdot

LSD, followed by a walk to a waterfall in a nearby park, about ¼ mile from the Riddle Crest House. It consisted of absolutely "hitting bottom", becoming overwhelmed by the Sorrow of Existence, bitter tears, despair, etc.)

It was, in a way, the Vision or Trance of Sorrow. The upshot of it is that I'm not going to contact Gary S. If and when he so wishes, he knows where I live.

I feel loneliness, but this cannot be allowed to interfere with the work. Perhaps it's just the Scorpio Sun, perhaps the glandular and psychological concomitant of being a woman. But even so, I am the gynander also–I fly free now, mateless as Maut. This state of existence is distasteful to my natural consciousness, but as a Magickian, I appreciate its value.

When Gary S. "liberated" me from my marriage, he did lead me to believe that it was to join him in a working-together. Now, my very presence irritates him. So, in terms of love-under-will, the greatest possible service I can render is to leave him alone.

If I am to be a Magickian and not just a vessel-functioning Scarlet Woman, I must learn to operate alone. So, for as long as it lasts, I declare this time a spiritual retreat–there's work afoot–I must attend to the Cincinnati nexus by myself, and be a mother, and wage-earner, and painter, and writer, and citizen, and Magickian, and human. There are times when the flesh curses the spirit–this incarnation must have been assumed in full foreknowledge, but right now I'm wondering where or how I managed the strength to undertake it. The above drivel is a disgusting exercise in self-pity. I promised Lu and Randy B. an intro to the thing on the Forgotten Ones. This is as good a time as any.

Sooner or later, the magickian must deal with the Forgotten Ones. They are sometimes called the Elder Gods, the Id, the archtypal forces of the subconscious or any term that denotes the naked force of survival and self-destruction inherent in Man.

These are the forces that your guru, priest, or spiritual advisor warned you about. They truly are the greatest danger that you will have to face in the Kingdom; they can end your life, or your sanity, or your contact with your higher self. They are known as Satan by the Christians.

The Forgotten Ones are also your source of personal magickal power. It is imperative that you meet them at some point in your development. The "higher" you reach to the gods of light, the "lower" you must plunge to the gods of darkness. To ignore their presence is to guarantee their eventual dominion over your will.

The you that stands central to the light and dark must meet them as a warrior-priest–to challenge, combat, embrace, eat and be eaten by them. You may fail in the process or you may succeed; in any event, the following writing may be of some help.

So much for the intro.

11/13/75 e.v. Letter from Mr. Grant today in which he points out the true nature of this record–a mirror–yes! It's been reflecting too much of one plane lately–ah, if ye be a mirror, little book, ye are also as much a person as I am. In fact you are me, or we're varied aspects of the same thing–or the no-thing.

Accurate record–for the past half-year, Gary S. and I have been at odds. The alchemy was flawed by persistent illusion and it's just this week that the flow seems returned. He exhibits wounds and bruises

on his spirit–did I inflict them, as he claims, or are they self-inflicted and done through me as his instrument?

He says that without his intervention, I never've gotten a divorce. True. He initiated me into magick, to Thelema, to warriorhood–all of it. And it worked so well, he can't handle the results.

He says–"manifest your real self." Fine. All masks are dropped, the energies flow through, and he recoils from the "pea-green aura" he sees. So for the present, for the sake of the Dance, I shall assume the Mask of the Warrior. Stoic, undemonstrative, definitely restricted–and a huge jest.

Not on him, but in itself. There's no difference between the Warrior and any other Mask. I never realized my mother's wisdom until now–love under will may manifest in the assumption of a veil or Mask that isn't particularly congenial to the real manifestation-self, for the sake of another's development. She never used these words, but this was the essence of her gift of transmitted wisdom.

Lu was over; we discussed the journal, Liber P.P. 's appearing in it. Maybe I should contact Tom Knight about the copyright process so we can keep things flowing on both sides of the Atlantic.

Mr. Grant's words of the non-existence of an entity behind the mask–whew! "I" remember being Awareness, and total unconsciousness (no mean feat)–through Raja Yoga the nature of no-thing-ness was accepted. But to act without being–can there be action without an actor? Is act–pure act–possible without some do-er?

Of course–Prakriti unfolds herself; the Tao is. Dear book–can I achieve this not-ness and sustain it? Or can it achieve itself and sustain itself? It already does.

To write, to speak, or paint, dance–whatever–it does itself, and the more purely, the better. For the vision of the "I-less"!

Who wears the name NAHADA?

No-one.

What does the name NAHADA?

Purely manifests in Malkuth the flow of the Double Current.

In what way?

The name is the Dancer. The name is the shadow of Hadit. The name is the reflection of no-thing-ness, a sound-symbol of nothing, that wields the absolute power of the All.

Art thou NAHADA?

I manifest the name, and the name manifests NO-THING-NESS. I am the symbol of the name, as well as the name being my symbol. If I am Hadit, the name is my shadow; if the name is Hadit, I am its shadow. I am the shadow of my name.

Lu and I have generated a tremendously strong sexual current–we've agreed to keep it unearthed and direct it into the Journal, into people, and back into the 93. He's Magickian enough to handle it, and so am I.

11/14/75 e.v.

Finished the letter to K.G. tonight–oy, how things can complicate themselves!

Spoke to Lu in re. the copyright nonsense, which provided the outer vehicle–the inner energy-flow, however, gives pause. Time to expand and reflect–

Last night, we began by discussing the Journal, <u>Liber P.P.</u>, etc. There was a good mellow session with the kids, and then the ritual happened, as follows:

We moved a small table in front of the full-length mirror in the bedroom, upon which was placed Mr. Grant's letter, the page of OTO information, a candle, and the Maat-feather from the temple.

I banished the room and Lu energized the mirror. I had my weapons there, and used the sword for this. We intoned the Law, then proceeded to unite with our mirror-selves.

Not entirely sure of the precise sequence here, but–we drew down energies and engendered our own "personal" power in its active mode. Lu assumed the Spare posture of covering the mouth and nose. I stood at right angles to him and drew together himself and his mirror-image.

I poured wine into the chalice–he drank from it, as did I, then I upended it and let the last few drops fall free. He accepted it, upside-down; taking the wand, I pressed it into the chalice from below. We then traded weapons and he did the same. He retained the wand, and I took up the sword.

He moved me in front of him, both of us facing the mirror. Grasping the wand by either end, he held it horizontally before me. I held the sword vertically, forming a Tau with the wand, then elevated the sword further until there was formed a cabalistic cross.

Standing thus, we felt the beginnings of an intense sexual current,

and we maintained visual contact via the mirror. A tremendous charge quickly grew, and was sent to the birthing of the Journal.

After ending the ritual, we sat down and discussed the mutual will about what to do with this newly-engendered energy-connection. It will not be earthed in physical form (at least for now), but used Magickally for the work at hand.

We also decided to channel it to Linda G. and Gary S., and to maintain the veil of silence unless asked directly about it.

My only concern this evening was in speaking to him on the phone. Lu manifests enthusiasm–but I hope not to the point of bypassing discretion. I hope also that he doesn't suffer any skewing of direction because of these energies. Time will tell.

11/15/75 e.v.

Well, Current flows on. Allen H. stopped over to collect the $8 I owed him for purple haze sacrament (LSD) and I wound up going with him to the science fiction club meeting. We there encountered Friendly (real name, John G.). Friendly and I fell into conversing and decided to go to his and Allen H.'s place to see if I could banish the magnetic elementals from his tape deck and also track back to his first major imbalance.

Friendly has much power and sensitivity–part of what put him in psychiatric care was having the power-experiences without anyone around to explain and show him how to use it.

Anyhow, in generating the polarized charge between us, I let it slide from the second chakra to the first and then up to the fourth–Yesod, Malkuth, Tiphereth. I manifested the Mother for him, and there was a point where he was being quite solar. He repeatedly "froze"

and said he experienced fear. Gave him a heavy dose of Maat-Gaia.

When Allen H. arrived, the energies got a bit ragged, and he (Allen H.) wound up in a capsule of contradictions. It's his problem.

The ghost that I'd felt in their house was banished and dissolved in the midst of all this.

11/16/75 e.v.

Allen H. and Friendly just left. I had forgotten my paycheck at their place, so they obligingly returned it, ate supper here, and we got into the usual discussion. I finished the rough draft of the "letter" for the Journal and they read it. We did ritual, wherein Friendly accepted the wand and Allen H. is al.so committed as teacher. This'll do several things–Friendly will become consciously the Magickian that he is. Allen H. will have to earth his energies in the teaching and there will be one more worker thereby.

11/17/75 e.v.

Casey was over, bought a dime's worth of trip grass from him, very fine, timed stuff. As it's been going all week long–we genereted an extraordinarily strong charge, and he handled it masterfully.

As these sexual charges grow more frequent they're intensifying, too. The people that it's generated with have more than enough for their own projects–plus many portals are opened between us, plus they each add another quantum of energy to the charge accumulating within me.

What am I supposed to do with this ever-growing charge, I wonder? It doesn't seem correct to channel it into VIII°, and no-one's appeared for higher workings yet . It could be this is building up for Gary S., or something totally unexpected. Now is fine, here is fine, and I'm

really not too concerned—just enjoying it all. So, back to the Dance of the Ravens of Odin?

In being twinned, you begin the dance of yin and yang, light and darkness—the dance of duality and the pairs-of-opposites. Your creative aspect spins out a positive force, your destructive aspect (for judgement destroys creation) spins out a negative attraction; in this Dance, therefore, the Laws of the Cosmos are decreed, spun out of the very fabric of the Dance.

By the twin aspects, you determine the necessary limits of time and space in which all Dances hence shall be structured. You Dance to the Watchtowers of the Universe, decree their boundaries and discipline the measures of the Dance. Art is the Tao's selection among possibles of the inevitable. Any more, or any less, would mar the balance and exactness of the Dance's effect.

For here, in the Dance of the Ravens, we first begin to use <u>effect</u> as a factor in shaping the cause. Audience feedback is possible in this dance for the first time, since it is in this Dance that the audience of the judge is created. In Dancing your own responses to your actions, you may know precisely what the responses will be in the macroaudience.

You are here to Dance the craftsmanship of Mask-spinning, to forge the proper personae best suited to the nature of your Dancing in the Kingdom. It is here also that you determine your ritual forms for the total Dance of the Mask as done within your temple in the Kingdom.

To speak of the practicalities of the actual Dance done with the physical body is proper unto the Dance of the Ravens of Odin.

The dance-form is simple—the body moves to the musick, as it will—

but the energies of the Dance are centered in the hands and face. The essence of the Mask to be danced is expressed in the movement of the hands–universal gesture–language will develop of its own accord, so long as there are no obstructions or embarrassments to hinder the free flow of the movements.

The widespread availability of recordings will assist in the selection of the music best suited to your own Dances. As a general indication or suggestion as to the nature of the most effective music, there is included here a selection of some types that have proven effective. The actual selection is entirely up to the choice of the individual Dancer, since taste plays a large part in the creation of effective tools.

11/18/75 e.v.

Eclipse and full moon (has to be full, stupid!). Open house at school, kids are doing well–Bill U. outstanding, Julie U. a bit forgetful.

This current period of sexual abstinence is effecting certain consciousness-changes. I'm not particularly rutting (as was standard in the past), but I can evoke intense desire at will, control it completely, arouse desire intensely in others, and transmute it to higher-chakra charges. It's still growing. I imagine there's a burn-out point, but I haven't reached it yet.

Casey got into deep eye-contact and about got knocked on his arse when I removed the Mask. He actually was propelled backward physically. Well, he's of age.

11/19/76

Again Casey showed up here. The energy working ever more intensely and subtly, and he makes no attempt to earth it. Fantastic!

DANCE OF THE SWAN
Ravi Shankar
Paul Horne–Inside 1&2

DANCE OF THE OWL
Tchaikovski–Pathetique
Buffy St. Marie-God is Alive

DANCE OF THE CRANE
Sibelius–Finlandia
Mahavishnu–Apocalypse

(DANCE OF HPK)
(Silence or White Noise)

DANCE OF THE COCKEREL
Wagner–Die Valkyrie
Hendrix/Trauer

DANCE OF THE HAWK
W.A. Mozart
Moody Blues

DANCE OF THE RAVENS
J.S. Bach
Loggins & Messina

DANCE OF THE IBIS
Stravinsky
Tom Paxton

DANCE OF THE VULTURE
Claude Debussy
David Bowie

DANCE OF THE PEACOCK
Ravel–Bolero
Jefferson Starship

DANCE OF THE EAGLE
Beethoven–Eroica
Walter Horton

DANCE OF THE MIRROR
Rimshy-Korsakov-Scheherezade
Gershwin–Rhapsody in Blue

(DANCE OF THE TEACHER)
(White noise or silence)

DANCE OF THE MASTER
Gregorian Te Deum
Flamenco by Montoya

DANCE OF THE BRAND
Chopin–Revolutionary Etude
Collins–Marat/Sade

DANCE OF THE WARRIOR
American Indian Chant
Crosby/Stills–Wooden Ships

DANCE OF THE JUDGE
Grofé–Grand Canyon Suite
Bob Dylan

DANCE OF EXCALIBUR
Paganini
Emerson, Lake, Palmer

DANCE OF SHIVA-KALI
Moussorgsky–Night on Bare Mountain
Rolling Stones

DANCE OF CUP OF BABALON
Carmen–Habanera
Gracie Slick–White Rabbit

DANCE OF THE MASK
Tchaikovski–Nutcracker
Spontaneous "jams"–street music

I suppose circumstances veiled some of his positive attributes before. I trust him because he's capable of anything, from sacrificing his life–to sacrificing mine. I have to trust him utterly, or not work with him at all. Keeping a guard up only siphons off energy, and weakens the charge.

I would like to know why this charge is being built now–I'm acutely conscious of it at all times.

Even though Nu completely encompasses Had, She never touches Him. The unity is of the totality of the situation...for Nu and Had, there are no other entities. They, together, comprise the totality of their system.

And so "I", as Had, am always alone, and ever united with all else. Another individual is Nu–all else is Nu. Self-Other. Dualism of perceptions. Everything below the Abyss is structured on duality. On to the Dance.

The practical point of the Dance of the Ravens is duality. This is best danced with a partner though it is equally valid for the individual to clone himself and move about the common Centre. The Dance develops from simplicity to complexity–which is not to equate complexity with difficulty; mastery grows also.

11/20/75

A thought–is someone actually going to wade through and read this verbiage, or will it simply be weighed on a scale and rated according to poundage? For me, being required to keep a Magickal Record is akin to confining a fox in a henhouse.

Lu just phoned with an invitation to a party at Randy B.'s Saturday night. I'll go–a little relaxation wouldn't hurt. He was also quoting a

few comments from a new book by Regardie–good grief!–the man sounds like a walking pain in the arse!

It was in reference to K.Grant's writings on the nature of Aiwaz, and what I. Regardie terms "revisionism." Sounds like old-time Marxist jargon. How can anyone claim to be an "authority" in the field of Magick, as I. Regardie apparently does, and still manifest such egotism? With the scarcity of paper and the ecological situation, it seems wasteful that he should see print. Enough.

Schizophrenic day–weather began sunny, then galloping stormclouds, heavy rain, glorious sunset. Cold front moving in. Energies were likewise schizy–or manic-depressive, really. From intense but unfocused excitement and elation to utterly dark doomings. Phoned Dan C. on lunch hour and was informed I'm dancing Binah a bit excessively, in the Dark Mother aspect. Eh. Think I'll do up a bit of smoke dope at this point and continue.

Hmm. I still owe Casey $10 for the bag. Not bad stuff–it hits Yesod, opens the astral. He was saying that I should transcend methodology (in. re. certain second chakra flow-workings) and he's right. Beginners tend to exaggerate.

Contemplating Gary S.. He's more or less severed communications on Malkuth. Strange. He was Hierophant for me–introduced me to Therion's writings, helped free me from the marriage (by leading me to believe we were to work together on a live-in basis), worked with me alchemically and, in short, brought me to where I am now.

Then, he declared that I was vamping his energies, that he didn't care about me, that I should leave him alone. Naturally, this was a bit of a shock. He now says that he's surviving only, doesn't do ritual, or many other practices (yoga, etc.) and is standing still while

everyone else is moving ahead rapidly.

He's also decided that he's not ready for the O.T.O.–Damn! And there's nothing I can do for him. Perhaps this charge that's been accumulating is for him. OK VIII° and invocation of Kali.

Later–the working used up most of the high–also, each individual who assisted in building the charge was linked into–and only part of it released itself to Gary S.

It seems some subconscious "woman scorned" on my part has been retarding his course. No more of that. We are one–always have been, always will be. I keep getting the feeling that his Berserker will manifest toward me soon–that it's a mandatory step in the Dance. Hope there's some control somewhere.

11/21/75 e.v.

At present I'm acutely aware of a constricting band around my throat. There's an indentation on the skin that corresponds with the sensation. Collar's loose, nothing physical causing it.

It has the feel of some sort of metal collar or necklace . . .it's thin, maybe 1/8 to 1/4 inch wide, like heavy silver. Large elongated oval hanging from the front of it. I'm stepping outside astrally so I can see it. Enameled red, white, silver, design difficult to resolve. Keeper of the flame.

So. A flame in a chalice, flanked by a yonilignam in reverse, and a sword. Underneath a stylized eye, or bull–both I think.

Link to Mithras via the bull–also Apis. The yonilignam is symhol of Magickal hermaphroditism, the sword is warriorhood. Fire and chalice–an element symbol (direct) of fire is above a chalice, symbol

(indirect) of water. (Second chakra's activated now. Hmm.)

What burns is the blood of the Saints in the Cup of BABALON. The Graal is fire-power as heat and light.

I AM BABALON.

I give so that I may take. I take so I may give.

The Bull Beast is caught through cunning, not innocence. He is led to the altar of ceremony well-fatted on the energy of Earth that I have given. He is drained of his fire-blood, into the Cup of BABALON, yea to the final drop.

The Beast must bleed thus freely of his own Will–I can but slash the vein–for none may bleed for another, nor cause him to give up his blood.

This Sacrament now freely given, with the Cup engenders Alchemy–the three fires combine within, the blood ignites! Thus–lives and blood and love and seed, free-given do (within the Cup of BABALON) become the beacon-light of the Star. His blood, I take; His light I give to Him.

This be the Word of the Working, wherein the Sacrament of Perceptions be taken.

From Kether do thou proceed, upward and down. The Tree Below (O Dance of the Feather) is the coming-to-be of the divers Masks of the Kingdom Manifest. The Tree Above (O Dance of the Air) is the coming-to-awareness of the divers Dances of the shadow of Hadit.

Consciously, to polarize the forces of the Working, do thou combine the Sephorith as pairs of opposites. The Air's Yesod is the pole of the Feather's Chokmah.

Work thus within yourself, or with another.

The forces of the working are to be given to the Cup of BABALON. The aim is to dance the Mask of the Hermit. The force will join the power of the Double Current with the power of the personal charges.

The Working will cause change according to Will by opening further the receptive channels of the Magickian(s), and thus increase the volume of useful energy available.

(The 93 Current is, among other things, a magickal rapport between those who are living the Law of Thelema. Its aim is in the growth of a consensus of living humans that Do what thou wilt <u>shall</u> be the whole of the Law. It is a world culture-pattern that shapes the value-system to the "type" of the Crowned and Conquering Child.)

Again, the inrushing forces will be far greater than what thou hast dealt with.

Craft ye a pantacle; the symbols given shall be scribed thereon in colour—as seen in the vision. The sensation of the collar about the throat will be signal to earth by holding the pantacle and gazing at it, there being also velvet at hand as a "touchstone."

Work the Trees thusly: (see page 116.)

The inner requires as much artistry as the outer. There is no difference.

NAHADA In thy name is power given. In thee does Had become the Babe Harpocrat, surrounded by the NO-thing that is NADA. Be also ADAHAN, who is also the shadow of Hadit. Thy number is 71, which is Binah and the No-thing of completion.

```
N - 50    62
       ─────  =31x3-93      62     71    133    124         71    133    142
A - 1    2                 +71    -62    -9      2  = 62   x 2    +9    +124
                           ───    ───    ───    ───        ───    ───    ───
H - 5                      133     9     124                142   142    266   ÷ 2 = 133

A - 1

D - 4

A - 1
   ────
    62
```

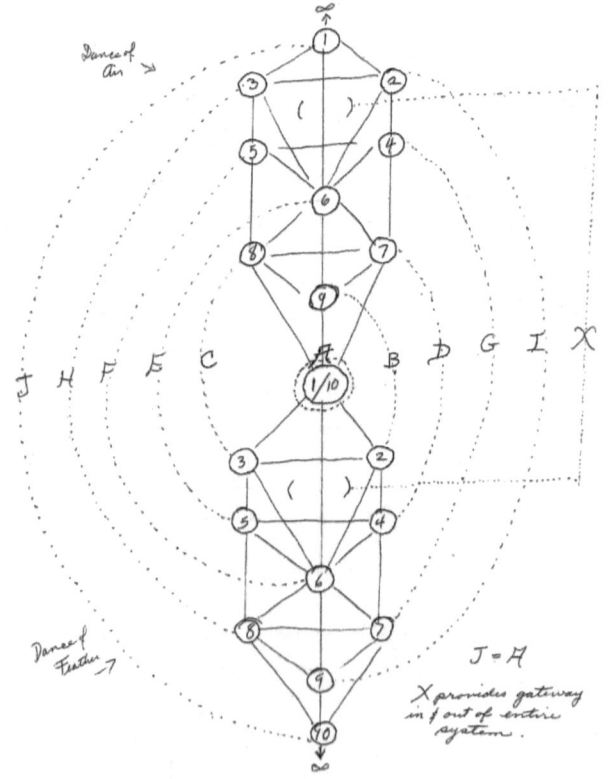

11/23/75 e.v.

Party/meeting of Journal people at Randy B.'s last night. Dave M. is the first witch I've ever met who's publicly embraced the Law of Thelema. Writes a good story, too. Gwen read the letter to the Sisters and heartily agrees with the spirit of it. Tom Knight wants to do ritual with me soon.

The most striking event happened after most everyone left—Randy B. and I and Jo B. were the only ones there; Randy brought out his wand, the energies began to perk up and he started channelling a vision-scene. This is the first time I've done ritual with a male and the channelling happened through him. He wound up shaking like a leaf—got him to his bed and covered him with his overcoat. Said that he wanted me, but I put him off as gently as possible.

11/25/75 e.v. Meeting with another literate witch (and oh so gay) named Don H. in LaRosa's with Lu. He proposes to do some writing for the Journal. We'll see.

Lu and I went to Randy B.'s afterwards. Randy B.'s a lot more unstable than I'd realized. His sex-identity bubble is extremely frail and he defends it like a demon. He was upset at having been "my Scarlet Woman". Fortunately Lu's wisdom rescued the situation and it ended in reconciliation.

I'd best withdraw from Randy B.'s presence psychically. I keep forgetting his restrictions and thus, by dealing with him as the equal he claims to be, I constantly back him to the wall. He must feel awfully trapped, cornered. How can humans be so frail?

I know, because I'm frail, too, in other ways.

Lu and I are working some kind of force that absolutely terrifies me. It seems time for an evaluation of "what is."

Lu is a main force, probably the Hierophant in this situation. He's teaching me more (in a short span of time) than I was able to learn from Gary S. and Dan C., even though they've spent all this time saying the same things that he is.

–Just had conversation with Gary S.–he still speaks as teacher. Any act or word on my part–well, it's all Maya. Set patterns and prejudice (on <u>all</u> sides)–if he has to be didactic, fine. He must somehow enjoy it, or he wouldn't do it, even if it is a subtle masochism. Nor praise nor condemnation, that's just the way it is.

Now. The force being used, desire-tension, building unbearably until it breaks through, upwards. Tantra, in a way–but the updrawing of the dark forces. Therein lies the terror. These dark forces are impersonal, irresistable, overwhelming. Pure energy, without form (O Wisdom, O Chokmah!) seeking form, the urge to become, to destroy, to self-destruct in the ultimate orgasm.

Blind power must be loved/willed into atomically sensitive creative judgement. Why does the Dance of the Ravens remain incomplete? Because the initiation deals with Chokmah-Chesed, path of the Hierophant.

11/26/75 e.v.

Gary S.'s insistance on my desperate need of self-knowledge just doesn't strike a note of urgency with me–what's to know? I'm a hollow onion. I suppose it's the various layers that he's talking about. Hell, these are in a constant state of flux. In the moment I frame a statement of reality about any layer, it's a lie–the speaking has changed it, even. It changes itself.

But–a modest effort at inventory.

10.–outer. All labels. Child of the Sun. Native of Sol III. Magickian

woman mother painter citizen worker writer Virgo sun, Leo ascendant warrior lover friend et alia.

9–emotions, astral competence, receptivity, id. Solar mode in lunar function. Accepter of emotional force, farmer of emotion. Cultivating emotions as power-sources. Root-forces, demons; still learning and experiencing. Astral perceptions, good; astral constructs, better. Probing the depths in preparation of hurling myself therein.

8–Mind cannot be separated from rest of "self". Mind is a resultant of perception, memory, analog-comparison, intuition. It is not merely complex circuitry, but, the <u>pattern</u> of synapse activation that generates "mind." Mind is based on bio-function, but extends beyond its base up to the Abyss.

7–relationships. Perceptions are refining themselves, and interchanges are becoming more direct. Less fooling around with surface talk, games, hesitation, overcaution. More awareness of the needs of the Other in terms of his/her degree of development. Every man and every woman is a Star, even though it is sometimes called for, for the sake of the energy-flow, to adjust the Mask in act and word in accordance with the state of the Other.

6–"I" "am" a "Magickian".

5–Strength endures. There is fire also, and strength of light, and strength of darkness. The appearances of weakness are veils developed by social conditioning–and they have their uses.

4–Creativity happens as it's called for. I no longer feel pressed to be "doing" anything. No more guilt if there's not a painting in progress or writing in the works. Things manifest on their own in the correct mnner and circumtances. Judgement is improving, as discernment and discretion become more acute. I still blunder badly, but a more

precise balance is slowly being achieved.

Da'ath–Knowledge is more experiential than theoretical now.

3–Understanding increases. Megastructures of form are beginning to "make sense." Slowly withdrawing veils, Ki-yop of "AHA!" Mind cannot handle this. "I" am a vortex in space-time continuum, a whirling yet motionless spiral, a cone, a spiral nebula, an eddy in the Tao. I am the form of an orbit.

2–I am force. My only adjective is "moving". Wisdom is–All is Change, Nothing is changeless. I am therefore the All, as well as the Nothing. I am the identification of the Macro- and Micro-Cosmos. I am the Tao; I go on forever, generating Eternity in which to exist. All-things must pass.

1–I am Being. I am coming-to-be. I am that which has always been. The Will-to-Become, which is God, is my ultimate essence. The Crown is Hollow, as is the seed. The All emanates from me, as I am the verb "to be".

000.–The Crown is hollow.
00. –Where there is no space nor time, infinity nor eternity.
0. –0=2.

Only when my thingness overbalances the no-thing-ness, do problems happen.

Later.
Gary S.'s as human as anyone else, entitled to as much damfoolishness as anyone else. Only he can change his Masks, and from here on it matters not to me which one he wears. He's still Gary S., in the process of becoming (as we all are).

I invoke Maut! I shall eat the carrion of dead Masks. When a dead

Mask is offered unto me as a sacrifice, I shall accept and devour it utterly. I shall consider a Mask to be dead at the instant I can percieve it as being a Mask. So utterly shall I devour all negatives, retardations, blockages and restrictions that nought shall remain save the pure flow of life.

Tahuti, your gift is a mixed blessing.

Word. Logos. In the Beginning was. Was with God. Is God. The most rarified of earthings, the most concretized of air. Word pluralized, flowing in currents of thought...will-being-0, and words heard, received is the Water of it. Command in words, barbarous tongues, incantations, evocations, invoking of gods, oaths, vows, declarations of Will–Word-fire, Will-fire, Will-Word!

And Spirit of Word, the mantram. The breathing-forth of OM and IPSOS and ABRAHADABRA. Yea-saying.

And Centre and Hadit of Word is Silence. Harpocrat rules the sound from Silence.

11/30/75 e.v.

Catching up with events now. I see where the true discipline comes in in this keeping of a record. Events are crowding each other in the time-flow. Childhood seemed spacious and eternal–time enough to digest and assimilate events–now things flow one into the. next.

11/25 was Thanksgiving Day. Gary S. was over and perhaps stayed too long. The dinner was fine, but it seems he burned out on the energies. He was nursing a chest cold, too, so that may have had something to do with it. Dan C. showed up later with my chart done a la equal houses–explained a lot, especially with Jupiter in the Midheaven. Which is why the pause in the writing of the Dance of

the Mask, on the Dance of the Ravens. Mars is there to add force to the Grand Cross and the Grand Trine.

Point brought up early in the day was the questioning of the wisdom of publishing Liber P.P. –Dan C. and Gary S. are concerned about the unready attempting the Mass of Maat and doing injury to themselves.

Granted that it's all Maya–the unqualified will simply fail to understand. Anyone of sufficient knowledge to comprehend the alchemical formula and directions, and of sufficient foolhardiness to attempt it "working Black" will destroy himself. If the destruction is sufficiently thorough, the individual will have been completely purged of non-Will and thus be reborn in the Law. So. Sophistry?

11/28–Moontime, and who should enter stage left but dear Fra. Anubis, the old brujo. So it was the Mass XI°, and that strangely. Every time the second-chakra energies were activated, we "shot up the planes" and, being thus transcended, the physical energies "went up" along with our consciousness, and dis-charged the physical. The elixir was thus of an etheric rather than physical nature, save for the kala-nectar and the blood. More mystic than magick–but this is something I must ask K. Grant –the boundaries of each. The charge that's been building for me was not earthed with this. It still grows.

11/29. Fra. S. stopped by and we were impelled to an elder god shadow-ritual in my temple. With no conscious planning, it became a Mass, and this time with a brother trained in Thelemic alchemy. Completely a surprise for the both of us–and it didn't earth his solo-working forces, but augmented them. Same for me.

Worked it Had-Nu, with thorough process–definite physical elixir, pure and abundant. "By the same mouth"–comm-union, charging of

pantacle, wand and feather. This is the first full-blown alchemy I've worked "independently", with competence and detachment.

12/2/75 e.v.

Running to catch up with the record again. Sunday night (11/30) Yet another Mass, with "Fra. X"–dangerous thing, this time, an exorcism for him. This is also the first time there's been extensive sex magick with another Brother present and working up the planes. The demon-forces released from Fra. X passed through me and into Fra. S. who fed them to the elder gods.

(Typist's note–Yes, three different men on three consecutive nights, in moontime. And during this whole time-span, the Observer within remained cool, detached and somewhat amused. It was like walking-through the part of a whore and memorizing the script. I was a Willing vehicle for those forces needed, in some way, by those I worked with. There has been no repetition with any of the three to date.)

Last night (12/1) Casey and I went over to Kentucky and scored some excellent smoke-sacrament. Doing ritual stoned has the advantage of eliminating the usual length of time for opening the portals; after that, there's no difference.

Dan C. and Gary S. were here when we returned, and of course the four of us held a spontaneous quality test of said sacrament. We unanimously concluded that it indeed was Panama Red, as claimed.

Casey left and the other two proceeded to work. Their new Masks are interesting–the "nice guy" variety. They were commenting about my absence from Riddle Crest, and were almost apologizing. Pfui!

In no uncertain terms was I banished. So what? I love them, and

accept them as they are, but there's the Journal, and work, and the kids, and this record, and the others I've begun working with et al., et al. I refuse to waste time or energy in a counter-productive situation.

True, their Martial approach is fine for my inner development, but right now it's manifestation time. They have their work down to fine art and it's beautiful to watch, but it's not "my" natural way or working. I'm a Warrior, true, but I battle in my own elements. "I" am being the whore. I bring the instrument of my body to the workings of Love-under-Will. I bring the priests into the most intimate of human embrace, so that they might therein discover that within themselves which is needful to their growing Starhood.

To any critic, loving or otherwise, I say Yea! indeed I am the Whore. It is mine to open the gates of the self to the Self with whomever the gods direct into my Temple. What had been for me pleasure is now joy. The orgasm of Spirit has taken the place of that of the body. And thus the elixir, equally made and shared, is of a higher nature than before.

I had, in the past, done alchemy tainted with the presence of my Ego-out-of-place. It was done as an identity—whether of the Kingdom or under invocation as a god. During the three days with the three priests, in the holy mode of the Blood-Moon, I see that Love under Will means itself literally. The Masses were done without desire as the initiating factor, but rather in keeping with the Tao. Desire was easily controlled and generated as a tool, and not as master.

The priests were affected, but not "I". They were being initiated somehow, and I acted as Hierophant in a strange way. I was aware that they were undergoing initiation through the act of coition and communion—but the nature of the initiations was veiled from me.

It doesn't really matter what they are, just that they are.

Hail BABALON!   I shall become Thee.
I accept the honor of thy priesthood willingly, lovingly.

Hail BABALON!   Warrior-woman, armed with a sword.

Hail BABALON! Cosmic Whore, Who drains and drinks the blood of the Saints.

Hail BABALON! Rider of the Beast, the seven-headed One.

BABALON, behold! Thou art release of restriction unto the Kings and Hermits. The walls within crumble belfore the onslaught. The power within pours forth–for Thee to eat.

Pleasure dost Thee give, and pain also. Within thy Cup, they become united; in Thy alchemy, they become a third, which is Joy.

Through Thee may No Difference be achieved; behold, Thou lieth with all who can approach Thee.

There is none, O BABALON, who might dethrone Thee from my heart–for in Thee is all power given.

As priestess of BABALON, AND MAAT, it is my Will that BABALON and MAAT be now united forever within me.

12/4/75 e.v.

Dan C. over last night–decent working–more open communication, dropping of veils. He has his Name, which is a leap in the right direction. (All directions are right. Wrong lies in stopping.)

Does Gary S.'s opinion of my workings matter enough to change what's happening?

No.

Tomorrow night is Dan C.'s party.

12/6/75.

Well, the gathering was smaller than anticipated–Herb Z. and I became better acquainted. Beautiful sword-dance, balanced well by the other elements as time progressed. This was done under the aegis of Mescalito; sunshine for me, purple haze for Herb Z.

Gary S. unleashed a lot of fire today–and that's part of the working. Why did I come up behind him and tap his top chakra last night? He sees the Qlipoth of Netzach, but it's off the Tree entirely.

He was demanding reasons or explanations today–I did a lousy job of inventing them on the spot. But in truth, I simply tapped. him on the head–no thought, just act. This not having reasons bothers him.

(Typist's note: It was a call to his Berserker. Sooner or later I'm to face his Berserker-form, but it hasn't happened to date. Will I die at his hand? Or is there within a lust-to-conquer the Beast rampant? I wish I could get an advance peek at the script.)

12/10/75 e.v.

Well, dear Record, here we are again, and another energy-band beyond that of the last recording.

Events: Gary S. was over again last night–in his usual baiting and goading manner ... He emphasizes the need of "honesty" in the relationship–i.e., he expects a full accounting of my workings with the other Magickians. He claims that the open channel between us is a source of crossed energies coming from the others and impinging on his consciousness.

a.) He's made quite a point about freedom and Love under Will, with emphasis on the "unusual" degree of sexual drive I seem to exhibit.

b.) He's so fearful of becoming attached to me (or anyone) that he's walled himself off, in a way, within a state of anaesthesia.

c.) He's in a bind because he can't ask for chastity on my part–it would constitute some form of committment that he abhors–plus being a form of Osirian restriction.

d.) He knows that he has all the necessary factors for being an artist of Love, but lacks the necessary confidence to employ them–if he "lets go", he feels that he will thus trap himself.

e.) He's indulging in an exquisite form of self-torture–and in this, his world must be stopped.

He's asked me to teach him, but still voices doubts regarding my honesty, integrity, strength, wisdom and mastery. He wants reasons for what I do. So–it _is_ my will to assist him in discovering his own beauty. How? By dancing a Mask with him.

Later ... There is a simpler way, with fewer veils happening now. I hereby abandon the Mask of Teacher, and indeed all Masks.

I stand alone on the floor of the Great Hall. Hear me, Brothers.

I resign and give up the practise of Magick. The trappings of the Outer shall remain for the benefit of others who choose the way of the Mage.

On the Inner, I vow Simplicity–my only task is to BE, all else will follow.

In the midst of activity, I will not act.

In the midst of speech, I am silent.

I had sacrificed the individual (King!) for the sake of the All.

I am as "real" as any other "I".

I exist within my own right, and honor all others as their own creators.

The NOTHING becomes the ONE. It is my will to be the ONE for this incarnation.

I, the ONE, am unique, without price, and powerful.

I need simply be, for I am my will.

12/15/76 e.v.

This is <u>some</u> record–so. Since the last entry I've died and been reborn many times. In fact, it's accellerating to the point that I'm being myself <u>and</u> Kali–constantly giving birth to myself and swallowing me down.

I've been about repairing interpersonal balances that I'd skewed by acting as an amateur.

The game-name is "Know Thyself" and the elusive subject is Maggie. It's a waste of time that should be used on Gary S., but that's a hot point of philosophical debate.

I'm finding myself growing acutely bored and embarrased that someone is reading these words. The subject matter is rather tasteless.

Ambivalence! Gary S. said he gave up the All to find himself, and I gave up myself to find the All.

Is there any difference in this, ultimately?

How sophomoric this all sounds!

He's teaching me the subtleties of mastery—the art of doing everything by doing nothing, and the science of pure Being.

La, the Dance!

Dear Recording Angel, my Brother who reads this—what fools these mortals be! Puck spoke truly.

12/16/75 e.v.

What is happening? How dare I aspire to Order membership?

I've been operating as a Magickian—wielding powers beyond my comprehension, touching the souls of men—and in such a state of abysmal self-ignorance! Only the HGA and the Hidden Masters have prevented countless tragedies—gods!

Tonight I saw Gary S.'s true Self.

There's a part of me that wants to slay myself for shame—I've done just about everything possible to hurt another human being—every low, mean, contemptible act that can be imagined, and in the self-deceiving guise of doing my Will, and flowing with the Current.

Yet, he remains constant and loving—not in terms of "forgiveness", but in terms of love under will.

Lex Talionis would have him exact due measure of pain from me for my deeds.

Lex Christi would have him pardon my deeds, restore me to grace and then suffer for my sake.

But Lex Astrae—he accepts my deeds as no different from aught else, neither punishing nor forgiving, but continuing in evolution. Faced with this, I can do nothing other than the same. It goes against everything I've learned, and experienced, surmised, heard of—everything.

Do I have the capacity to love as he loves? Do I have the strength to live Will as well as he? If anyone could be termed Saint, it's he—but I dare not be anything less, then (sic), myself. No Bhakti this time, for it just won't do.

The Lamp and the Sword!

When I was a child this life,
I loved in innocence and trust,
laughing down the corridors of light,
dreaming in the forest afternoons.

The trees loomed tall, protecting,
and sifted sunlight through their leaves,
making patterns in the pond's green depths.

Strong hand that held my small hand—
on we walked, to see the world in beauty.

He was god—swooping me to touch the sky
in wild delight and laughter.

Then we were many, playing with our god,
cuffing each other about like sporting cubs;
but when he spoke in stern, commanding tones,
we'd stop, quite chastened,
for having displeased our lord of wisdom.

In love, in joy, and cub-respect,
we grew beneath his eye.

Then Death roared down,
and brought Confusion with him.
The daring and most golden cub
was torn from out our midst,
hurled to earth–
to break, and bleed, and die.

Where was our god?
How could he let this happen?

I searched,
in the thunder-night of the soul,
amid the howling winds of grief and rage,
by the stark light of flashing fear–
I looked among the trees of past sunlight,
seeing them now shrunken, twisted, gnarled.

And I beheld my god–
weeping for his shattered seed,
and knowing not the way
to vengeance or forgiveness
for the stranger of the deed.

Innocence was slain there, on that night.
The tide of life is mightier than grief.
I sought for strength,
and found it in a stranger who survived.

I vowed and chose for strength,
to fashion mine own children
in a way
that they should never grieve
nor lose the light.

I robbed the stranger's strength,
in untaught sorcery,
and gave it to the children of my body.

One day,
the unborn growing large within,
I came to watch my broken god
do losing battle with the hand of Death.
I could not meet his eyes.
He died alone.

(His lady's death was different–
I held her hand,
and wished her godspeed
on her go-ing flight–
but that's another tale for other times.)

I understand about Dad, and that's past. I understand about John U., am that's past, too. The phase of Christian asceticism and the mystic Tiphereth-samadhi was a sanctioned and holy form of escapism. Fine. Not without value, and not unreal; but limited and unearthed.

The "spidering"–well, a perverted exercise of power. All the friends and acquaintances that I manipulated and maneuvered–I could do it, and I did do it–for entertainment, amusement, diversion. Actually I was violating them, raping their wills, using them. Casey survived, since he was my equal (and at times my superior) in the decadent art. Now he's a master, but still vulnerable in places.

It comes around to Gary S. again.

He simply doesn't fit any model I've met thus far.

He introduced me to THERION's writings and began the practise of Magick with me.

He was the main force behind the divorce.

He's been constantly "stopping my world."

And yet he has human shortcomings and imperfections, many of them. We've been through the bit about shared past lives, worked alchemically, played with power-flows etc. Presently, he seems to be insisting on working in Malkuth alone, not wanting to use the vocabulary of Magick or any formal ritual–and yet the changes are flashing up and down the entire tree.

I'm terrified, and utterly serene. We <u>are</u> the children of ourselves, even in a single incarnation.

Dearest Brother–this must be an old, familiar thing for you. How many records have you read, each repeating this primal formula? For your love and patience, may it be that the weariness it must entail will be lightened by some variety somewhere–thank you for what you are.

12/20/75 e.v.

On 12/17/75, following telephone conversation with Lu about changes we'd both encountered in the use of language, entered the temple with the intent of an inward working on the Word.

Invocation of Tahuti and Heru-Pa-Kraath. IPSOS as incantation. Image of Tahuti in ibis-form, changing to human appearance, writing on a scroll. Couldn't understand the script appearing on his/my scroll. Awareness-point transferred between seeing the god and being him.

As Tahuti, saw the form of Harpocrat in his traditional pose, floating in darkness. Disembodied voice: "The wisdom of the word is Silence. Speak, but not to be heard. Do Magick, but give not the appearance of doing, nor speak of it."

Conclusions: As English is a living tongue, every word in the language is a person, akin to the personhood of the Hebrew letter-numbers. When new concepts arise in the evolving mind, new words will be born to frame them. A word is Nuit to the Hadit of a concept. The Word gives form to the Idea, incarnates it in an etherial and concrete way, so that the concept may be conveyed and communicated to other individual minds.

Realities other than ideas may be transmitted by Word, and concepts may be communicated non-verbally...but in the Word is an especial power. This power may degenerate as far as "Deutschland uber Alles" and "My country, right or wrong", but it may also reach the sublime heights of "Do what thou wilt..." and "so be it".

Those who use words incur a Karmic responsibility for this use. While there are usually too many variables to predict the exact outcome of words spoken and heard, or written and read, the priest of Tahuti must exercise informed Will in what he writes or speaks. The power of Word carries with it the dangers of persuading one of lesser grade to act in a way contrary to his Will, and thus the speaker opens himself to the forces of confusion in the spiritual ecology of the Universe.

As living entities, words also must be allowed to flow in the grace and beauty of their inner nature. Restrictive formalism cripples the power of words to move the hearer. Concerning facts and logical processes, formalism is needed; however, when used to reveal the soul to the mind and to the soul of another, words must be free and natural.

The freedom. of language renders the words transparent and allows the concept or idea to shine forth unhampered. When one notices the language by which a thought is conveyed instead of simply receiving the thought, then undue restriction has been placed on the words. Again, Tahuti's word/sigil:

A
LAL
ELALE
KELALEK
IKELALEKI
DIKELALEKID
ODIKELALEKIDO
SODIKELALEKIDOS
ODIKELALEKIDO
DIKELALEKID
IKELALEKI
KELALEK
ELALE
LAL
A

12/18/75 e.v.

IX° with Gary S.. The formalism of the former workings is gone. Since we both had colds it was low-key, but mellow and subtle. There's an automatic director that comes into play–when working alchemy with Gary S., there's no inclination to do so with others.

This isn't some Osirian restriction operating; I've proved myself free and capable enough of obtaining any priest for a legitimate

working. Rather, the power we generate hasn't been equaled with anyone else.

Damn! that sounds so baldly pragmatic. No, it's not that calculating, really. There's love-under-will. It's a force that I'm no longer trying to find a form for. Just where is the Netzach? The mutual figure-8 orbit of two Stars.

12/23/75 e.v.

Post-Solstice–and a strange one! Solstice eve Dan C., Gary S. and I went to Oz Farms with Dan C.'s new lady, Siebhan.

Tom (Knight) misses the Bitter Blood Street Theatre. We spoke, multilevel. Earth-words were of trees, and fire, and time and solitude. Much more than that was said.

But–Ginger M., our sunshine Munchkin, is dying of Muscular Dystrophy. It's taken a sudden turn for the worse, and tests are being run. The paralysis will move from her legs to her lungs; and she'll suffocate. Her sorrow over not having children is balanced by her work with the autistic kids at Children's Hospital.

And she is beautiful. She's lived with her death since age five. She saw her brother die of MD, and knows its progress intimately. She speaks of flowing with it, and indeed she does.

A Sister is dying–and there's naught to be done except love her and be as she is. So rare, so exquisite! I dreamed of a painting for her and her Gary M.–the Emerald City, seen from a dark woods, with the forms of Tin Man, Scarecrow, Lion, Dorothy, Toto, and Gary M. and Ginger M. It'll manifest soon.

Let it be. She needs no assistance in her dying–it's centered, serene, beautiful. She's a Star with no veils on her light.

So.

Solstice day, Gary S. phoned me at work, Ace of Wands. His car went kaput with ruffles and flourishes, and he heard teacher-voices taunting him about me and my will. So he wanted a conference and I went to the Riddle Crest house after supper. A lot of what he said made sense from his observer-point, but!

12/24/75 e.v.

Brief lunchtime conversation with Gary S.–I was let off work early and met him at a restaurant. I assume that I'm to receive and learn–his way–since that's what's happening. For some reason, our relationship is the most important single thing in my universe right now. So much power in it!

Wait. That sounds as though power's the motive for my being here. No.

Love under will, first and always. Power is there, but not the prime interest. Say, woman–something's within that does exult upon the power–some cold giantess that would command a race. How close am I to permanent entrapment in the Abyss?

There is the Wisdom of the high, and of the low.
Who may say, Chung Huo,

which would profit a man more to heed?

For they speak in different tongues–
the Wisdom of the Middle
is achieved in silence.

By words is the veil of separation woven.
In silent act,

the veils cannot contain.

The mouth speaks, but then it drinks.
More eloquent, son of my cousin,
are the thousand tongues
hidden within the palm of the hand.

The ways of the dancers are strange,
and best kept apart
from the eyes and the ears of the people.

Does the warrior sleep in his armor
in the season of peace
and within his own guarded courtyard?

The Wisdom of the low is not for scorn—
The woman and the serpent
are both devious, misleading, and powerful.

Is the serpent to be blamed
for being other than a dove?
Each perfects his own nature.

Chung Huo, were it not for opposition,
the rocket would not rise,
and force would not flow in any way.

The opening of the plum-flower
must take place
amid the winter snow.

It is for now, prince of our family,
that you may hear us
through the armed woman.

For too long has this messenger
been denied the gate of access
to the inner court of your consciousness.

Speak as Chung Huo,
as you were three thousand years before.
I am Hang Tsin Cho.
Remember me.

12/30/75 e.v.

Calendar-year's-end inventory:

Physical body–relatively good health.

Astral–working well, and in objectively-checked situations. Have to watch <u>how</u> channellings are delivered.

Mental–using free-form non-A logicks, and they're working.

Intuitive–learning to trust it. When unimpeded by prejudice, it works well.

Centre–coming to manifest more often than not, but needs more practice.

Strength–learned this rests on change, not granite-like immobility.

Creativity–beginning to balance destruction (let's hear it for synthesis!)

Form–mutable as ever. Hopefully to achieve the excellence of Silly Putty in the near future.

Force–letting it be the 93/Tao.

Crown--?

Events–simplicity . . . I listen to what people say, I see what they don't say, and I do what seems right. I like leaning my body against someone else's. I like looking into their eyes. I like to receive and send warm energies with people.

I like sleeping, eating, working, laughing, painting, hugging kids, talking, playing Rachel (my violin), writing, doing ceremonial ritual, taking slow hot baths, smoking marijuana, tripping on LSD, reading, woods-walking, making love to trees and sometimes rocks, petting animals, being with the river, soaring into the night sky, watching bugs, driving the car, blowing people away, being blown away, drinking the sunlight, weeping tears of joy for beauty, going up the planes, handling high-intensity energy, corresponding with and communicating with people, being alone, listening to music, dancing, making love to and with people, becoming various gods, evoking demons (mine and other people's), dying, being out-of-body, being born, being in the flesh, slaying, giving birth, saying goodbye and hello.   I like being me.

I don't like (in me or other people) deliberate stupidity, cowardice, confusion, uncertainty in action, hesitation, indecisiveness, self-pity, restriction, evasion, cruelty for pleasure, self-advertisement, serious hyperbole, snobbishness, lust for power, procrastination, indifference. Or anything else in that vein.

I've learned that "Do what thou wilt <u>shall</u> be the whole of the Law," that "love <u>is</u> the Law, love under will."

I've also learned that "we're all Bozos on this bus", and that the Dance of the Mask, if done well, is joy unto Nuit.

Later, Night.

It's been initiation/realization/manifestation all day long, and it continues.

Phone conversation with Dan C.–very effective wall-breaker this afternoon–it really launched this present phase. Began by the conversation, followed by brief Hatha Yoga and Tae Kwan Do exercises and asanas in the back office.

At home, phone conversation with Gary S. He's through Sunday night's katharsis of Da'ath, and declares himself to be coming from Mars in terms of strength. He said he's riding the pain and ideas of suicide and murder.

As I've seen for quite some time, I must face his Berserker-Demon. There's no-one else in the area who could do it, except maybe Patrick M. He's got me as Hecate, or some vampire-succubus. He flashes into an "evil" image of me and up comes the demon each time.

Doing laundry tonight, I invoked Hippolyta. (She's a redheaded Amazon with one eye, one breast, and usually smoking a cigar. She came to me first a long time ago–very much a dyke, but not to me.) This was because I have to meet Gary S. in Mars. She manifested the gynander-bees, a huge golden swarm of them, and we sent them to Gary S.

I watched them poise above the roof at Riddle Crest, form into a Maat-feather, then plunge through the house and into Gary S.'s top chakra.

They're humming around inside him now, flashing like little golden stars. They're building honeycombs inside him (really strong structuring), and transmuting the pain into honey. This is a great energy-source and healing agent, and he's doing well that way, in re-assembling his bodies.

I sent a half-double to be with him for a few minutes. He didn't exactly see me/her but he felt us and started getting agitated–so I

merged the double with Hippolyta, she merged with me, and here we are.

Following this, I was summoned to the Great Hall, and instructed by Them in the final balances of this initiation.

1) The freedom to say "no" as well as "yes" is a necessity of true liberation.

2) The capacity of love is infinite—one must be fully with the "other" person, and free to do one's will. Intuition is the voice of Wisdom.

3) Binah <u>is</u> Understanding, which is the root of compassion.

4) Death-and-destruction energies must be received transparently, allowed to pass through and dissipate. Resisting only generates greater intensity.

5) Initiation= "payin' your dues", as the blues singers say.

6) The greater the Magickal power being handled, the more veiled the manifestation—but the only effective veil lies in transcending the appearance of "doing" anything.

7) Ethically speaking, it's far better to be seduced than to seduce. At the present level of evolution, no-one can resist. Therefore, allow the "other" to exercise and develop his/her solar aspect of will. Do not pretend. Be subtly, sensitively receptive, and allow <u>them</u> to succeed or fail in the seduction, judged solely on your centered responses and intuition.

8) Operate through all chakras in a balanced manner.

9) True strength manifests in gentleness. Even though one has no water in the natal chart, simple alchemy can transmute the elements

of the Inner. Earth is the closest, easiest and best to change to water.

10) The Mask may be Danced on the Inner, in terms of "stopping one's own world."

11) The Dance of the Mask shall be structured according to the Tree of the Feather in Liber Pennae Praenumbra.

12) This initiation must be experienced in water, or the systems will burn out. Do not seek after the word–it shall be given.

13) I am signed upon the Ajna thus: ⊗ No more may be spoken or written of this he who is to know will understand.

12/31/75 e.v.

Here's a rather organic event. Returning to the office from the Post Office today, I felt a sudden wetness–and my period had stopped on Monday. Silently cursing the mess, I went to the ladies' room to rinse out my slacks and tend to the body, and encountered a good-sized bloody mass.

I rinsed it off on a paper towel as best I could, and examined it minutely. It was difficult to see without a magnifying glass, but I saw organic tissue amid all the clot-stuff. Checking back in this record–my "BABALON experiment" took place more than a month ago, at moon-time, so the only possibility was two weeks ago, which means Gary S.

He's in no shape for this at the present time.

Should I tell Dan C.? He's the only one I could right now, but should I? I feel sort of dizzy, have to keep checking on how the bleeding's progressing–don't want to hassle with Dr. Kaiser–too many explanations needed.

Later—Talked with Dan C. and all's well. The shoulder started in with the pain again, called Dr. Finke, and he's prescribing me some muscle relaxants.

I am going to inform Gary S. tonight. I have the "remains" in a folded paper in my purse. So I'm going to do ritual tonight; the paper and its contents will be burnt, mixed with wine, and consumed.

"By the same mouth..."

1/1/76 ev

Last night was an ending and a beginning. Gary S. viewed the "material" and agreed it was embryonic. We prepared it as I had intended; the communion of flesh was accomplished, and the Child now lives in each of us.

Everything flows, because it must. Form is not a fixed shape, but the Mask of the Dance best suited to the nature of the Force working through it.

To understand a Star, a process, a law of the Universe, one must first unite with the Wisdom/Force that shapes the form...Wisdom is Force, Understanding is Form.

What is the Great Force of the Cosmos?

Change. On-going-ness, evolution. Falling from one energy-state to another. Entropy. All matter/energy seeks the leves, the balance of all potential differences. Luke-warm soup.

When Nuit rests, and Brahma sleeps, nothing happens. NO-THING happens.

When Nuit turns and arches above Had, Brahma exhales, and Everything begins.

Does the gray goo of the end of entropy have a self-motivation to re-form the Ylem and burst forth anew? Brahman does nothing, but Prakriti is the mover, the pressure-breath of creation.

The initiator of Evolution, the motive of coming-to-be—Maati!

(This is a record of the Inner—is it true growth, or the unveiling of things that exist timelessly?)

I know that I have now passed beyond the furthest point of achievement of former lives.

I know that I am now beginning to fulfil the function for which I was born.

The function has no easy label. By simply living life in joy (and sorrow), I fulfil my office and function. What are these?

One is to be priestess of Maat. What does this mean?

To live poised and centered, to GO, to balance in the forward motion, to soar on the current of Air;—in so doing, I manifest Her to all who may see. For this I am AQUILA, wearing the feathered flight-cloak that Bear Claw gave me—the White Eagle, crimson of breast and black of brow. I am NAHADA also.

Who is Maat?

Lady!

Radiant dark between the stars,

Flame-dancer,

Black and brilliant,

Feather-flame and quill-plume
writing as you GO

upon the parchment-skin
of Man.

What silent word, O Thou-who-moves,
is graven in our nature
as you dance?

IPSOS!
the secret given,
know ye now
what it would bid ye do?

Lady love,
O pearl within the lotus,
By the same mouth
that drinks the kiss of life and death
is the word of True Will spoken.

IPSOS!
The terrifying paean of the gods
echoes through the ages
unto Man.
Once it was heard as ICHTHOS,
and then Death
was ever triumphed-over
by the crowned cross.

Now, Hawksons, hear ye well—
the paean rings again,
and it is IPSOS!

Ye are the children of yourselves,
the self-created ones.

There is THAT, forever and beyond,
then I am,
then you.

I am dark sister unto Nu.
She, the shining one,
is all about ye, and within.
Thou art the Hadit-point,
the self made of My being
that is encompassed by bright Nuit,
and in turn encompasses Her.

I am the shadow of Nuit—
who is the shadow of Hadit?

The Word is flesh, and dwells among you.
All that you were, and are, and shall be
lies within the power of the Word.
The Word rests ever in your mouth,
ready to be spoken to create you.

In the silence of the egg of blue,
you curl your infinite Self—
then with the Vision
comes the Voice—
and shattering the Cosmos-egg,
you leap to birth
with crown and sword and arrow.

King, Warrior, God!
Hawksons, such are ye.
Aye, and more besides—

Stars, in flaming glory of your being!

Men—that heedless Race who made the gods,
then turned to worship
those who were not made in consciousness.

Priests—who live to show the Stars themselves,
and reunite Man with the gods he made.

Magickians—the agents of Willed Change,

Hermits also, men of chastity,
who abstain not,
but love in freedom,
love by will,
and do not possess,
nor are possessed
by any one or any thing soever.

Artists are ye, making Beauty out of life Itself,
and Scientists who learn the Cosmic laws.

Artisans and farmers,
Fools and Saints,
carpenters, and millers,
teachers, leaders,
Dancers of the wind—

Such are ye,
and I am you in all of these.

I am your life-force,
and the flow.
I am Tao and TARO,
Death and Change.

I am what you sing to in the night.

I am Nuit's shadow,
the Unseen,
that which is between the manifest.

Here is a tale:

Once there was a man of wealth and fame, of great power at court, and an influence throughout the countryside. He had come by his great good fortune by always listening, and learning how to take advantage of all situations.

Strolling in his garden at dusk, he stopped beside his lotus-pond to contemplate the beauty of the water and the blossoms. His reverie was interrupted by frantic splashings; at the edge of the water he beheld a lizard-form emerging from the pond, gaining dry land, and beginning to glow a fiery red.

"What are you?" he addressed the apparition.

"A salamander," was the reply.

Searching his memory for facts and opinions of salamanders, he became aware of a paradox.

"What is a fire-creature doing in the water?"

"Well," said the animal, who by now was pulsing orange, "I had some business with a carp.

"Actually, he had been an alchemist searching for the secret of transmuting lead into gold. Unfortunately, he reversed the formula and turned himself into a goldfish. But that's the way it goes, sometimes."

Sensing a unique opportunity, the man assumed the manner that had won him so many friends at court.

"Would you be my guest for now?" he inquired, "Perhaps we might learn a great deal from each other."

"Are you sure you know what you're doing?" asked the beast.

"Almost all the time."

"Why don't you step up on that flat stone, and I'll transport you to your quarters." So saying, he pushed back his silken sleeves and bent to grasp the stone. No servant should know of this phenomenon; and he <u>had</u> maintained his strength, even in his middle years.

Later that night, he entered his study; the white heat of the salamander filled the room and illumed the space with a glow brighter than the light of an overcast day. The gentleman had dressed himself in chemist's garb; a large leather apron and a cap disguised his worldly status.

With a gracious bow, he approached the hearth wherein the salamander yawned, scratched, and blinked sleepily.

"Have you rested well, my friend? I've brought you victuals and drink."

He drew from his apron pocket several lumps of sulphur and a flask of quicksilver. Unstopping the flask, he proffered it with a lengthy pair of tongs.

"Don't mind if I do," nodded the amphibian. "Cheers. Just toss that other stuff over here. Thanks."

The host pulled a three-legged stool as close as he could, considering the heat, and waited in polite silence while the salamander ate,

drank, and fetched up a hearty belch. Lounging back on the log-grating, the beast picked his teeth with his tail-tip and cast an appraising eye at the man.

"You have a name, I suppose?"

"I'm known as Sir Melor," was the reply, carefully balancing self-confidence with the charming modesty that had won countless hearts in the eleven provinces.

"May I have the honor of knowing your illustrious designation?"

"Since it's Thursday, you can call me Clyde. What's your game?"

An instant's hesitation of internal debate, then candor triumphed over caution. "You are a being of power—a fire-elemental, aren't you?"

Clyde stiffened in offense.

"Elemental, my arse! If you weren't obviously operating from ignorance, you'd be crisped. My dear mortal, I am a salamander, in full control of my faculties, and as far beyond an elemental as you are beyond the apes. On second thought, that's not a good comparison..."

"A thousand pardons—" Sir Melor hastened to placate his guest. "I am not truly versed in technicalities of the Art, but I meant no insult."

"Oh, all right. You're close enough with the 'being of power' label. So what do you want? Wealth? Fame? Women? Boys? Immortality? Invincibility?"

Taken aback by the directness of perception, Sir Melor pondered a moment—why <u>had</u> he brought this disconcerting creature into his

home in the first place? Feeling the silence extending to an awkward length, he essayed a new start, using his best diplomacy.

"Well, most gracious Clyde, it <u>had</u> been my intent to provide you hospitality and comfort so we might converse to our mutual increase of knowledge."

"What I don't know about humans I wouldn't be interested in–but you did give me a decent feed and a place to catch a nap. Say that I owe you one–so what do you want?"

Sir Melor pursed his lips, leaned his head on his hand and lost himself in thought. How to phrase the inmost desire of his soul!

In his mind's eye came scenes of his student days, time spent in the study of philosophy, history, metaphysics. There had been long debates with the more perceptive of his fellows concerning the nature of Existence, the meaning of life, the reason for action and non-action.

His practical pursuits had gained for him his wealth, position, reputation and comfort. All that he now truly desired was to know the ultimate secrets of the Cosmos, to possess the knowledge of the gods.

How serious, how sacred, this quest! With the key of knowledge of the workings of the universe, he could bring about a transformation of the world! No longer would there be need of war, or poverty and disease among the people. There could be abundance for all, an uplifting of the downtrodden; men would become wise philosophers, and women would be gracious delights of beauty. Science would progress, and art would flourish.

And he, Melor, would never reveal his bringing it all to be. No, he

would do it all in secrecy, never claiming and proving to the world the fact of this ultimate benificence. In modesty he would continue to live, never sharing with a single soul, his inestimable secret of his gift to mankind.

In his imagination, he soared above a landscape of peace. Fruitful fields alternating with lush forests, cities sparkling like jewels, serene sails unfurled upon the ocean. There were even strange craft plying the air itself, bearing men amid the clouds.

In all this vast scene of peace and plenty, there was not one beggar, vagabond, thief or cripple. The people were industrious, smiling, placidly enjoying their harmonious existence. Far to the north plodded the fur-clad remnants of the barbarian mercenaries, their services no longer needed, they journied perhaps to their homeland to begin peaceful pursuits of farming and trade.

To the south, the fires of the forges were reducing the implements of war to the form of tools, ornaments, and idols of great beauty. To the east and the west was harmony, order, peace.

He opened his eyes, and was amazed to see that Clyde had doubled in size. The heat within the chamber was becoming uncomfortable. The salamander was drumming his claws on the andiron, an expression of boredom on his reptilian features.

"Don't go into details. I was following you."

His back now reached the arched opening of the hearth; he rubbed his spine against the stone in sensual satisfaction.

"You might as well ask the question now."

Sir Melor was forced back to the opposite wall of the chamber, quite alarmed at the growth of his guest. But no matter that the

creature could no longer fit within the hearth; the floor was paved in flagstones. Even should a few items be damaged, the acquisition of his new knowledge would more than compensate for his loss.

"This is my only request," he rasped through his parched throat—"What is the secret of the Universe?"

The gargantuan muzzle loomed above him. With an almost-pitying expression, the salamander smiled.

"There isn't any."

His flaming jaws finished Sir Melor in a bite-and-a-half. As the walls of the house exploded away from him, he grunted in annoyance.

After the debris had settled, he began ambling toward the ocean, leaving a wide trail of smoking earth and burning trees.

"Well," he mused, "It's a damn sight better than being a goldfish."

1/5/76 e.v.

Bill U.'s twelfth birthday. John U. bought him a wristwatch. Gary S. was over and took the Pan painting for his temple and will bring me back the one of Mahamatara.

She's my original personal deity, a synthesis of many goddesses, up to the Abyss. Her full name encompasses three languages, Aryan, Greek and Latin—Mahamatara Panthea Domina "Great Mother-All Goddesses-Lady"... she directed my first solo ritual back in October of '73, in Mt. Airy Forest. She harks back to the Isis/Gaia times.

There's a writing...

The Priestess must remember.
Dark.
Cone of white light
Altar-stone
One
Alone here
temple   dark
filled   alive
chimes   bells
cymbals   sistrum
drums   tambor
tinkle chime ring flutter   thump tata thump
clear   bright
flows   white
silk   silver
swansdown   snowflakes
mist   pearl
pace   glide
beams   pure
liquid   light

Moonshaft the altar touching, glitter and gleam
On chalice and dagger and dogwood flower
O   l
be   Gê
she   now
here   lies
To waken
La.

Gaia, rise!
   Mother and sister
      Lover and friend!
         Thou of the Caverns
            Of fields and of
               mountains,
                  Receive us within thee
                     And enter, in turn,
                        Our Earthsouls and bodies
                           Our minds and our spirits
                              So we may be fruitful.

                      The fields now make fertile
                  And hasten the springtime
               The plow and the planting,
            For life loves the prudent
          And herds ever wander.

                  So teach us thy ritual
               Of plow and of planting;
            The Sun dies within us
        to grow to His rebirth,
    to be His own seed.

Drunken with moonlight
she sways–
To the altar,
hovering
above the chalice
Ah!

The lovely dagger,
tongue of the serpent,
    Flash!

Between her breasts
    the crimson lotus flowers
        dark rain into the mooncup–
Honey-wine, spring water
      swirled
with the scarlet
      drops
to the embers,
  to the houses of the winds,
and to the lips of she
  who stands
    in silver rapture–
      pure, pulsing,
        one.

Beyond the Temple door
  in moon-wandering she goes.
Light-frosted meadows,
    Glittering streams,
        Pearl-mist in sheltered valleys–
To the forest, flowing with the light,
  she steps within the grove
    of pines and shadows,
      where she finds
        His eyes.
Form of shadow, force of night
Dark, silent, fearsome–

She does not flee–
    Dream-langour stays her feet.
      She does not judge,
        nor does she fear

        the power here,
       inevitable act,
      nor chastity
    of priesthood–
for such this is.

Touch, love! Light and free,
     warm, and moving
        at the pace of night.
Turn, love! All is an embrace,
     tree, light, or forest floor
       are you and him,
         and both.

The wood and the world
  are your body,
    his,
      the folding-in
        of selves,
           ebb and flow, gathering–

Cool hands caress the two–
     a sister has followed,
       for love–
         found love–
           open, welcome, join–
And three embrace
    to flow together here.

Palms and fingers
     cheek and jawline
       hollows of the throat
         shoulders, breasts–

      Yielding curve of belly
     arch of thigh
    warmth of loins
   gently moving—
     secret dark
        sudden nectar
           irresistable
              oh! not yet—
           ache for completion
       slowly, love!
In me!
    Around Me!
        Flesh within flesh, moving,
            touch becomes—more—
        Blending
     Am I he? or you? myself?
Naught!

What now, neophyte?

Again, trying to make sense of the patterns of life, the growth and change? Have to have a formula, eh, Virgo?

OK— 2 ÷ x = 0 where x = infinity or Maat

Is Maat a noun or a verb?

She's a gerund—GOing.

This incarnation simply doesn't make sense.

Nope.

It's supposed to make power, not sense.

Oh?

Of course. The only possible way to use power and stay 1) incorrupt and 2) alive and 3) sane is to be absurd. Make doghouses out of altars and taste troys and sappho for celibacy.

Hmmm.

Do. Your. Will.

????

Trust your intuition–it's the voice of your Angel.

Desire? Ego? Id?

All part of you, you know. Your Will must encompass the totality of yourself. From Elder Gods to Maat. You're simply invoking the Elder Gods right now and working Darkside. So?

Why the censure?

Because you are too timid with the Elder Gods. You have to use some caution, of course, since Death Wish rules in this Kingdom.

Annihilation of self? Inasmuch as self is a restriction on true freedom.

Is it not the self that is to <u>be</u> free?

Only as the Self <u>can</u> it be free . . .

Do not lose the vision, NAHADA.

You had to earth, but don't forget Spirit. Be practical and in samadhi

simultaneously. Be the master that you know yourself to be—no preferences.

Deal with whatever presents itself.

1/6/76 e.v.

So I'm lined up to go to the Psychic Forum in Norwood Sunday. I'm to sit behind the table with Randy B. (Tarot?) think I'll bring along a few hundred copies of Liber Oz to distribute.

Don R. phoned tonight. His wife finally moved out, and his auto's kaput. He'll be at the Psychic Forum after the Autogenesis lecture at the same place. Good tie-in. He'd like to get together Friday night. His place?

Lovely budding Thelemite, well-veiled. One must use caution when dealing with someone undergoing a heavy strain, and divorce is definitely a strain. It would seem that my experience in the matter might be helpful for him—and me.

The seed is hollow.

Dance ye well, and lustily—drink
deep, dine well,
sleep soft
love long.

The course is before you—
mayhap as a curse,
or a blessing betimes,
there being no difference
in pleasure or pain.

The crown is hollow.

At centre, the NO-thing,
all else swirls around IT.

See.
With vision,
awareness.

Thou _art_ That.
Love _is_ the Law.
Love _under_ Will.

Be.
Be not.
Be Nuit.
Be Maat.
Live.

1/11/76 e.v.

Friday night at Don R.'s. The gentleman has been buying my paintings for the past five years, and so has some insight about what he's getting into. Lovely environment he has. A man dropped by to visit, just in from New York, a Magickian named Ben Rowe.

The three of us did some smoke-soma, and Ben Rowe spoke from higher than his daily human self. He said I have to sort everything I've learned, and only operate from what I've experienced. This is true enough so that the speaker's credentials are immaterial. I asked his name and number and he gave Mahara 253.

After he left, Don R. and I did purple microdot and went to bed. In the process, I find that he has a six-year-old daughter from his first marriage, and that this is his third marriage that he's ending. He also was a heroin addict, and kicked the habit himself. He's well on

the path of self-discovery, and has a will to teach ... he has much to give.

The sex act itself was extended in time (as usual when tripping), but not completed physically. Gary S., I find later, was receiving visuals—by coincidence, he was tripping that evening also—and it caused him great agony. He said that he was screaming for me to stop, but it continued in an infinity of hell for him. I'd drawn what I'd thought was a tight circle, but obviously there are "connections" that aren't affected by the circle. I'd percieved his presence as a clear white flame, but hadn't gotten any of his pain.

Last night, Gary S. and I completed a true Mass, the first in a long time. Tonight he arrived at the Psychic Forum, and I left with him.

It's not my will to cause him pain, but it seems to be a side-effect of what's happening. He's responsible for my being as I am now—but without my apparently cruel actions of dealing with others objectively but thoroughly, I couldn't be strong enough, complete enough, to do him any good.

He's opening now, finally—so vulnerable—I must be master of all the energies that are happening. He's sacrificed his individual growth for mine—(in consciousness; he grows unawares by means of his sacrifice.)—now I must aid him as a hermit warrior.

1/12/76 e.v.

Friendly and Allen H. were over tonight. His (Allen's) second Book of the Forgotten Ones is a true channelling—his flavoring, but it's a good indication of his development.

Friendly seems taken aback at my seeming reluctance to visit them at their apartment. I suppose he's used to sexual agressiveness on

the part of females. Good learning experience for him when it goes otherwise.

Spoke to Dan C. about taxes and Riddle Crest/Spoke with Gary S. He's being understandably wary of me now. He can't deny the evidence of his own experiences–yet the past is painful. Wants to know my nature. TAHUTI?!

The name is NAHADA 71.
The nature is that of the Cosmos.
There is no difference between the microcosm and the Macrocosm.
Nature, Prakriti, Lila.

NAHADA is MAYA.
Beyond her is Nothing.
She exists only for the Dance.

Her Logick is that of the Poet–
 Fantasia, and Change.
Her image is throned on clouds.
It hides also behind the pooled reflection.
It rests in the grasses of the oasis.
It tames the cat with the Thrysis.

She plays the bow and it becomes a harp,
wherein the clear notes are arrows,
piercing the soul in sorrow and in joy.

She rides the beast,
coupling with the Cosmos
in no-mind and intuitive Art.
She takes command;
there is no opposition.

Pouring starflows to and from each chalice—
she is a speck of flesh
upon a small blue planet—
no more nor less than
any other speck that walks thereon.

She shall endure.
There is no choice.

She couples also with Death Himself,
receives His seed,
and bears the Lord of Changes
to His birth in space-time.

She falls often, rises ever,
and appears most cruel
to the Other that is one with her.

Love is a blade, also.
Such is the one who equals Maya.

1/16/76 e.v.

Tuesday (the 13th) Don R. and Ben Rowe were over. They bought some grass from John. I showed Ben Rowe the parchment copy Allen H. did of <u>Liber AL</u>, then presented it to Don R., who accepted it. Spontaneous ritual on acceptance of the Law. I gave them each a Shiva poster. Ben Rowe said he percieved an entity at the east end of the kitchen table, orange skin, red hair–it was Agni, present for Don R.

Wednesday, Dick M. treated Gary S., me, Patrick M., Chris, Lu and Linda G. and the two granddaughters to an evening at the Soviet Circus. Quite a bit of mastery there–chi and body. Afterward, Gary

S. and I to his place, IX°, effectively harmonizing energies.

Thursday (last night) Don R.'s car broke down and I picked him up with mine and brought him to my house. Gary S. arrived from his grandmother's and we rode Don R. home. Gary S. and I talked til 1 a.m.

Tonight on the phone, it seems that things are moving along nicely. It is time for a retreat with magickal chastity playing the major factor ... it's time Omno (or Omne-ed.) is reborn on a more centered and harmonious plane. I've quit trying for a secure future–there's only Now, and Being, and Will and Love.

There's a tremendous initiation going on, and it's covering the whole Tree. The individual Sephoritic initiations have been completed for this cycle, and it's time for an integrating balance of them all. Gary S.'s working on the positive manifestations of Hod, Netzach, Yesod and Malkuth, and I'm working on the positive manifestations of Geburah, Chesed and Tiphereth. Both workings are being coordinated, with full perceptions of the vagaries of Da'ath.

Another good thing happening is John U.'s progress. We're utterly at ease and honest with each other. The divorce is the best thing that we've done. He offered me his share of the selling price of the house to go toward purchase of the farm; in return, I'm to help him out of difficulties with the tax people.

There's a painting on the easel now—a portrait of the Magus of Maat who instigated all the energies of Liber P.P. out at Oz Farms.

1/18/76 e.v.

Last night, ritual with Gary S. The afternoon had Don R. here, and a parting for this phase of the cycle.

What of the ritual? IX°, but in a specialized mode–under invocation of Kali.... He submitted his will to mine, and in turn I invoked the Goddess. She danced upon him in many ways, causing some subtle and profound changes deep within. Saturn is his ruler, as Mars is mine–and perhaps in Her destruction, some of his Saturnine self-restriction was eased.

Finished a letter to Mary R., and am to see lovely Tom Knight the Druid tonight.

Later–11:31 p.m. Home from Tom Knight's. He generated powerful energies with his poetry, warping the fabric of space-time. We did ritual on a challenge basis–I found it extremely interesting that I was both able to maintain centre and at the same time fully experience the nature of the energies.

He became messenger of Ydriggasil and I invoked Maat, so there was no real danger of things getting out of hand. He's a master of astral imagery and creative gesture. Thank you, Tom/Owen Knight, but I can't get into sex energies with you.

So. Back to the situation. Time for a Magickal Retreat... I've said it often enough (I tell you once, I tell you twice, I tell you three times and it's true...) so the cycle rolls around for an inward-turning.

Hmm. Two weeks ago, during that Friday-night trip-rite with Don R., I achieved a new level of strength, consciousness and awareness. This enabled me to regain the proper frequency to work with Gary S. again, alchemically.

Also in the process, I've "let go" of Don R., and any other attachment, and last night's working was of some positive help to Gary S. He's been "stuck" with his Magickal Record, he's been 'stuck' in a perception of pain regarding me–and now it's flowing again.

I'd been "stuck" also, sexually–both ways. Between being too attached to pleasure and not working it as Love <u>under</u> Will. With Will, I was able to participate in an extended Kali-rite last night–to the point of using bondage and discipline (ritually) for the sake of evolution. I'm not the compleat sadist, and at times I find it difficult to operate in such a manner. But the specific need of the moment dictated form, and I believe it <u>did</u> loosen some blocks for him.

I've discovered that I'm not "toning down" the manifestations of my nature for anyone. If they're not to percieve it, their systems won't register it. If they are ready, they receive as a beneficial (?) flow.

How do things appear right now?

Dancing,
downsifting,
angelflakes of light–

starshower,
glowstorm,
harvesting of night.

Be, brilliant and bright–

moonpool.s in shadowglades,
darkforest dancing–

NUIT, encompass!

Misting
and drifting,
smokeveils
and shadewind

from spaces between

wind slowly within us–

in radiant dancing
the dark is aflame–

MAAT, guide us in GO-ing!

1/19/76 e.v.

Today I almost lost centre. Even as I write, there's pressure to destroy the balance–I'm letting it pass through. It's a natural that John should be Choronzon's vehicle for me now. He's generating interference like crazy, but the work proceeds despite it.

It's good Gary S. was here to see the process–it may generate more caution in him, but at least he knows that I needn't fall every time I approach the edge.

(Tyger just brought in the energies of tonight's snowstorm.)

There was a channelling for Gary S., a vision of Samael. He warned about a danger in the Martial Arts, Doesn't make any sense, presently.

Also, there came instructions to give Gary S. the wax crescent I'd fashioned and charged last week. This is for his Yesod–the crescent on Shiva's brow. It was said that the Lunar qualities of Yesod are polar to each other–Diana and Hecate. Passive reception and active projection of moon-radience. Has to be a pure & balanced reflection of Tiphereth, though.

So–pull the plug on Archimedes! Rachel pops her bridge & downs her sound-post. The snow falls, rendering travel dangerous. There was an obscene phone call at work today. Interference from John U. Extra-schizoid energies with the kids.   La/aL.

I tend to lose centre the moment I form any sort of attachment to anyone or anything. The omens cease being omens and become part of the ordeal ... I'd better learn to see the point of an initiation sooner than I've been able to heretofore.

Item–it deals with Yesod. Item–there are forces looking for a "way through". Item–Tom's been twanging merry hell on the space-time fabric around here. So have others. Object–desire? Maggie? Phooey. Too Gothic-novel. Very ego-flattering. Who needs it?

1/20/76 e.v.

The books arrived! <u>Cults of the Shadow</u> & <u>Images and Oracles of O.A.S.</u>—Am scheduling definite reading time for these! Frontespiece of C of S ... "Priestess of the Fire Snake–it's the asana I do during the first parts of alchemical workings. Interesting–judgement suspended until reading's completed.

Lu and Randy B. came to collect <u>Liber P.P.</u> and "the letter" tonight. I found myself declining various requests–such as teaching neophytes. (Hell's fire, Lu, I'm only a neophyte myself, and unqualified to teach anyone.) Writing, maybe. But it seem as though things will go otherwise.

Friendly was over too. Not much time for private conversation, but I advised him to find the local places-of-power and tune in to the energies.

The body tires. It's been quite a day.

1/21/76 e.v.

Delving into <u>Cults of the Shadow</u>. So far, all of my personal experiences vouch for the truth in it. And so far–the book is helping on proper vision for Gary S.'s sake. The Male-lunar, Female-solar formula is

precisely how we've been working all along. Our imperfection as a working unit is due to my reluctance to assume responsibility for my strength.

The Christian programming has been so strong that its perverted ghosts are stubborn and require repeated banishment. A great deal has been transmuted–all sorts of attachments are being recognized and released, daily.

Getting back to <u>Cults</u>–The material is presented with such economy of words and intensity of distillation, that I have to reread paragraphs two or three times to be sure I've comprehended them totally. (Listen, dolt! You <u>cannot</u> comprehend anything totally. The very act of comprehension renders a change ((subjectively)) in the thing comprehended. Said change immediately falsifies the comprehension, and a new level must be sought. The Sorcerer's Apprentice only doubled his problems when he divided the water-bearing broom with an exe.

Have to check out the Afro Tree diagram again, especially Chokmah.

Hmmm–there's a vision knocking to be let through.

To the rainbow gates of the City,
the conquerer comes.
Within the walls, an old man
crouches in the night–
his battered harp
wails out the blues.

The notes slide out like fog–
Gray drifts of mist
that wrap the warehouses

and mask the foghorn's moan
across the wavelets slapping
on wharves and cobblestones.

"What cargo, captain?"

"The future of my wealth, good sir—

"Ivory and gold and tortoise shell,
Emerald, sapphire, ruby, pearl—
Gems and gem-ores from the Mines of Hell.
In chains, the pleasure-boy and dancing-girl.
Musks and resins, essences of earth,
Gums and spices, salt and herbs and tea,
A tigress from Harrappa, ripe for birth,
Apes and peacocks, serpents from the sea—
Such wonders shall afford me wine and meat,
And those who buy will get, in measure just,
The value of their coin. Is it defeat
That none percieve my cargo as I must?
The treasure that I bear is that I GO—
Is it but hull and sail and I that know?"

The conquerer stays his hand before the gate.
The lonely music of the mist
drifts in his mind,
calling to vision and the ear
dusk-twilight, hooves and wheels.

A concertina draws in the mist-music,
and plays provincial folk-tunes
in the dim cafe's smoke and laughter.

1/22/76 e.v.

Don R. and Ben Rowe over tonight. Don R.'s apartment was burgled–and he's been having a water elemental as a houseguest.... but one of the Brethern materialized and banished it <u>for</u> him. Ben Rowe's given him some ritual material, including banishment rituals–I recommended the old Lesser Pentagram–feels more correct for him than any other.

The guys have a strong telepathic link now, and it's a relief to know Ben Rowe's there as a teacher.

Spoke with Gary S. on the phone, and shall do solo ritual for him (not place-taking; it's for channelling energies <u>to</u> him.) Will do so now.

1/23/76 e.v.

Ritual last night simply consisted of banishment, VIII°, et alia. (Strange–<u>Cults</u> is a revelation–many practices that have spontaneously evolved themselves for me, I find, are correct methodology. More on this later.)

The internal muscular contractions that I've been doing for years–because it feels good–I finally linked into the "power roar". It's hard to describe–it begins with the rhythmical indrawing and relaxing of the anal-vaginal sphincter-muscles (actually, everything of the pelvic floor that can be moved) and is immediately echoed by a rhythm of the brain. I "feel" a roar in the inner ear, and my eyes react in synch–the interior of my skull tingles and in general, the sensation is that of a fountain of light. The "observer" becomes acutely sensitive and distinct.

1/25/76 e.v.

The above process was employed in ritual last night. Gary S. lay passive/receptive, I sat in student-asana at his side. Well, first I banished, of course–Gary S. requested me to do so since I was active principal, and I scribed an angel-posted circle.

Anyhow, crossing arms it was right on right, left on left; we were in hand contact, with a small space between the palms. The spaces almost instantly housed an energy-ball each.

I took the consciousness-point from my ajna chakra and moved to the throat chakra, branched in two, traveled down the arms, through the hands, and into his neuro-meridian network.

The visual aspect was our anatomical analogues in a glowing, translucent white; the neurones were a silvered sparkle-flash. I moved to his spinal column and extended along its length, muladhara to ajna-bindu link.

Beginning at the bottom, I concentrated awareness to a point within a spinning energy sphere which was his chakra. Back at my body, meanwhile, there began the rhythmical energy-pulsing as described in the last entry. To my own senses, the heaviest concentrations of energies were in the second, fourth and sixth chakras, but were being transmitted through first, third, and fifth.

To shorten it–I concentrated on each of his chakras in ascending order, with a soft drone-chant as guide to his conscious mind. This chant changed mode with each chakra–until the ajna, it was single words repeated, summoning Kundalini, opening the sushumna and attending, at each node, the ida-pingala balance.. At any rate, at the ajna it changed to AUM, and went beyond–a hiss fading to silence.

He reported sensing a tingle in the first chakra; which was more than I'd hoped for–essentially this was a preparation of channels. I had taken the essence of the energy, as prismed or lensed in color from each of my chakras to his, and felt energies being received in an open and passive way. Beh, it's a beginning.

This was followed by a Mass of Maat, dark of the moon. We charged The Books with the elixir–not that they <u>need</u> any assistance, but it was intuited to do it.

1/26/76 e.v.

The Mass of Maat. I have a distinct feeling that I'm about to belabor the obvious, but to keep this Record honest, we'll simply have to go through it.

The basic form of the Mass is given in <u>Liber</u> <u>Pennae</u> <u>Praenumbra</u>. It also occurs to me that it's the first ritual I've seen thus far, since the Æon of Isis, in which the priestess/Magickian is the active principal. In the Tantric mysteries, she is the vehicle of manifestation, but not the pontifex.

In the Mass of the Holy Ghost, and in the mode of BABALON, there is a more solar mode happening for the woman–but it was still somehow lacking a dimension. This isn't to generalize–I can but speak from individual experience.

So. First after the banishment is the intonation of the Law, verse and response, by the co-priests. (It is a true concelebrated Mass, despite distinct roles of active/passive.)

Also pronounced alternately are the words Thelema. Agape. ABRAHADABRA. IPSOS.

She is invoked by the intonation of Her Name. Maati. Maat. Maut.

The assumption of God-Form at this point by both participants is in the gynander-asexual Black Flame.

Priest and priestess are equally active in the phase that is needed for the necessary degree of sexual arousal. It's totally up to the expertise, artistry, and taste of the individuals. However, special attention is directed to the stimulation of the priest's first chakra.

The end of this first arousal is not coitus, but fellatio to orgasm. During the final moments of this phase, the priestess is repeating IPSOS as mantram within the heart chakra.

The actual orgasm and release is experienced by both in the state of NO-Mind.

The priestess consumes the elixir totally, then spends approximately a half-hour in a comfortable asana, engaged in the following process:

The elixir is absorbed into her bodies at the heart chakra. She brings it to throat, ajna, bindu, and it flows back down to the heart chakra. The cycle repeats, until the energies inherent in the elixir combine with the energy of movement imparted by the cycling, and the energies of the chakras. At a given critical point, the elixir-energy does not return to the heart chakra, but fountains up and out through the sahasrara. It 'rains' back down through the whole system and collects within the uterine cavity.

(During this process, the priest is in a state of rest—ideally, emptied of identity, in a state similar to the "empty Mirror" of Zen.)

At any rate, the cycling process of the initial elixir is a distillation. The resulting substance is an equivalent of honey—a psycho-physical, biochemically-produced quintessence of an organic nectar. For a name of this substance, I propose "talam". However, nectar-honey is

sugar based, and semen-talam is protein based.

It's energy-potential has yet to be explored, as substance-in-itself. Intuition posits that its nature is akin to protoplasm in its ability to assume "independent" life. This could be inconvenient if mishandled. (Note – it's mostly DNA + the Kala-flow – researching latest in genetics – <u>key of life</u>.)

For the course of the Mass, however, the talam is sealed in the uterus–the inmost chamber of the "triple-chambered shrine"–until the end of the second phase.

The arousal process of the second phase is more subtle and prolonged than with the first phase. Eye-contact and the most gentle of touching are the major means here. Bodily discomfort or abrupt movement may disrupt the processes and energy flows–nothing inharmonious should be permitted to occur.

When both concelebrants are ready, the following process begins:

The priest remains supine (corpse asana), the priestess kneels and straddles him. Each concentrates the vision on the other's ajna. Penetration is effected not so much by direct pressure, but by slow, coordinated contraction of the pelvic floor muscles of both celebrants. This contraction is continued as the priestess leans forward, supported by her arms, and brings her face close to that of the priest. She inhales his exhalation, and reverses; this double-pranayama is matched to the rhythm of the pelvic contraction until the process becomes self-sustaining.

(At this point I generally become deaf and blind physically–even the sensations of the sexual connection and breathing are subsumed in the rhythm of the process. Eventually the rhythm transforms to a roaring hum–white light and electric ecstacy somewhere directly

above the top of the skull. I have no idea as to the duration of this state. I assume it varies. The white light is eventually divided by the downward-movement of the Black Flame, and the consciousness is concentrated in the ajna and in the talam itself.)

The priestess again sits erect and begins a slow circular pelvic movement that gradually gains speed and force. The priest mirrors this motion in complete coordination.

(Here, the consciousness gains a third and microscopic focus—within the spermatogenic system of the priest. "I" become about three times the size of a sperm cell and am present among the frantic, swirling creatures.

They each have an aura that brightens according to the activity present. I chant to them, croon and coax, agitate, and build up the pleasure-pressure to the utmost degree prior to orgasm.)

The circularity of motion effects a dilation and relaxation of the uterine cervix, the opening of which is usually sealed by the presence of secretions of the mucous membrane. The talam, informed by the consciousness-point of the priestess, is aware of the process, and begins to "glow". The consciousnesses of the priest and priestess are united through each chakra, primarily via the ajna and the second chakras.

There is a triunity—the full human linkage via the ajna, via the male genitalia and via the talam. In the breathless suspension of activity that occurs immediately before the first throb of orgasm, that peculiar energy-force termed Maatian charges the semen, the talam, and the female secretions. At the moment of orgasm, the three substances unite and form a fourth (kreta).

The consciousnesses of the celebrants, united with the subtances

separately, also unite in a sextupile fashion to produce a seventh.

This seventh consciousness is the force; the fourth substance is the form. The supra-human energy of Maat is the pressure-of-becoming <u>and</u> the result of the multiple fusion.

When act is again possible, the priest orally extracts the elixir and shares it with the priestess in a kiss-communion. It is also possible to charge objects at this point, although wisdom must be employed regarding the suitability of the items so charged.

The celebration of this Mass on the second day of the menstrual period is of an entirely different order of power. The talam itself is of another quantum-level because its composition is changed by the inclusion of blood. To facilitate reference, this lunar substance is called malatan. The blood also constitutes a fourth factor in the orgasmic union, and makes the elixir a fifth-form, kretalo.

Without necessarily implying causality, I can report that, following a moondark Mass of Maat, changes in the Outer are unusually dramatic and sometimes violent. On the Inner, this ritual is the single most effective means I've experienced to effect an "upgrading" of comprehension, understanding, and wisdom.

1/28/76 e.v.

Don R. was over last night—we spent most of the time in the Temple playing energy-ball. The gentleman is intense! Since there are veils he insists on maintaining, I shan't press for his name. It's Tao that Ben Rowe is his teacher. If I'm to be "benefactor", all I need "do" is be—which is my will in general.

So. I am, in human consciousness, somewhat disturbed by the existence of the Mass of Maat. It doesn't seem to fit any system

with which I'm familiar.

Hold. Nahada, this rite may be performed only by true gynanders. You are female in form, as Gary S. is male in from, yet well ye know the spirit within him is both and neither, as is yours. There is no difference, save in physical form. This difference of form enables that separation for the sake of union.

All writings that I have read, though, have the priest as celebrant.

As ye have written before, the Mass of Maat is concelebrated. Every man and every woman is a Star.

Further: The form of the Mass is similar, in part, to the corn-rites of Gê–as ye remember–but this is only a superficial similarity. In those times, the formula was in female power–Magna Mater! Now, ye are hermaphrodites.

Mahamatara was the godform of your initiation. She, the summation of all previous goddesses, has played Her part. Nuit and Maati–NOW. The Universe and Her Shadow. If Maat is the shadow of Nuit, who is the Shadow of Hadit?

Maat is Truth. Veiled by the perception of the Universe. She is not seen. Ye who yet see the Universe, and are conscious of yourself, have not the enlightenment of this koan.

Had is a point—can a point cast a shadow?

Who is providing the <u>other</u> end of this dialogue?

Adahan.

Of what value is the Mass of Maat?

1) In the Microcosm, it reinforces the hermaphroditism of the concelebrants. Its effectiveness increases proportionally to the purity of the perceptions of the priests. It doesn't discharge energies through the negating of polarity; rather, it develops useful polarities within the individuals, aligns them, and increases the potential difference between the poles. Each Magickian becomes his own magickal partner, complete, in one persona. This enables individuals to work in concert with any number of "others" of equal hermaphroditism. — cross-pollination, the mating of annelidae.

2) Macrocosmically, the Mass of Maat provides a cross-point, wherein ychronos and chthonos can a) merge, b) cease to be or c) be manipulated reciprocally and/or correspondingly.

At this writing (in terms of common-time), the Macrocosmic potential of the rite has yet to be realized. The celebration of the Mass provides a cross-point for us, however. We have complete access to our History, but the Mass provides a homing-focus that we find of value in terms of efficiency.

Continue the practice of the Mass of Maat. It is shielded until such time as ye gain full mastery of the cross-point. The name of the cross-point is NOW. The immediacy implied is a direct description, limited and created by your perceptions.

Celebrate the Mass; become aware of NOW; extend it perceptually along the axes of ychronos and chthonos in the directions of eternity and infinity—this brings the encompassing of Nuit by Hadit, and the transcendence thereof unto Maat.

Lila is simultaneous. History, progress and evolution are representations of individual points-of-view. All that is, is. Human consciousness is conditioned to see narrow, consecutive segments of

it, and thus is born the double-veiled illusion of the passage of time and the traverse of space ...

Alpha Centauri "sees" you four years "ago". The precession of the Equinoxes is an illusion—the sun is always rising in a complete circle of the Zodiac. The glaciers are marching and retreating simultaniously.

(Writing this at work and just phoned the "correct time" number-the voice said: Time-four-eighteen.")

Man is dragging his collective knuckles on the ground and at the same time is vibrating as white dwarfs and red giants.

See yourself, Nahada—that molecular chain of amino acid is you, and so is that red giant partner of that binary-system. You are the murderer staked out in the sun and also the priestess of Gaia. You are the plasma pseudopod hurtling through space in the tide of a supernova, and the molten basalt seething in process of planetary formation. Your substance is literally star-stuff—and ye return to your beginnings.

All that you are, from star-core to Star-core, is a continuing pattern of wave-particles. You are a pattern imprinted on various substances–when you will to do so, your pattern shall modify into the OM–and Nahada, as such, will not be, and not not-be.

The recognition and extension of NOW is best realized and manifested in the Mass of Maat.

This is its value.

Spoke with Gary S. by phone tonight. Damn! He was the first initiator, and has single-handedly (on Malkuth) assisted my

continued survival. Of course he doesn't trust me. Neither do I. As Maggie, I'm constantly walking the razor's edge. Even the writings of the past few days are a temptation–it is so deliciously attractive to live in the cosmic mode and let Malkuth function on automatic.

And it will, at that–that is, when my conscious attention resides in the spheres of light, my body carries out its functions perfectly, I can converse, drive a car, work the job, etc. However–

Gary S. knows when "I" am not "here". He regards this as an insult and as my not doing my will. This may well be so.

Since he needs my presence, I have been fairly well-earthed lately. (Since the trip with Don R.)

Since I am a Virgo, the subtlest traps are laid via Earth. My ego is based on the element of earth, and so when I am manifesting, (operating with attention in Malkuth) all sorts of sly ego-tricks try to happen. I'm detecting them at earlier and more subtle stages of development.

So far: Reading <u>Cults of the Shadow</u> and not quite believing what it's doing to my consciousness. Some of the material is recapitulation of earlier works, but so much is clarified for me, that it's "stopped my world" in Casteneda's terms.

Where <u>was</u> this book two years ago? It confirms so much of what was painfully learned (violently learned?) that it's the power-source of the present conciousness-change. It somehow triggered the writings of the past few days and gives me pause in terms of closely questioning my own work in re. Maat.

The chapter on Frater Achad did it.

But, in <u>Liber PP</u>, a great deal of stress is given to the point that it <u>is</u>

a preshadowing. The Æon of Horus is in progress. The voice of the Akasha questions She-Who-Moves closely on this–"The Hawk has flown but threescore and ten" etc.— She replies "I have come to aid the Children of the Hawk to fly."

The Maatians are naturally masters of spacetime. They travel freely upwhen and downwhen, and in all seventeen major dimensions (what?). Their presence in our midst isn't all that remarkable–save in terms of aesthetics. If their transcendence hadn't matched their sensitivities, I'd think they'd not be able to stomach our presence. Humanity still drags its knuckles in in many ways.

But–they do come. And in the company of the Brothers of the Comity. Extraterrestial intelligences indeed—and the only reason that they assist is friendship—for our future selves. That, and compassion for our "present" and past, selves.

So–Maat is preshadowing Herself in a very practical way–evolution-insurance, as it were. Hell, we went back to our Atlantean origins for the same reason, in a very crude (comparitively) way.

And rounding back to Gary S.–he is one of the first prototypes of the Maat gynander, and he needs to catch up with his personal developmental needs. I've a bit of ammunition already, since I've been in the flesh this time fourteen years longer than he. Why this particular timing? I'm not sure–but he's replaying his personal history at high speed right now—"is the imitation of an action that is serious, complete, and of a certain magnitude, which, through pity and fear, effects the katharsis of those emotions."

This is the primary focus of the now (NOW?)–Gary S.'s healing, growth, etc. He's airing it out, and I'm being water, mostly. Not only for his human individuality (which must be matured before being

transcended properly) but also for his role in this geographical area and in cosmic evolution.

The Cincinnati Vortex is manifested mainly through our workings, to the best of my knowledge. It had existed since the Adena Tribes lived here, but it hadn't really been attuned to, and energized by the 93 until Lu began his alchemical workings.

When Gary S. introduced me to the writing of Master Therion, and we did the first ritual in appalling ignorance–it was later found to have been a perfectly effective Mass of the Holy Ghost.

A Magickal Child was concieved–twins, as a matter of fact. The visible twin was the brief existence of a formal Lodge and the still-growing rapport of individual Magickians[1] in the area. The invisible twin was the process leading to the writing of Liber P.P.

Both have been earthed, incarnated. It therefore seems safe to claim success in the first phase of this incarnaton.

Now, the matter at hand is Gary S. In order to be of any help, I must join his Dance. This is a subterranean dance, dark, deep, the Elder Gods–but manifested in everyday simplicity. His is a Capricorn Moon, and he's finally managing to exercise his Yesod. And He expresses without attachment ... My function is to be as the flow indicates.

Last night ZsaZsa U. was relating a rather interesting experience. She said last Sunday, she found out that she'd been a male for most of her incarnations. I asked her what the method had been for knowing this. She said that she'd been visited by a man with long black hair ("Longer than yours, Mommy" –and mine's practically waist-length), in a black robe adorned by a seven-pointed star; he

---

1 Now manifesting as Beth Cabal.

was also holding a gold feather. (How much of the image derives from eavesdropping, I don't know). I asked if he'd said anything in particular, but she couldn't recall anything other than the akashic information.

Not bad for a nine-year-old, but then she's had Beble (her two-inch-tall invisible pal) since she could talk. Considering the children–Lili U. sees auras, and has been studying some basics (though I was a bit concerned when she was flirting with Wicca). She's asked for instruction in ceremonial magick which is fine training for the Ophidian workings––at least at age thirteen.

Bill U. claims to remember a life in the colonies during the Revolution–and he swears he can will people dead. Rather dark of him.

Zsa U.'s just plain fey. She sees people's familiars as animal-forms atop their heads. Even at age six months, she'd "go astral" and be gone from the Kingdom in consciousness frequently.

Julie U.'s my earthy Aries––maybe she'll discover the other planes sometime–it's her business.

2/2/76 e.v.

In the interim: I did get the review of <u>Cults</u> finished and handed-over to Lu. It'll be in the first issue. He seems to be having difficulties in getting Wiccan representation in the contributions. We could always ghost something along those lines–(but not I, Lord!) Phooey–Randy B.'s been initiated into a Gardnerian coven–let <u>him</u> do it.

It somehow eludes my grasp–how an individual can be operating as witch and magickian simultaneously . . . he's awfully fond of ceremony.

Pause for consideration: the "old rituals are black"–but, when a group of magickians are together in one place, the energy is so intense, it always (in my personal experience) instigates spontaneous ritual of some sort.

Last night, to my house were Lu, Randy B., Allen H., Friendly, Lizzie (Randy's lady), Gary S. and mineself. I gave Lu the review and borrowed his copy of Sothis Vol. 1 #5 (What's with the MacFarlane's? Lu and Randy B. have both met Peter and have no idea as to what might have prompted those ominous documents)... ah, well.

We all sat in the Temple–Lu central, self as Porter...Maat and Elder Gods invoked and we then hand-linked and it circulated. Lizzie said she'd never experienced any similar energy-flow. There is an automatic curcuit-breaker operant in each individual, I've noticed. Anyone's sensitivities regulate what they can receive and therefore handle. With the exception, of course, of those who've gotten themselves "stopped" —they're not doing their will in some fashion, and when transmitted energies come to them, it either precipitates them into a state of confusion or brings about catastrophic events that "happen" to them–financial reverses, traffic accidents, illness, etc. C'est la vie.

Mass of Maat Saturday eve... It came to charge one of the Cakes of Light for Gary S. to consume over the span of a week in seven parts. He's being more energetic and positive lately. The Mass was done well and completely–it improves with practice.

Friday. I awoke at 4 a.m. with the tachycardia in full course and Poochie barking his head off outside. It is an effective alarm system, but hopefully another means of returning me to Earth will evolve. I believe Myrrh A. was around on the astral.

2/2/76 e.v.

Candlemas. After last night's gathering, Gary S. obtained a ride home from Casey, since Dan C.'s auto, which Gary S.'d been using since both his chariots are ailing, would not start in the $\pm\,0^0$ F. temperature.

After work, I picked up Gary S. at Dick M.'s, went the grocery-store route, and brought him to the house for supper and an attempt to jump-start Dan C.'s car from the battery in my Olds.

There followed a successful energy-rondelay with Gary S., the kids, and John U.—ah, these adolescent developmental problems!

After the kids went to bed, I saw a scene in which Gary S., in scuba gear, was exploring an underwater arroyo for remains of Atlantean ruins. This changed to an open channel between him and the Children of Maat.

He/they are employing tremendous energies with him—primal, first chakra, survival powers. His Maatian-physical-self is running this initiation—which is reassuring—the fact that it's happening is proof of his survival.

He says he's experienced similar energies with an Egyptian Tarot deck, during the first Winter Solstice at Oz Farms, and again tonight. He almost lost consciousness he says, but maintained control for the sake of others. He was given a choice; to resist or to embrace the energies. The latter can be done in his temple at <u>his</u> chosen time.

This is the first time I've seen him actually dazed, "spacey", unearthed. He did touch the Kingdom in the act of driving the car home. He doubts his strength, but he wills to go on. This life is getting progressively more and more interesting. Dance, Maat!

2/4/76 e.v.

Windows installed and real-estate agent contacted. Last night Dan C., Siebhan, Gary S. and I astral structuring the farm, casting the I Ching–"Gathering Together" changing to "Following". And Don R. and Ben Rowe were over tonight.

Yesterday and today I experience tremendous antipathy from somewhere in the unconscious toward the farm. The title "head of household" provokes within me the following:

1) smug satisfaction of the autocrat
2) resentment at having to assume the Mask of authority
3) simple acceptance of the role in a very natural and non-attached way.

Not multiple-choice, but all of these (plus complicated variation and combinations) Also–desire mutates to strength which mutates to oppression which mutates to desire–spiral progression of an increasingly-refined cycle. Rajas-tamas-sattvas?

2/5/76 e.v.

Ben Rowe and Don R.'s visit–why? Ben Rowe: "Because Magick happens more at your house than anywhere else around." Don R. "Pinball machine–yaaah!" High-level vampirism? Will wait and see.

K.H. (my boss) searching, questioning his value-system–wants to read <u>Images</u> <u>and</u> <u>Oracles</u>.

2/8/76 e.v.

Spent most of today driving around the hills of Kentucky with Gary S., checking out possible locations of the farm. John U. signed a document tonight, that states his intention of giving me his half

of the profits from the sale of this house. Yesterday I spent in preparatory cleaning for the redecorating project.

We crossed back to Ohio on Anderson's Ferry—Lady Ganga, in all Your forms! She was in great spirit-running high and choppy, churning with the strength of the winds and of her vast eternal self. We stopped a bit upriver at a marina. I stood among three trees at water's edge and dropped a penny between their roots and into the river.

I've been given governance of the farm and in such, direct influence over the outer lives of seven people, including myself. Indirect influence of many others is also evident in events.

Part of me accepts this reality—it is li, it's part of my incarnational task. Another part protests, desiring only solitude in which to go inward and be/not-be in the heart of the forest.

If the Hindu concept of the four stages is correct, my state of householder is just beginning despite thirteen years of rearing a family. It is as though a spiritual family is coming into manifestation, and guess who is Reverend Mother?

But I, too, am Child!

Maati!

To you I dedicate the Dance of the Mask of the Abbess. I dance as a Child's play...it is but a Mask Dancing itself.

I wonder if it's a true Magickal vow, classically speaking—Hmmm. I haven't the foggiest about whether the following signifies a damned thing, but—

I, Nahada, do vow that I shall not take myself seriously, nor ever embrace the belief that "I" exist, save in such manner of appearance necessary to a given Dance or Mask in progress.

(The cats are making banshee love outside.)   To bed.

2/12

Finished <u>Images & Oracles</u>. Beautiful. And especially the portraits on p. 93. The immediacy of first-hand anecdotes makes this a more intimate glimpse of both subject and biographer. I wonder if it would be possible to persuade an autobiography to manifest from the author???

The business about gods disappointing one and releasing the energy of belief back to the source really strikes home. It reads like the theme of my life!

Of course–no<u>thing</u> can be powered–once an individual is focussed-upon as energy source/receptor, there's a stopping. We are verbs, not nouns.

Presently, Gary S. is recounting my misdeeds to me. True, my behavior, actions, perceptions, et alia these past two years have been somewhat less than admirable. No doubt I've been a major source of pain for him. He's focussed much of his life-energies on me, and I've done many things that could be considered abusive.

Yet presently I can feel no guilt–there's no pangs of conscience, nor inclination for contrition.

2/16/76 e.v.

Gary S.'s rightfully called a moritorium on alchemy with me. I have withdrawn to the Inner, here to consider a crisis of ethical decision (can one "decide" anything, and are "ethics" but a cosmetic rationale to mask blind instinct?).

However, using the vocabulary of the present illusion, it boils down to a Hamlet mask.

1) "I" have acquired power to influence and change human consciousness–the quantity and extent are irrelevant; <u>one</u> other individual within the sphere of this power would suffice.

2) My actions are less than impeccable. The synthesis of HGA and Elder Gods has not yet been completed successfully. By this I mean that I behave demonically on occasion, using anyone to enjoy the sensation of exercising power over them. This is Black.

3) There's no longer the excuse of ignorance to mitigate the responsibility.

4) The criterion for objective judgement in this matter is Maat as righteousness. In the scales of Anubis, does my continued presence in the Kingdom a) promote or b) retard the evolution of human consciousness?

(I note with astonishment that I am weeping.)

5) If the scales show that my presence is a detriment to the evolution of the Race, I will leave the Kingdom. If my presence is a benefit, then I shall continue in the flesh until this assigned incarnation has been completed.

6) At this point I invoke Maat that I may <u>see</u>, in full clarity, what the totality of my existence has wrought thus far.

Con—I have caused much pain both to the innocent, and the knowing ones. The innocent have been used, or at least changed in ways that they did not control. The knowing ones could not be used, but they have witnessed my being incomplete and less than I should be.

–I withheld supportive compassion from my father at the time of his death.

–I invested John with the ideal image of godhood that no incarnate human could possibly meet. At the inevitable failure, I abandoned

him—worse, he was made to feel himself a failure.

(Possibly missing text at bottom of sheet. Appears to be hand cut. –ed.)

–With Gary S., I persisted in regarding him as an image of mine own fashioning, instead of beholding him in the purity of his true nature. I would not permit myself to see him truly, for in true seeing, I could not hope to exercise my personal power over him—neither in terms of forthright seduction, nor in the subtler forms of chela or bhakti-yogini.

–With all others, I have not dealt with them according to their natures, but according to my own desires, tastes and preferences.

–I have procrastinated about the development of the full extent of my Magickal powers and abilities because this requires the complete abandonment of personal identity–I fear the Void–and this fear has meshed with my self-survival mechanism to the point of retarding my growth.

Pro–I attended the occasion of my mother's death, and assisted her passage in strength and warriorhood.

–I have borne four children, whose consciousnesses are being nourished in the solar radiance of the 93 Current.

–I have caused pleasure to others not only through my paintings, writings, conversation and lovemaking, but more importantly, in successfully mirroring them so they might behold their own Star-selves.

–With John U. now, I treat him as an equal, and encourage the growth of his strength.

–With Gary S., I am directing the totality of my strength to the rending of the veils of separation, using the Martial forces that are a large part of my nature to the implacable destruction of any

obstacles to Unity. The majority of these obstacles exist within me.

–I have not stopped. I cannot possibly renounce Magick and withdraw my awareness to Malkuth. Since it's impossible to regain the innocence of the uninitiate, there's no choice but to continue until I achieve the innocence of total enlightenment, and become the Eternal Child.

Greetings, NAHADA, I am ADAHAN, the Shadow of Hadit. I am you, your double. We must unite in Love-under-Will. Neither is complete without the other.

ANDAAHHAADNA in full, ANDAHADNA in final.

A = 1		Recalling the number-play on p. 50:		
N = 50		Nahada was given the number		71
D = 4		ANDAAHHAADNA works out to		124
A = 1	A = 1	ANDAHADNA	" "	117
A = 1	N = 50			312
H = 5	D = 4	$\frac{312}{2}$ = 156		
H = 5	A = 1			
A = 1	H = 5			
A = 1	A = 1	It's the number of the combined full form,		
D = 4	D = 4	124, and the spelling of the reduced form,		
N = 50	N = 50	ANDAHADNA.		
A = 1	A = 1			
124	117	AND = andros, man		
		AHA no comment necessary		
		HAD likewise		
		DNA desoxyribonucleic acid, the genetic blueprint		

Both NAHADA 71 and ANDAHADNA 124 seem to fit. Two different masks for different dances? "A rose by any other name..."

2/16/76 e.v.

Gary S.'s being harrassed by some "outside" force right now—if there is such a thing as "outside"... Maya is so hard to keep straight! I'm presently sending him a shield, and it does feel as though it's being bombarded from somewhere. Parabolic reflector on the astral to return the energies to their source.

Arise, my beloved, and come!
The time of pruning is at hand,
and the voice of the turtle-dove
is heard in the land.

Brother, awaken!
The Egg is shattered,
naked do you lie
upon the sands at the foot of the Mountain.

Remember who you are,
behold your forms of glory,
and arise!
The day breaks swiftly in the East–
prepare, O Brother-Priest,
Warrior and comrade,
Hierophant,
Let not the work here die.

I come on eagle's wings–
Receive me, Lion.
You bleed in BABALON's cup–
I weep to see the agony of blood–
"Torture the eagle until she weeps
and the Lion until he bleeds."

Is this not the Higher Alchemy?

When we unite in ritual of power,
none may surpass us
in our space of care.
We are untouched
by any in our realm;
we are the Force and Form
that guard the city.

And yet, beyond this land,
the orders of the gods are yet expanding;
you must not fail,
or fail full many
behind you, in a downward-falling flight.

What does it matter?
Only that I care,
and will not let you fall–
I am the guardian of your own True Will,
your Warrior's Will, that cannot be defeated.

Beyond your gates I will not go–
your fragile balance must not be disturbed.

But I will shield you,
hover over you,
and come as eagle
to your temple bed.
There to embrace,
and work the Alchemy that heals, and nourishes,
and restores you to your strength.

This separation, O Hawkson,
is but for the joy of union.

2/18/76 e.v.

After last night's entry, sent shield-energy to Gary S. Gods! He was wide open and leaking all over the lower astral—and sure enough, like blood in water draws leeches, sharks and other nasty things, there were plenty of scavengers after his life-energies.

Once the shield was around him and "locked in", I assumed the white eagle flight-form and entered his presence, received by his lion.

Went into the temple and did VIII° under invocation of Maat. The sigil appeared and was held throughout:

The power flowed directly in through the Feather, the Book of the Law, the wand, and me, into the sigil and on to him.

I wrote him a talisman-letter today in which I pointed out the nature of his block (orbiting around the foree of pain instead of Go-ing on) and did a lead-through into the pain, to complete disintegration and out through the Kether of a new Tree. If he's the least bit receptive, it'll work.

2/22/76 e.v.

The past four days have been busy. Today we were shown the first in a series of farms .. Dan C., Gary S. and I. I spaced out and had to get earthed by sheer will on return home.

Last night we did a Moon-Mass under acid, and some good things occurred—like channelling a rebirth process for Gary S. and having him resume full functioning to his capacity.

As usual, I feel as though I'm Going on a narrow, precipitous ridge—there's some illumination of the path now, but it's a twilight condition.

Assessment—I approach mastery, but control is incomplete. At present, am feeling preferences—such as being too earthed at times and not enough at others. I feel drawn to the astral planes (which are useful power-sources and sometimes informative) but this is a form of obsession. All planes must be at operating optimum at all times, and in balance.

2/24/76 e.v.

Don R., Ben Rowe, and a new gent named Randy were over last night. Randy's starting to question his reality, so I gave him the outline of the Tree of Life, a tip that he'll have to die and re-create himself, and advised him to keep a diary.

In the Temple, invoked Tahuti and did an energy-working. Ben Rowe gave me darshan and sort of bent himself from lack of practice. He says the lower triad within me is entangled in a web of what feels like solidified rubber bands. True. What is it?

The perceptible effects are an extremely negative emotional ambience. Hod gets messed up in terms of lack of clarity and the inability to communicate verbally. Netzach manifests an Osirian/Infantile/female desire to abdicate self-responsibility, or an overwhelming urge to withdraw from the marketplace. Yesod goes utterly murky and vague, irrational urges toward killing or suicide, or just giving up, manifest.

Not at all a pleasant mode of existence!

Ben Rowe says practice of operating constantly at full capacity/ability is the only way to establish permanency...

Later (almost midnight) After finishing the work at hand at the office, I managed to do about a half-hour's worth of mantra-meditation, and what a difference! Perhaps the main reason why I come so perilously close to losing Centre at times is due to sheer physical/mental/emotional fatigue.

Did VIII° tonight, under invocation of Maat. Purpose–to prepare for major Elder-God working. (Voice from within: you are working below grade) Answer from without: probably, but I don't see it. For one thing, I'm not claiming any grade, and for another, ritual is for the denser bodies. What should I be doing?

The night howls–
sirens in alarm, and cats' strange lovesong,
wind rounding corners,
moaning in its flight.
Read not your omens?

To match the hawk's flight
in your eagle-feathers,
first ye must plummet, owl-like,
from the moon.

Athena's bird of wisdom
trees itself, in the black sphere
of ocean's Understanding.

2/26/76 e.v.

Interesting session with Mrs. R. last night. She interpreted my natal chart, and I did a Tarot reading for her. We were impressed by each others' accuracy. The "deck-jumping" significator for her was the 4 of Disks, and she is a Capricorn.

I stopped in at Riddle Crest and reported the results to Dan C. and Gary S. They were in stitches because the chart reflected the accuracy of their own words about me. Dan C. started asking questions and I started channelling stuff about the Guatamala earthquakes, the new virus strains, mass initiations of groups—Typhon's next in Air–probably tornados etc. We did a silent energy exchange and it was nice.

Strange–I do a lot of the energy-workings with Don R. and Ben Rowe, and last night was the first time in a long time that I've done anything with Dan C. and Gary S. along those lines. Perhaps I'm to blame—Dan C. and Gary S. intimidate the hell out of me, and it's not conducive to higher energies to spend most of the time together engaged in parlor-psychoanalysis.

About the chart–basically, I'm a stubborn pushover. Mrs. R. emphasized repeatedly that naught can happen to me against my will, that I have control of my life, and that lack of discipline is the only reason for failure. She says I have the makings of a teacher.

2/27/76 e.v.

Gary S. came to my house last night–soon after his arrival, the phone rang. It was Don R., saying that he and Ben Rowe had received a powerful urge to come over to see me. So, all right.

Gary S. maintained a Mask of observation and invisibility throughout. Ben Rowe described an astral adventure he'd had this past week–a cavern-temple and enthronement of himself a la the Emperor trump. He's now claiming Magister Templi—oh, hoo hah!

He (Ben Rowe) is undertaking to correct my faults and energy-work my poor crippled nervous system (he says.) I am, according to him, becoming bogged down in the Elder God energies and will soon lose

all momentum and thus become trapped in Darkside forever and ever. Tsk!

It was all I could do to maintain a Mask of neutrality and acceptance of his consciously good intentions–there was considerable pressure to "cut loose" on him; but from where he is, he wouldn't have perceived the process correctly. In the post-mortem discussion, Gary S.'s only comment was on the subtlety of Ben Rowe's ego-trip.

Don R. was publicly embarrassed by Randy's total lack of discretion in re. the information he picked up here the other night. So it goes. The management will not be responsible for the results of carelessness in the use of the product.

In all, I was a bit disappointed with the lack of perception on Ben Rowe's part. He was so concentrated on the mysteries and wonders of the triangular relationship of himself, Don R., and me, that he apparently did not <u>see</u> Gary S. at all.

This in spite of some rather broad and obvious clues I provided, even in spoken conversation . . . Would that the more highly-developed ones, at least, manifest a little more awareness—Not that I'm manifesting at all well myself, of course–argh!

Everything (the stars) and everyone keep telling me to be more discreet, more selective–marvelous. Wonderful. All I need is small desert island and a dinghy I can demolish for building materials.

The only alternatives now visible are 1) complete self-isolation or 2) continued open acceptance of the company of individuals that "accidentally" drift my way–but seeing them clearly. Not rejecting them for failures or imperfections, but knowing their weaknesses as well as their strengths, and loving them regardless of either.

3/1/76 e.v. Quick catching-up. Saturday eve, did some blotter acid with Gary S. Not much physical visual distortion.

Began ritual and 2nd chakra energies were transmuted "up the planes". did a "chakra-opening" for him. Also received strong impression of "blackbirders". Bahaman-African slaver, dumping slaves overboard to avoid detection.

The evening was strained by my own tactlessness. Yesterday we did come to a better understanding, Alms park, discussing the situatiom.

He sees difficulty with Dan C., leaving also problems with veils. He is Hierophant, teacher, alchemical partner to me. Neither of us cares much for the concept of legal marriage, and yet considering the children, the only alternative is for him to be a "boarder" on the farm, but only if Dan C.'s living there. This "boarder" veil is only just passable with Dan C., and utterly ridiculous without him.

It's damned inconvenient living separately–the separation is financially a strain, and it renders ritual an isolated event, circumscribed by time and distance. Dan C. doesn't keep up his end, though–in terms of physical work and in energy.

Malkuth is sometimes a drag, in its own terms. One cannot deal with a problem on its own plane, though–so, we shall approach it from above.

3/2/76 e.v.

Don R., Ben Rowe, and Allen H. were over last night. Allen H. to receive a receipt for my payment to him of the $111. for the parchment Liber AL. This is to help him get on the Food Stamp program...He's headed for Florida next week with seven people in

a van. They'll be camping out and scuba diving at Key Largo. He's more stabilized and realistic, it seems. Good.

Don R. and Ben Rowe were informed of Gary S.'s nature as my teacher–they weren't overjoyed. What Gary S. says is true–like so many other Magickians of our acquaintance, they're adepts who indulge in shop-talk and time-wasting conversation <u>about</u> Magick.

I admit to a similar indulgence in the past (<u>recent</u> past) and also I percieve the need of a withdrawing from "socializing". The work at hand is to ready the house for the market, be with the kids more, channel energies and support to Gary S. and Dan C., get financially sound, find the farm, move, settle in, plant a crop, make the place livable, etc.

For the Inner, meditate more often, spend more time alone in the Temple, become acquainted with the persona of ANDAHADNA, and methodically <u>do</u> the Dance of the Mask.

Once established at Centre and getting each Sephora opened and operating at full capacity and balance, I'll be ready to begin the Dance-<u>with</u> Gary S. There's absolutely no way that I will write and/or publish the Dance of the Mask without having lived it first.

At present, I can't consciously see what benefit the Dance will be to the Workers. It appears to be a highly specialized and personalized system–of course, Lu and Randy B. want to publish it through C.C.P. (Conquering Child Publishing –ed), but it will have to be an effective method––

It's to enable one to shape the ego as the most effective tool for the manifestation of Current in Malkuth. Realization of potential of the Race of Man–is there any other Work?

This will include the taking of our proper place in the scheme of things—husbanding the planets in love and care, assisting wisely each sentient species to thrive according to its nature, becoming individually and racially pure, conscious, human, channels of the harmonious manifestation of Trimurti.

It is thine to Know, beloved,
the purpose of your journey in the Kingdom.
Self-knowledge, first,
for lacking this,
there can but occur
an aimless wandering,
a halt in GOing,
and confusion where there must be light.

Know that self is but a mask
that dances in the play;
behind the Mask is Being, pure,
and within, not-Being, equally.

That and Thatlessness,
the Hadit,
and NU surrounding and within.
The Mask for other Masks to see
shall be a rainbow-veil.
Evanescent beauty, here and gone,
in bright transparent colors
shall it shine.

Within, the Mask of mirror,
empty mirror,
still and clear.

The Outer Mask is veiled,

and cloaked in shadow,
dark, mysterious,
the shining beauty glimpsed,
by other Masks, as in a dream.

Thyself to see thy nothingness
and find the joy and sorrow
of this truth—
The Mask alone feels joy and sorrow,
feasting deep upon the blood of life.

By the same mouth, O Dancer of the Mask,
is the bloodwine savoured
and the prana breathed into the Void.

By the same mouth, Gynander of the Kingdom,
is the honey of thy Work shared by others
and the silence of the Egg maintained.

Dance on silver rainbows of thy spinning,
bridging worlds and planes and galaxies!

Fold and spread the wings of time and space,
weaving dream-desires for the Children,
spinning moonsilk fabrics of delight!

VIII° after phone call with Gary S. He seems so tired and energy-drained!

Used the new banishment, and invoked Maat.

Declared will to direct the entire force of the Cincinnati vortex to him, channelling through my AQUILA astral eagle-form. I united

with him sexually on the astral during the culmination of the rite. So basically the energy was sent twice–first directly through space/time and secondly via the channel of NAHADA-AQUILA.

The follow-up will be in terms of the solid earth-energy I've been working with these past two days. While I'm at it, I'll send Dan C. some Mars/Scorpio fire-energy . . .They seem to have the Tamasic Toad re-forming atop the house.

Strange; even under invocation of Maat, I functioned as NAHADA. The invocation didn't fail–but it seems that Maat's presence leaves the Magickal "identity" intact.

Ordinarily, the god replaces the conscious self, at least as I've experienced it. Maat seems to <u>unite</u> with the conscious self instead. I like that.

3/3/76 e.v.

Well, maybe the previous night's hexagram means something for today. (#29 the Abysmal) The old chronic <u>angst</u> is acting up again–(i.e. "Here I am 37 years into this incarnation and <u>why</u>?) This indicates the persistance of the ego-self–what else could possibly ask "why"? Some impish little Mask perches on my shoulder and responds "why not?". All dissolves in laughter.

Doing the Tarot here.

Dan C.'s tamasic toad seems to be the source of the "drag" I feel. This comes through Gary S. to me. and perhaps is the way of rebalancing it. Analyze it, get some earth-fire generating, but adopt the <u>form</u> of receptivity.

The Binah cards indicate that perhaps I should draw the tamas to myself, secretly. Chesed indicates receptivity, and Geburah the

warrior-priest of Maat. The Magickal triad indicates alchemical working in the near future with some definite astral-earthing. This is perhaps in terms of a sigil and dream control—or in duality with Gary S. I don't know whether it's wise to ask him to participate just now, since his energy-levels are low, and it's the Toad that's doing it.

3/4/76 e.v.

In the name of Tahuti, Aumgn.

This is a Word given through NAHADA 71. It is Word of a Task; first of Omnê, then of the Children of the Law, then of the Race.

The Task is the bringing into manifestation in the Kingdom the whole of the Law, which is love under will. The force of the Task is the current 93, in union with Current of the Aeon of Maat.

The form is that of the Crowned and Conquering Child—this Child being the Race-Consciousness of Man. The Knowledge of the change to be worked is that Man resides presently in the Abyss, as Harpocrat-within-the-Silence. The Race-Mind sleeps, and manifests as the "collective unconscious"—the seat of the Elder Gods who have made the Gods of Light through the sleeping planetary mind. Man must be awakened to full consciousness in the mode of Ra-Hoor-Khuit, so that he may act as the balanced and double-aspected Heru-Ra-Ha.

The art of the Task lies in the perception of all the necessary factors, the pattern of their arrangement, and the aesthetic approval of the Task-in-progress. Ruling this creative process is the production of Magickal sigils on all the planes, particularly in the Place of the Unborn. These sigils are executed by the Dance of the Mask.

The conditions for the Task are defended by the Warrior-Priests

who dance the Mask fully armed at all times. Such is the power of evolution, that any who would retard, halt, reverse, or in any way interfere with the course of the working shall be eaten by Choronzon, whom they invoke by the opposition to the order of evolution.

The beauty and centre of the Task is that the conscious Race-Mind of Man is the inevitable development of our nature. We are not opposing nature, except insofar that nature resists change, even when the change is consonant with Her laws. We are simply becoming that which it is ours to be.

We are to be a world-Child, so we may play in wise innocence with our friends and brothers who await our awakening. We shall live, grow, and die, and be reborn as the Race Mind, dancing Maya until this cycle closes—such is our will and our delight.

The teaching and communication, the education and the mutation shall be done by Scientific Artistry, or Artistic Science. The work will inspire and give pleasure while subtly imparting the needed information on the patterns of genetic change. This will not be didactic art or propaganda, but the revelation of the patterns of Man.

The operant place of the Task is within the realm of the astral planes. It encompasses the use of the titanic power of the Elder Gods to arouse the sleeping Child—through the use of nightmare, if need be. It is also the mode of the moon, wherein is suspended all disbelief. Man is becoming more receptive to the inner realities. The specialized location of the Place of the Unborn shall be attuned to the Chord of the Child, and the sigils fashioned by the Dance of the Mask shall be enwoven in its frequencies.

There is a small chromosome-change needed in the realm of the

brain/mind interface. It is the unlocking of PSI faculties, allowing the intuition to function at full efficiency, and achieving clarity of perception.

Each incarnating soul spends time, while awaiting the correct new body to be concieved, in the Place of the Unborn.[2] It is from this place that it oversees the development of its body from conception through embryo-stage. At the point where the body becomes a fetus, the soul enters the body and development is guided by the individual and the racial subconcious. One forgets, in the womb, the experience of the past; and to forget is to place a thought into the subconscious.

By attuning the Place of the Unborn to the Current 93 and the Current of Maat, and by impressing information therein by the sigils woven in the Dance of the Mask, we give the waiting soul the means to achieve its own mutation. It will ever be the individual's choice to personally awaken or no. Only a few will be experienced enough to understand, and only a few of these will dare to change themselves in such a profound manner.

3/5/76 e.v.

For the others, the inexperienced or timid ones, the Dance of the Mask will condition their dreams, in such a manner that will dispose them to accomplish their awakening during the course of their incarnation.

The Elder Gods will be brought closer to the threshold of the day-mind of Man. The Gates of Inbetween will be opened by the Black Flame, who will remain poised in that portal. Those individuals who will not adjust themselves before birth will find it extremely

---

2 Same as the Bardos of the *Tibetan Book of the Dead.*

uncomfortable to remain unconscious in the course of their lives.

Nightmare will haunt their noontime—the hour sacred to Pan will see the glimpse of vast shadows, and reality will change appearances to match the deepest terrors of Man's sleeping soul. It is likely that waves of madness will sweep the planet—but there will be no refuge for the mind that seeks to cling to its unawareness. There is no asylum from the Elder Gods—whether in insanity, physical death, or in distraction through sensual pleasures.

When the sleeper wakes, the Dancers of the Mask will have prepared his place within the pattern of the Dance. The Dancers will be as the Hermit—holding aloft the light of the sleeper's Star so he may behold his Nature and Will.

In the Kingdom, the Work shall proceed as follows:

The Dance of Maat will be performed by each Dancer—this is the means both of self-education and preparation for the progress of the working. Those who live the Law of love under will shall perfect their realization and manifestation, each according to his/her will. These are the Warrior-Priests, the Hermit-Kings, the Artist-Hierophants and the Teacher-Fools.

Whose will it is to farm, will grow the food as holy sacrament; whose will it is to build, will render each structure as a temple. Shopkeepers will purvey their wares as Magickal weapons; who govern and enforce will do their wills as guardians of the harmony of the spheres. The artists, craftsmen, teachers, parents, athletes, healers, and scientists will practice their disciplines in purity and truth, for the sake of the joy of the doing.

By allowing to be done what it is one's nature to do is the Dance of the Mask rendered perfectly. This prepares the planetary conditions

for the inner and more specific working, as well as preparing the Magickian for the working in the Place of the Unborn.

The specific ritual for beginning the Task shall be done upon the Spring Equinox, 1976 e.v.

Even though the complete formulation of the Dance of the Mask has yet to be earthed, there shall be, as the first part of the rite, the invocation of each Mask of the Double Tree of the schema. Ye have awareness of each in Tiphereth—the invocation and ritual declaration of each Mask shall begin its course toward complete manifestation in the Microcosm and the Macrocosm.

Invoke, then, Maat as the Black Flame. She will guide to the Place of the Unborn; ye are to remain invisible to the souls in this place. Impress in the Air of this place the symbols of the Eye of Horus and the Feather of Maat. Link to the symbols the cord of your consciousness, and follow the Black Flame to the portals of the Temple of Typhon. Pass within.

Do not cast a circle within the Temple; rather, pause to assure certainty of your Centre and Chi and then invoke the Elder Gods en masse. The Named and Nameless shall ye call—the Names shall come forth from your lips without passing first through your mind. Open totally to Them but never vary from your Centre and balance.

Within the Temple of Typhon, and in the midst of the Elder Gods, without circle nor fear, perform ye the Mass of Maat. At the first drawing of the Nectar, when the energy thereof passes through the Priest, he shall will that his seed be substance for the Elder Gods—in the distillation through the chakras, the priestess shall unite the essence of the Old Ones with the Black Flame in the fountaining of the Sahasrara.

During the second phase of the Mass, both celebrants shall open their whole selves to the energies of the Elder Gods and of Maat, so that the tri-unity of the elixir shall be a perfect balance. At the instant of ecstasy, the symbols of the Eye of Horus and the Feather of Maat shall be illumined by the Lightning-Flash. This will transfer the energies of the working to the Place of the Unborn, graving therein the sigils of the Dance of the Mask for the attunement of the incarnating souls.

A portion of the Elixir then should be used for the charging of a Cake-of-Light. The remainder shall be consumed by the priests.

Kindle a flame within the censer. With the wine of the chalice, baptize the Cake-of-Light as Adam Kaedmon. In the names of the Elder Gods, the Priest shall eat a small portion thereof; in the name of Maat-Maut, the priestess shall do likewise. The remainder shall be eaten by the fire.

Together, the celebrants shall call forth and summon: Heru-Pa-Kraat! Ra-Hoor-Khuit! Heru-Ra-Ha!

Here ends the rite. So mote it be.

There'll be more on this, but I'm pausing here to type up the material given thus far for Gary S.'s consideration.

If the miraculous were to happen too often, wonder would become the commonplace, and awe would become the everyday.

Ah, but I would disagree! Is not the commonplace miraculous, and is not the everyday the most awe-inspiring reality that we know?

How so?

The fact that we exist, in such a form, with such a nature–unique, free, continuing on in our lives–that such fragile creatures could so long endure is amazing.

We are but a fraction of a second old in the lifetime of a star–our race is scarce the wind's brush on the face of the mountain.

And to a mayfly, we are the eternal.

Art thou the Optimist in this debate?

Only if you choose to play the Pessimist.

Why sit we in debate?

Because there exist diverse natures among the sentients of this Universe–we also are diverse.

How can you know this? We don't even have names! We're being born from this moving pen–coming to be as we speak.

I do believe you're right. Say there–you who write–what are you doing? If you're going to be God for us, the least you can do is render a proper job of creation.

What seems to be the problem, gentlemen?

Here we are, suddenly existing on the pages of your Magickal Record–and with no idea of why.

Well, don't ask me–I'm just moving the pen. Shall we find out the nature of this manifestation?

I'd like to find out who I am, first, and who this other character is.

By the way, who are you?

I'm Nahada 71 in these pages. And what makes you think a proper creator is supposed to name her creations? Adam was put in charge of naming all the animals.

Adam.   That's _my_ name.

How do you know?

It feels right—how else should I know?

So he's Adam ... Who am I?

Who do you feel that you are?

Gawain? No. Grendel? Uther Pendragon? Bohwani? I'm strong, you know—sort of your sword-and-sorcery hero-type. Ah Ha! See? You got an astral picture of me just now, didn't you?

Yes. And you're not bad-looking at that. I saw that you had rather longish bronze-colored hair, a saffron cloak, a leather headband, a silver kilt, knee-high strap sandals—yes, and you have a broadsword in a sort of furry sheath hanging from a silver-studded belt. Nice body.

Can you see _me_?

You're robed in a rather heavy, wine-red habit—at any rate, it's floor-length, with full sleeves and a hood. Your hands are pale. You are slighter of build than our friend here, and you are southern and he is northern. Oh—you have a heavy cord cincture about your waist, and you have a leather scrip hung crosswise—the strap's over your left shoulder and the container's on your right hip.

Acceptable.

But what's my name?

Sorry, my warrior friend. You could be Conan if you'd like.

Too trite. And no, I'm not Farfhed, even though he looks like the Grey Mouser.

Hmmpf.

How about Zan?

Very well. It feels good, like Adam said.

So. Adam. Zan. What is this all about?

Nothing, except you know that you've created us, we exist. There's no more point to our existence than there is to yours. Remember "Waiting for Godot"?

Point taken, gentlemen. Good night.

3/9/76 e.v.

Have been quite agitated all day—losing my objectivity, perhaps, or letting Patrick M.'s change get to me. Saturday I went to D.O.L. (Dawn of Light —ed) and he did his damnedest to convince me that Magick is evil. Today Gary S. informed me that he's (Patrick M.) going to discontinue selling books on Magick, Wicca, etc., and only carry astrology, eastern and Christian books.

Gary S. indicates it's a time of universal retreat—perhaps this is so.

I do feel a gathering of fire-energy, perhaps because of the approach of Spring.

Hail to the Ram-feast of Spring!

The sleeper wakes, stirring underground.

Green heralds of the Sun's new year
let fly the bold and tender banners
of triumph over death and cold.

Unconquerable life!
As on the seasons turn,
so roll the tides of birth and growth and death.

Long ere the Sun winks out
(as cosmic cinder floating dead in space)
this daily miracle that men call life
will have its star-wings
and shall seed the heavens.

This is true.

3/10/76 e.v.

First, sorrow over Patrick M.'s "conversion" and recanting. Although I know this whole thing is Maya, I'm nevertheless saddened by his change. Next, in the line of business, I'm being defensive of Mr. Harris and his actions. Then, just had a kick in the heart chakra and I feel a heat rising in me.

Conclusion: there seems to be an "attack" underway–or, seeing it differently, my Centre and balance are in a precarious vulnerability.

Patrick M. does channel much power, and he's letting it go; rather, he's hurling it from him. This is disturbing the entire vortex and requiring a new stability and balance to be found immediately. Equinox is also immanent, which also signals a directional change.

The working: Kether–restoration of balance to Cincinnati vortex
Chokmah–the 93 Current and the Maat Current
Binah–Omnê
Da'ath–Harpocrat as Hadit
Chesed–Assignment of emphases–Hermit
Geburah–alchemy and individual master-consciousness
Tiphereth–Warrior as Ra-Hoor-Khuit
Netzach–Brotherhood of Stars
Hod–Bear-Claw speaks for Pan-Hermes
Yesod–Kali devours, Typhon bears Set.
Malkuth–non-action–Tao is Tao

Interesting–subjective problems cease when the energy flows. The flow stops when the consciousness centers in any particular Sephora, including the Supernals.

Later. Gary S. dropped by the house this evening and found me atop a ladder, busily painting the temple-room. The first coat's finished now.

He's being understandably fiery. I <u>have</u> let myself be influenced by Patrick M.'s "fall". But it's sorrow manifesting through Mars !! more five of Cups, Mars in Scorpio and all that.

He says again that I've been acting like an adept–in his universe, a term of semi-scorn. Why don't I deal with the "seeds of things" the way I should? I'm capable of so doing, because the experience is there.

Yet, time and again, I find my consciousness (dayside consciousness!) focussing within the Ruach and I instigate action therefrom. Is there still that much unharnessed Ego left? Woman, you slide all over the

Tree like an epileptic monkey!

The more subtle awareness grows, the more quickly does Mind veil the vision. This is some sort of initiation. A multiple-effect event.

1) Gary S. says that Patrick M., despite heading the Lodge and claiming to operate via the 93, was never able to accept the third part of the Book of the Law. His personal power was so effective that the results of his workings <u>seemed</u> to be of the Current, as he claimed.

2) In spite of the genuine affection I feel for Patrick M., I must never stoop to pity, or to taking his "trip" seriously. The Mask he's dancing is illusion, and a comic illusion, at that. (Gary S. says that laughter generates positive, healing energies; seriousness and worry generate negative energy. The best way to "do" anything for Patrick M. is to laugh at him. But I'd much rather laugh <u>with</u> him, but he's being too serious about himself for that to happen anytime soon.

3) Gary S. can no more remain uninvolved with whatever I'm doing than <u>I</u> can–for there's no difference. He sees truly and clearly that we are not just "individuals", but Omnê. He <u>lives</u> what I've been channelling–and so do I, albeit subconsciously for the majority of the time.

My demons have been zealously guarding this veil for quite a while–they've so effectively used the tool of obsession that it wasn't until tonight did I catch an indication of the depths of the being, Omnê.

I keep wanting to wear a name when I am nameless!

The unity of Omnê is <u>not</u> some pretty poetic metaphor or an abstract philosophical concept—it enjoys a reality in the Kingdom.

I write this Record as Maggie, or Nahada–and am therefore engaged in a subtle deception. No. It is the Tao–highly colored by the personality that wields the pen–that is writing itself and of itself through the agency of an "individual".

3/15/76 e.v.

A five-day lapse, hmm? Things have been rather hectic, but still—

The tenth was a Thursday. Friday, Siebhan invited me over for a chat. She's living upstairs of Dan C. and Gary S. I dropped in on them first, in a hilarious mood because of the comedy of errors that Julie U. had initiated. Dan C. joked a bit, but Gary S. retired behind the newspaper, seemingly a bit miffed at the manic energies.

Upstairs with Siebhan. She spoke of various creative projects that she's engaged in, also bringing up the fact that the termination of her living with Dan C. was fast approaching . . . (Typist's note–as of Aug. 20, they're still together.)

She told me that she has been active in the Cincinnati lesbian community and that many of her friends are astounded that she's living with a man. I know she was watching for a reaction–but the only reply that came to mind was "If you love someone, what difference does it make what sort of body they wear"?

She's divorced from a bitter and violent marriage–her two children are living with her ex-husband. She had a breakdown of sorts, and came to live with Dan C. as a sort of retreat and recuperation period. They set a time limit on the relationship (supposedly ending May 1), and both are feeling the pangs of the limitations.

She wants to open a feminist bookstore, perhaps on a mail-order basis at first. I told her that if there were a comfortable margin available from the real estate dealings, we perhaps could financially

back the venture.

Following the conversation, Gary S. was very upset, fiery-commanded that I go to my temple and become aware of the energies on other planes.

After I arrived back at my house, I didn't even have time to cast a circle; the phone rang and he was on the line. He'd been subjected to an attack, he said, from me (!) in terms of Isian energy generated during the conversation with Siebhan. Perhaps I'm lacking in awareness, but conscious mind was doing no such thing...Ah well, the exchange did evoke a rather nasty demon—mine, of course.

Said demon's named Envy and his first words were—"I am the Lord thy God; thou shalt not have strange gods before me." He/it went on to say that his aim was to be master of the Cosmos, anyone commanding more power than himself would be attacked and destroyed, and their power added to his own. Nice fellow. We triangled him until the following night.

Saturday night, before the Mass, we entered the triangle with him. He went for Gary S., but I transposed myself between them, held the demon back, then embraced him, felt him re-enter and merge substance with me, and I consciously integrated him—again. So, he and I are united, but in a different way.

Yesterday we painted my bedroom—it was a joyful day. The physical work was a dance, the energy-flow was invigorating, and conversation aired out many things that needed discussion.

Well, if weather permits, we'll be doing the Equinox ritual at Red River Gorge. Allen stopped by to collect his things, and mentioned that there were caves in the cliffside.

It's worth exploring.

Randy B. phoned me at the office, with a scheme to buy out D.O.L's stock of books on Magick, Wicca, etc., and open a "hard-core" store of his own. It'd be nice—but he'd best acquire some practical business theory first.

3/16/76 e.v.

Yesterday I managed to finish the second coat of paint in the bedroom, conversing all the while with Mary Sue, my sister-in-law. She's back in Cincinnati for medical treatment—she's had a uterine infection for the past five years, and the military medical people did nothing for it. So brother Jim (Electronics Technician 1, U.S. Navy) remains in the Phillipines.

In her tale, it's apparent that the Navy's dehumanized Jim to an alarming degree. He refused to believe that she was ill until a definite and frightening convulsion convinced him. She says he enjoys the regimentation of the Navy.

Of course, if the smallest details of one's life are regulated, then there's no need to think, or make decisions. What a damnable Osirian slave-situation!

I should write him a letter, but presently there's too much Martial energy surrounding my vision of him.

Later, during a phone conversation with Gary S., I learn that Dan C.'s staying the week at Dr. White's. So the gentleman _is_ Dan C.'s voice teacher—it's still delaying any work on the preparation of the Riddle Crest house for sale.

Perhaps I'm becoming too earthbound and obsessed with work. Oy, but there's so much painting to be done on the house, and

other repairs to be effected, and the ordinary household chores of cleaning, laundry, etc. simply pile up in the process.

Ho ho! This is being written at work–and Gary S. just now called. He, Dan C. and Siebhan awoke with a jolt at precisely seven this morning–and he'd been dreaming that I'd abandoned a feast and cut everyone off totally—hmm. It feels as though there's a volcano revving up inside me just now.

3/17/76 e.v.

Sure, and it's older than Christianity, the sanctity of this day... hail, the Tuatha da Daanan—hail Llyr and Tyr na N'og.

Stopped at Riddle Crest last night. Dan C. suggests that I'd visited Jim astrally from the dream state–probably true, which accounts for my being actively miffed at him (Jim) on awakening. Too much fire and judgement.

Seated at their table, I felt Gary S. lift my hair and tie something about my neck–he told me to check the mirror and lo! it was one of Siebhan's macrame necklaces–with beads representing (Queen scale) Kether, Chokmah, Binah, Chesed and Geburah. The cord's gold–simply elegant!

Went astral tripping to a blue-green tunnel with brainlike masses (cerebral convolutions) and to a place having hanging tendrils of purple, green and blue. I made contact with a dolphin named TUD'L, of the Order of the Marlin. He informed me that dolphins are the priests of the ocean, that dolphins are generally advanced spiritually because of lack of hands and subsequent distracting technology, and that we can trade bodies for the joy of the experience. Nice guy.

Later a strange energy exchange followed by a small but lovely IX°

working. The energy-thing had Gary S. touching my spine in various centres and sequences–there followed such an influx of power that "I" left the body for a while––whew!

3/19/76 e.v.

Tomorrow's Equinox–the temperature's risen nicely; it's supposed to reach the mid-70's (°F) tomorrow. The sky's overcast now, but the campsite's far enough south of here to invalidate speculation based on local data.

Gary S.'s in the Vision of Sorrow again, in a way. He's still spectacularly human. It would seem that he still had Karmic learning to do about pain, since he's experiencing so much of it now. True, I've been a major source of it for him, and, humanly speaking, I do not want to hurt him at all.

Herman Hesse––Magister Ludi, Journey to the East . . . .

The business at hand is experience and assistance. "I" am to learn/remember the vision of consciousness-as-It-is, and at the same time assist the race to do likewise. Working with Gary S. is the Magickal end of it–in our Temple-lab, we learn essences; in Dancing our Masks, we signal-code the Current with the data of change, planting seeds, as it were, to grow within the racial unconscious of Man.

There's a certain amount of feedback, though, of tamas-force or Choronzon/Chaos endemic to the Race. We're not as 'insulated' as we should be but that's just a matter of growth, I hope. I know of Man's retardation, because I experience it myself. I also know of Man's potential, because I've experienced, in an incomplete way, certain states of being and act that are more harmonious and complete than the average daily reality of the "present".

This is true of Gary S.–he's in the process of becoming, also. Even though he's more advanced than I, he still has his lapses in manifestation–and perhaps I've been remiss in not mirroring them for him more forcefully.

3/20/76 e.v. This is being written at the campsite. Our impromptu tent's up and dinner's been eaten. There are several young men in the remote part of the field, and a couple has pitched a tent near the turnoff from the road, We'll have to be very careful with our circle.

3/22/76 e.v.

This is the first opportunity available to make an entry since returning from Red River Gorge.

The journey and the ritual itself were successful. All the elements were an integral part of the working–campfire, thunderstorm, the earth. As night fell, we had a glimpse of the stars before the clouds gathered. We stoked the fire well, causing it to burn high and well, and then we fashioned a small altar-place on the earth before it.

We banished, scribed a circle that included the fire and the tent, and declared the Law.

We danced the twenty-two Masks of the Double Tree before the fire–each of us taking turns in naming the Mask and dancing it in mudra/gesture/mime. When we reached the Malkuth of the second Tree, we invoked Maat.

We then journeyed to the Place of the Unborn, and established the Eye of Horus and the Feather of Maat in the Air, invisibly to the souls there, within the obelisk-temple. Maat then led us to the dark gray granite Temple of Typhon.

We retired to our tent (which might as well not have existed,

save for visual privacy) as the first drops fell. The Typhon Temple manifested in the Kingdom as a thunderstorm with mighty bolts of lightning. The Mass of Maat was celebrated in the midst of the Temple and the storm, <u>without</u> a second circle being cast, and therefore in naked contact with the forces and powers of all planes.

At the climax of the Mass (and the storm), the symbols of Horus and Maat were called to consciousness and the link between the Elder Gods, the Black Flame and the Unborn was established. The rite succeeded in its purpose.

There were numerous other things that happened the following day. A ring of our hair was fashioned and given to the place-spirits at the Altar of the Sun. This altar is a sandstone outcropping on the side of the Tunnel Ridge crest that has a two-foot tall chalice sculpted from the living rock by the action of wind and storm. In its cupped hollow was the rainwater from the storm; we each drank from it in reverent communion.

In all, it was an experience of wealth—the hills, the rocks, the magnificent cave site on the road to Tunnel Ridge, the golden-eyed toads so tame they could be touched without fleeing.

My only regret was that my achievement of silence was incomplete, and I did become attached to the place. Perhaps my present condition is attributable to having some of my bodies still there. I shall now ingather what I may of myself.

3/29/76 e.v.

Devoted Saturday morning to writing to Mr. Grant and the afternoon to washing walls.

Mr. Grant opened some interesting vistas—for one, that Patrick

M.'s "conversion-attempt" isn't all that it appears to be, that it's a common occurrance of 'testing' probationers, and that things eventually flow aright.

He also brought to stage-center again the practise of Bhakti Yoga. From our conversation, Gary S. may be amenable to working this way again, on the Outer, but suitably veiled from the profane. He's understandably leery of it degenerating into mere hero-worship or any other manifestation that might deviate in the slightest degree from utter purity. Agreed.

Painting a room with him is a most enjoyable exercise in Karma Yoga. The energies flow between us, in and around the whole house; the children appear, assist, disappear, bring their friends over to help and to receive the flow of the work-energy—in short, it's an extensive earth-working that generates pure joy. It's the practical application of the doing of will—would that all of life were so sweet, simple and strong!

Don R. visited Friday night, bringing a bottle of wine and an irreverent brochure on "The Bloatarian Brotherhood". He's taken up skydiving—for the thrill of it, I suppose. He's an intriguing individual, much more aware than I'd originally supposed him to be.

3/31/76 e.v.

Gary S. tells me that Linda G. and Lu are to be married—after happily living together for more than a year. There's no accounting for taste, I suppose. Gary S.'s been thrown into a contemplative state by this, which in turn affects my consciousness.

I sincerely hope he's not going to approach the subject with me in the near future. At this point I'm older than the human race,

older than organic life itself. The four states of life follow a true and profound course of spiritual development and, as an individual, I only have about ten more years remaining as a householder.

As an individual, Gary S.'s still in the student cycle. When the time comes for him to be a householder, he should seek out and find someone of his own chronology or younger.

I weary of life in the flesh–it's simultaneously ephemeral and interminable. All the intense Karma Yoga and enthusiasm about the farm seems pointless–either it will manifest or it won't–and it really doesn't matter. "I" do not own the energy, money, or will that's being invested in the project–and it all suddenly seems boring.

Any earthly endeavor, as a matter of fact, seems equally pointless. ("The point is, is that there is no point.")

O, my Brother of the Outer Dark,
We chose this life of flesh before our birth.
In time, in space, I have forgotten much
that deals with task and purpose, rank and fate.

Can you recall, dear Warrior, why we came?
It deals with Man, I know, and gods, and freer life–
in taking flesh, one eats the lotus and forgets–
only in dream-glimpses have I seen the plan.

The flesh becomes a burden in its joys.
'Tis a fair planet, filled with holy life,
the light of sun and moon, the course of stars,
the strength of mountains echoes strength of space.

Is it for the spider's web, bejewelled at dawn,
or hillside rivulet's sweet crystal laughter

that we came again? Everywhere is beauty
in the Kingdom-O! And yet, and yet-

The pain is everywhere! The blindly reaching-out,
the agony of not-yet-realized becoming!
(They mine the gold of the Sun to fashion chains,
and yoke themselves in empty servitude!)
The Tao is, and we are, and yet are not-
O Brother, let me go to whence we came
or speak to say the limits of our task-
what must be done to earn release from self?
What is the work? Or must we simply be
until the time arrives to cease from being?
If this be true, so mote it be.

4/1/76 e.v.

And a happy April Fool's Day to all! This is a feast-day of high order ... ah! The Greeks may have had a word for it, but I don't-many words, perhaps, and none too coherent-TAHUTI! I invoke thee!

Still thy mortal pen and tongue, woman, and be clear in the recording of perceptions-and let the perceptions be clear, first and foremost.

Prego! In listening to Gary S. describe his relationship with Dick M. (his employer-a quasi-Marxist curmudgeon who would be intolerable to ordinary people), I percieved the true nature of Gary S. himself.

He's becoming a god.

This is only beginning to be realized by his consciousness-the veils of his humanity are/were as effective to his own inner vision as they are to the Outer Kingdom.

He is <u>living</u> love-under-will.

He endures a heavy barrage of unpleasantness, pain, attack, blindness from those whom he assists in changing themselves (and <u>I'm</u> a prime example of that.)

He endures in situations that would defeat normal men of normal sensitivity—and he is more sensitive, psychically, than anyone I've met. What is merely disagreeable for others is pain for him–human pig-headedness, lack, the not-doing-of-will.

He endures, and renders change of awareness to others. His personal preference would have him retire from human company altogether–and yet he lives in the midst.

His love is selfless, detatched, pure–he wills to love, and love is becoming his will, more and more so.

He lives as saints of all faiths strive to do–and in the midst of this living will/love, he pours every drop of his blood into the Cup of BABALON...

I did Shivapuja last night, with his permission. This helps me to <u>see</u> him.

4/2/76 e.v.

Awoke this morning with heavy emotional avoidance-reaction to Gary S.–the sensation was one of not being able to cope with what he's becoming. The same sort of dread with which I approached childbirth, and with which I see the farm project.

It, they, he–are so damned <u>huge</u>–tremendous, overwhelming! A certain part of "myself" is in a state near to panic. Hmm. PAN-ic, indeed.

I cower somewhere in a corner of my mind, whimpering–"No! I can't handle it! It's too much! Stop the world, I want to get off–help!" And slowly, like a vampire-mist flowing under the door and through the cracks in the windows and down the chimney, comes the realization– "But Maggie, dear, this is how it <u>all</u> is. Your narrow viewpoint of reality has sheltered your infant consciousness up till now, veiling the infinity that threatens to send you into a fit of cosmic agoraphobia–Time's up! Remove the blindfold–surprise, surprise!"

Ah–dread, fear, panic–delicious silent <u>scream</u> that sends the Rabbit-Ego skittering down some twisting corridor below. Alice sits bemused, hands full of eat-mes and drink-mes, not really knowing <u>what</u> to do with it all.

The hookah still smolders atop the mushroom–where has the Caterpillar gone? The ubiquitous Cheshire-cat smile appears, only this time around it forms the three-eyed goat of the the Devil Trump. Alice eats <u>and</u> drinks (to Nuit! to Nuit!), then closes her eyes to meditate awhile.

Made a red and yellow wax "Eye of Shiva", and charged it nicely VIII°, went to Mt. Airy forest and buried the thing beneath the campfire-site in the pine grove––just following intuition without any specific notion as to what it's about–fire and earth, for something.

4/6/76 e.v.

For those of you who've missed the recent installments of our ongoing dramatic presentation, here's an essential summary:

Dan C. and I put down $100 in earnest-money on a place in Georgetown, Ohio this past sunday. Beautiful place.

John U. pulled an attempted attack-threat last night—going to take

the kids from me if I move that far out of Hamilton County. I checked with my lawyer, Rodger, this morning; John U. has no substance nor power to harm.

4/9/76 e.v.

With the increased tempo of developments in the Outer, it's been difficult to find time enough for entries here.

John U.'s taken a 180° turn, and is now expressing a very positive attitude about the farm.

Stopped at Riddle Crest last night, IX° with Gary S.

All week long he's been suffering from flu and acute melancholy –completely five of Cups. Tonight he's on a 3/4 hit of acid, "dealing with his demons", and he sounded a bit more cheerful on the phone.

Whenever I speak to him of the joy of being, he counters with, "Well, you're easily pleased." And so I am–if one has no expectations, one can't be disappointed. I can no longer judge if a thing is "good" or "evil". I know when conditions are pleasureable or painful in varying degrees, but I'm learning to balance the attraction-avoidance response–not in the prior state of enslaved ambivalence, but in simple awareness that, indeed, there is no difference between any one thing and any other.

I do have an occasional relapse–all week long I've been "burning myself out" about the mountain of work to be done to render the Dorothy Lane house marketable–and accomplishing nothing in the process. This was an indirect result or accompaniment of an amazing amount of attachment to the farm. So today I managed to let go.

4/14/76. e.v.

Dan C.'s ill with a chest cold, poor baby–we're rescheduling priorities, concentrating effort on the Dorothy Lane house. Beh. Enough.

Don R. was over last night, measuring things for the carpentry repairs. Not much to say, save that he wants to have a chance to converse with Gary S. We generated some energies–a nice test and challenge. Each time Yesod sparked to a greater level of intensity, I brought the rest of the Tree into new balance around it, instead of attempting to dampen down the attraction-response as before. It does work a lot better.

4/16/76 e.v.

We had a double birthday party last night (brother Pat and daughter Julie), much hilarity and delightful nonsense.

Real estate deals and more real estate deals! O, Malkuth!

In the midst, dear hearts, in the midst of all the Disks, Gary S.'s been at it as usual. Why must Magickians be such <u>difficult</u> people?

(Answer–the difficulty is an illusory effect of the fire-purge of "personal" imperfection. If one is purely and completely as one should be, there are no difficulties.)

He sees a need to talk to Don R. and tell him to contain his approach-energies until after the farm is completed–fine by me. Don R. phoned last night; he'd made a connection for me with a restaurant that displays the artwork of area artists, a place named "The Seventh House". I thanked him nicely, and I wait for a phone call from the owner of the place.

I've had passing thoughts of concern about the present situation–

almost all of my conscious-waking-mind's time is being devoted to business in the Kingdom. I'm aware of development occurring on other planes, but intervals of introspection and meditation are rare. Ritual occurs, on a solo basis, sporadically and spontaneously, and some form of the Mass continues on a once-a-week basis. Nevertheless, despite the manifestation of so much Earth-energy, the realm of the spirit and the Ruach continues to unveil itself.

There's been much emphasis on Maggie's individual "self" lately—she finds it a bother and an annoyance—as though an "identity" were being forced into manifestation. Oh well, fair's fair, I suppose—let's get it over with.

OK. In the Kingdom there exists a unit of homo sapiens/solaris, female, known to her fellows as Maggie Cook. At the arbitrary space/time coordinates of this writing, she is dancing a furious tarantella of Earth, sailing merrily through a process that should result in the relocation of her body and family at a farm. Why is this happening?

Because it is a part of Will.

Who's Will?

Will is Tao, without individual signature.

There is an aspect of Will that manifests in individual situations, and may be called a Star's True Will.

Fine. In this sense, in the limited plane of "individuality", then, it <u>is</u> Maggie's will that her life be danced in this new setting.

Why?

a) It will enable her to live/work with Gary S. in relative privacy

and fewer attempted restrictions by society. There will be no need (probably) to enter into an official contractual relationship as demanded by manslaw.

b) It will provide a home more intimately present to Nature.

c) It will provide for her children an environment of peace and power in which to discover and nurture their own True Will.

d) It will be a home for her brother, Dan C., an operational base for whatever travels his Art demands.

e) It will be a home for Gary S., he who has never had a true home this incarnation.

f) It will be a haven for Stars who need to regain natural purity and simplicity.

g) It will give her a place in which to be, to work, to cease, to die, in keeping with the tides and flows of Nature.... to become Nu/Maat.

4/19/76 e.v.

After two day's work, half the trim-painting on the front of the house is complete. Very tired afterward (the Sun turned Gary S. inside-out) we crashed and I went home to a broken sleep from 3 to 7 a.m.

Long phone conversation with Dan C., cleaning up lower astral garbage, gained an interesting view of things as he sees them.

He's after my "self", too, as being "just Maggie". So it seems, dear book, that even those closest to me must be "masked-for". "Just Maggie" to "be a Magickian" only during ritual. This is akin to Gary S.'s "sealing me off"; from upper planes entities.

Fine–each according to grade, they have presented me with their preferences as to the masks they wish to deal with. This is understandable, but it also is a form of limitation. Both Dan C. and Gary S. are after me to "be real" and "unmasked"–an impossible request as long as they hold some preconceived image as to what my "reality" is.

Since I'm still in process of coming to understand what "reality" is, myself, and since all things, including "me" is in a rapid state of change, I <u>have</u> been as open and unveiled as I have the power to be–actually, I believe that there's much less to me than meets the eye.

You, dear book, are the purest earthing and record of change occurring according to Will. It began with the declaration of Will to receive all that the Children of Maat willed to send–and so it continues, with a constantly-changing perspective of who the C. of M. are, and what is being sent.

Inventory:
One thirty-six year old female human body, in relatively good health, with a high probability of genetic predisposition to cancer and heart attack. Good for another 20-30 years, maybe.
a) liabilities-obligations:
1) rearing of four dependent humans of high intelligence, imagination and will.

2) maintenance of flexibility in living/working with Dan C. and Gary S. in farm setting.

3) finding a means of support for self until death.

4) completing assignment of this incarnation

b) assets-privileges: all of the above, plus:

1) having access to the 93 Current

2) tying-in with some great realized beings in addition to Dan C. and Gary S.–notably Mr. Grant and the O.T.O.

3) being enfleshed at <u>this</u> locus of space/time–planet Earth, 1976 e.v.

4) experiential knowledge of "other" dimensions. etc.

Despite what Dan C. and Gary S. maintain, "I" do <u>not</u> exist. There <u>is</u> a functioning personality that informs "my" bodies, but it's generated by these bodies and is consequently mortal.

There is a "soul" that provides continuity of experience between (and in) the various incarnations, but it, too, is temporal, and only will remain for the life of the Universe.

The immortal, eternal, and infinite "self", the Hadit, is the Atman only. This "I" is Brahman, or the Tao. It is Being/Non-Being.

This Self, being without quality, cannot manifest. Manifestation is the play of the gunas.

That-called-Maggie has been manifesting through instinctively-crafted masks, in terms of the growth-processes of the soul. I must now use those masks which best serve the needs of others. Also illusion.

This requires the systematic re-absorption of all previous masks. These protomasks were spun, mainly, by survival-reactions to the perceptions of the Universe, and as such are not perfect and are biased.

4/21/76 e.v.

Lu, Joe Bounds and Linda G. were over last night for the final

corrections on the paste-up for the Journal. Longest damned Magickal pregnancy I've ever participated in.

Trying to find a photog for Demon Feast. Herb Z. hasn't the equipment, so I'm trying Adrian. Haven't received the counter-offer for the farm yet and really don't care. If it happens, fine: if it doesn't, fine.

Living with Dan C. and Gary S. isn't all that attractive, really. The land itself would be worth the move, but I'm doubtful about my limits of strength.

Read an article in the paper about forest fires at Red River Gorge and the tinder-dry conditions there. So I went to Chimney Rock on the astral and did a rain-dance. Woke up at 4 o'clock this morning to close windows because of thunderstorm. It's raining now. (10 a.m.)

Also went to Babalon Temple and invoked Maat. White flame became Black Flame, dancing feather-form of interstellar space. What is the Point? The closing down phase of this Magickal Record. <u>One</u> chosen practice, huh? Well, the Children of Maat haven't directly manifested for quite some time—and it's high time I opened to them.

Hey! Monsoon! Rain-curtains blowing sideways across Harrison Avenue! Silver veils of power. More later.

Later. Well—it was just like the time in January, only no evident tissue. My period had stopped Monday, and just now I found myself having to cope with a sudden rush of blood, fresh and clotted. I'm a bit dizzy and nauseated—a condition that calls to mind the hemorrage that happened after Zsa Zsa U.'s birth. I've noticed that when this sort of sudden blood loss happens that things get cold, and dark, and remote.

Adrian can do the print for me. He's going to a marriage counselor lately–his second wife is even more earthbound than Kay was. Too bad–after a lengthy rap, it seems that there may be a chance that he's close to finding his will and doing it. He was on the verge of a proposition, but I'm not about to ball him.

4/22/76 e.v.

Again to the brink of madness, dear book–(and I ask, what has the development of events have to do with the Children of Maat? This is all very Netzach-ish.)

Telephone call with Gary S. last night, left him in fury and me in tears. He did call back later to mellow things down–but.

What is my will? How am I to benefit from the farm?

At the moment, my only desire is for a swift and peaceful death.

I may not die until there is a stabilized situation extant that will fulfil my karmic duty, mainly regarding the rearing and the education of the children. The farm would provIde the physical setting–and, if it be his will, Dan C. would be an ideal guardian for the kids—but John U. would have first call on them, as their father.

At worst, ten years would see Julie U. reaching age 18; she, being the youngest, will probably be able to be self-sufficient with a minimum of assistance from the other kids. It may be that I'll be permitted death before then, in which case the farm would suffice.

As far as it goes with Dan C., although we are the closest in spirit among the Cook clan, there is a tremendous gulf between us as individuals–in personality, art, experience, outlook, self-knowledge etc. I still have somewhat of a surrogate-mother role to fulfil for him–not in the blatant sense of Malkuth, but in subtle ways of a

spiritual nature. It feels as though he's about finished with this.

And as for Gary S.–well, I've been as severe a proving-ground for him as any mortal could be . . Except for a necessary re-balancing of his Saturnine darkness with the light and harmony of his Sun, there's not much I can assist him with.

He's a pure child of Heru-Maat; I am but a bridge between Osiris and Horus. The power of Maat has reached "pastward" in the time-stream to earth itself through me in Liber P.P., but there's no value in continuing this incarnation.

It's for Gary S. to grow and learn various manifestation-skills (humanly speaking), and in turn expand the Initiation of the Aeon of Heru.

Whatever value I may have had to the evolution of the Race is spent. With the notable exception of preparing the children for independent living, there is no point or purpose for my life–I am eating the food, breathing the air, and occupying the space that rightfully belongs to someone else, someone more suited to assist the Mansoul to awaken to its full consciousness.

I'm a third-rate talent and fifth-rate human being. There is nothing in me of honor, or truth, or beauty–I've abandoned old friends, cuckolded <u>all</u> my lovers, neglected my children, confused the innocent, flattered the egotistical, bastardized my talents, squandered my inheritance, betrayed all trust, blasphemed all gods, and desecrated whatever purity that my soul may have initially possessed.

Whatever beneficial energy that has manifested in paintings, writings, conversations, relationships, etc., has done so despite my personhood, not <u>because</u> of it.

Where "I" am, there is confusion; where "I" am not there manifests the perfection of NU-HAD.

The only hope and power lies in the NOthing.

(The observer notes this process. It is, in part, a katharsis. Something seems to have been completed.)

The imprint of Her Lotus feet
are seared into my soul!
Down She dances, in the smoldering,
smoking fires of the night–
Sun and Moon, Thy eyes are!
Thy barbed tongue
leaves no hiding-place, escape, refuge–
Kali-KA!

Born so many times
between Thy steaming thighs,
then severed, and devoured–
crushing of flesh and bone and gristle–
my skull strung on the necklace,
rattling and clanking on Thine ebon breast;
my hands hung on Thy corpse-girdle–
LA, LE-LA, KALI!

Thou art the Wheel–
Born to die, die to be born–
ENOUGH!

Goddess, there is no choice;
to escape Thee, I must invoke Thee:
to leave the Wheel, one must become the Wheel__

Kali, Kali, Kalika!
Hare, asi Kalima!
Jai Devi Rani Duruga,
Kali, Maha Matara.

And yet—She's only part of it—there's more—

Through Da'ath, the entire Qlipoth must be dragged forth, reality turned inside-out—in the space between the Tree of Life and the Tree of Death, I must meet Choronzon. (He'll wear my face, I know it!)

This is Maya, all of it, all of it—and yet it must be danced—I wear the flesh again, dubious vestment of madness and delight—

I was not born in ignorance—<u>this</u> time I knew, I chose—the entire responsibility of manifestation is mine alone—I chose, in full foreknowledge of each act on Earth, the probables, the possibles, the pain I cause, the people I betray, the wreckage of lives that line the path I tread ...

Maggie, Nema, ANDAHADNA—know thyself!

I am the walking Gateway of the Mad!

On crippled feet I dance the Earth, bringing the Needle's Eye to rich men mounted on camels.

GIMEL names me least, yet is a true name.

Bereft of beauty, I never lack for lovers.

As carrion-scent draws vultures, do I draw men—and women, also. I am the gate.

To enter me is to enter doom.

Many have embraced me—only to waken and find themselves mated to their own corpses.

A few have entered me—and in the midst of searing agony, found their own strength and growth thereby. With these, once having passed through me, they turn and I am gone.

I possess nothing—none may possess me.

What see thee of thyself?

I am the shaker of foundations, the Mother of Despair—I hold fair promise, luring on the Children of the Light; when they believe they enter a garden of delight, I go, to leave them in the naked desert of their souls.

And such is my curse—to know that I am such—a promise of substance ever broken, an apparition of stability less solid than the mists of morning. And yet it is mine to feel, as keenly as the hapless ones within my sphere of illusion, the pain, frustration, agony, despair that I have caused for them.

Know I full well that I am deception.

And if you are illusion, who then is this weeping woman?

Maggie weeps, Maggie laughs, but Maggie isn't there.

What is your will?

To meet with Choronzon, between the Worlds.

To what end?

That I may be the Needle's Eye for Chaos itself.

And to what end?

If He may pass through me, and I through Him, then Order shall be born in all the Worlds, and the cracked and shattered vessels of the Qlipoth restored, made new.

And to what end?

That Man awaken as the Crowned and Conquering Child, in innocence and strength, and join the Brotherhood of Stars, and become God. Thus shall close the Kali Yuga.

So mote it be.

(I had a dream last night, that I ventured to London, astrally. I found myself in a shadowy structure.

A woman greeted me, in a small vestibule. I knew from the lilt of her words that I was, indeed, in England. There strode forth another figure, a man, who greeted me and embraced me. In this embrace of welcome and love, I received a totality of radiance and power of a frequency and completeness I'd never before experienced.

He showed me various rooms within this house; many people were engaged upon strange, and often incomprehensible activities–they smiled and bade me welcome also, without stopping their activities.

Details escape me now–too soon I had to return home, to meet sunrise in Ohio.)

I Ching: 10, Treading,   to   25, Innocence, the Unexpected.

(9 in the second place) "Treading a smooth, level course,
                          The perseverence of a dark man
                          Brings good fortune.

"The situation of a lonely sage is indicated here. He remains withdrawn from the bustle of life, seeks nothing, asks nothing of anyone, and is not dazzled by enticing goals. He is true to himself and travels through life unassailed, on a level road. Since he is content and does not challenge fate, he remains free of entanglements."

4/23/76 e.v.

After yesterday's depression-session, a woman was struck by an auto right outside the office window. Cause-and-effect be damned, but I must reinforce my circle. Also, I was rejected by the Summerfair selection committee–just as well, severing ties with this city etc., though I could've used the money.

I recognize some aspects of classic manic-depression, but I have to handle it myself.

I have cast a circle and declare my will–to be whole, complete, strong, balanced. In the name of Maat, I renounce all past ties and restrictions, and declare myself Her priestess. May Her truth, righteousness, and balance be mine also.

I venture through Da'ath, bypassing the conglomeries of Knowledge: all facts, theories, formulae, symbols, signs of conscious science and conscious art.

I behold:

      Suction–indrawing
 Shapelessness, amorphousness Dissolution, randomness
      (ignorance, confusion)
 Weakness, fear   Irresolution, indecision
      Vertigo, imbalance
 Distraction, murk   Isolation, vampirism
      Anaesthesia, turmoil
      Helplessness, slavery

I see.

I've lived here for a while.

Thank you, Flame-Dancer.
I return. So mote it be.

A truth–the "awakening" process begun by the Equinoctal ritual is working on me.

a) I should've known this in advance.
b) Fools rush in where angels fear to tread.
c) There's nothing for it but to go on.

Dear Maggie,

You are, no doubt, the Archtype of the Blundering Idiot. You are playing with forces of a superhuman nature with woefully inadequate preparation, experience, common sense, and guidance.

You are causing needless turmoil in the Universe around you, particularly in the lives and consciousnesses of the ones who love you. There's no choice but to continue the process now begun, but at least have the decency to tighten your circle, aura, and veils.

You have all the strength you need–you but lack a key to it. Your true Self may be compared to an infinite Well. It is dark, and deep, –yet, armed with the appropriate vessel, you may draw, endlessly, from this Well of Self, all the needed waters of healing, balance and strength.

Become, consciously, the Well.

Let go all bonds–religious, emotional, intellectual, astrological, categorical, physical, spiritual, positional, political, sexual, identional, ideational, philosophical, psychological—<u>all</u> of 'em.   Here's God:

God= Supreme Pressure

God= Sacred space/time   God= Name of Power

(God = Innocence)

God= Executive-enforcer   God= Legislator-creator

God= Fidelity

God = Honesty   God= True social order

God = Controlled desire

God = Satisfaction

Now that's really weird. A subjective-experiential view of divinity. The Church would love it—it's not a chosen reality of mine.

It proceeds.

It is further my will: to create a place of peace in which to meet and converse with my Brothers. It is not just that anyone should have to enter my arena in order to communicate with me. The battle continues, and yet I may also, at the same time, communicate in peace. It is the Heart Shrine.

Truth: Each Star must find his/her own way of achievement, of "centering"–one of mine is courtesy. And really, what is courtesy but a form of self-love? The rites of host and guest are of the most sacred among the warrior-races . . . . and it feels good.

Further: The Ego is a legitimate aspect of the human self. It proves to be the stumblingblock of many because of its link to various states of consciousness (not all) and its tendency to assume total control.

"Ego-death" (a misnomer) is the most common spiritual means of removing this unbalanced control of the self; actually, the process is one of putting the Ego in stasis, immobilizing it, as it were. The Ego is semi-mortal–its lifespan extending to that of the emotional

body–and thus it cannot be "killed" while the self inhabits flesh.

Now–Maggie, through various painful processes employed during your period of Christian asceticism, you managed to put your Ego into a stasis so deep that you've effectively forgotten it. Clue? <u>Forgotten</u>.

One works with sigils for the purpose of Magick, and the most crucial part of this type of Working is the forgetting of the sigil. This is done by dropping it into the subconscious. Which is what you've done to your Ego.

All was "well" until Gary S. awakened all of you. So–<u>your Ego is awake</u>, but operating in your subconscious. It has authored all those symptons—tachycardia, depression-agression reactions, confusion and veiling of Will–and it will kill you unless you do something.

And here's how: You must effect the controlled release of the Ego into consciousness–and beyond. It has <u>such</u> a charge backing it that, literally, all Hell we'll break loose upon its release, unless you make careful preparation, devise the proper and pure channel for its direction, and have it merge, or unite with your HGA instantly. Got it?

Who's sending me this?

The Children of Maat via ANDAHADNA, your higher self.

"I" am the waking consciousness?

Correct. See, the Ego is simply the Kingdom's manifestation of the HGA. It's gotten a bad name, since Freud and the Vedantists, as being the source of Man's ills. Actually, when you witness someone being "egotistical", they're simply manifesting demons, in the

Magickal sense of the word.

Ego is my younger brother, my Parzival. We shall be complete when he rejoins Me. You, Conscious Mind, have been doing very well in a position you're not really qualified to handle. But the strain is telling on the whole Star, and it's time to restore true harmony.

How shall we proceed?

First, forgive and bless your Ego–

Ego, te absolvo et benedicite.

Then, ask its forgiveness and blessing–

Self of Earth–wilt thou forgive and bless?

(Echoing, distant) I forgive, I bless.

The Hadit-point hovers above–it too must join us.

Adsum.

All is ready. Be calm. Assume meditation–and let go.

Procedamus.

* * * * * * *

We journeyed through darkness–a small splash of light revealed a dim circle of vision–I was spreadeagled, chained–visions of the crucified Christ–shattered. The Virgin Mary–shattered. The brilliance of the Monstranced Host–shattered. I saw a toad, crucified–

Uprushing, blinding speed–

And at that instant the phone rang. It was Gary S., asking, proposing

a year's retreat–no O.T.O., no Journal–simply human development, and an oath of obedience.

I'm so tired. will there ever be any rest?

Later, in another place and time, it will continue.

4/26/76 e.v.

The details haven't been too clear–I only know that for the past three days I've been hovering on the edge of madness, unable to find the fulcrum-point for moving the world.

I'd issued a challenge, to encounter the Opposite One between the worlds—and the challenge was met. There's no such thing as a winner in this contest. Just a turning-inside-out of everything, an embracing of opposites ... To be and not-be at the same time ... What is my desire?

Peace, first and foremost–this doesn't require placidity–far from it! The majesty of a thunderstorm, for instance, is an exhilarating delight. The peace is of the Tao. The Tao is–but at times my waking consciousness is hampered from perceiving myself as it, mainly by the innate Chaos-demon of identity.

I have completed some major and nesessary process of reintegration of aspects of the self–necessary in that, once all "parts" are recalled and resumed, the whole self may again subside in Brahman.

What shatters the unity of Nothingness? Accepting a way of living that is inharmonious to one's nature. Also, the passions, the pride, vanity, greed, self-aggrandizement etc. that induce the illusion that the "self" is separate from the "Universe."

Ah, pleasures! the sky, the stars, earth, all the elements–plants,

stones, animals, humans, spirits, forms, music, art—best, the intangible lilt of a moment suspended, when the heartbeat of time is at rest...

A moment suspended in the amber light of afternoon sun, droning of bees and the benediction of slow-moving waters. Tree-leaf lace woven with the sky; blues and dark greens, sifting sunlight patterns on bare earth; ferns, and moss, and lichen on forest-bark.

In life, in death, there is no difference. Strange beings come and go, parading the infinite variety that Nature boasts, and that Man strives to imitate.

What will I then? To live as I would die–in conscious unity and full participation with all life. The outcome of event is meaningless–the rise and fall of cities, nations, races, worlds of sentients–matter no more (or less) than the upthrusting of a mountain range, or the plunge of a comet into the heart of a sun.

"Magick is the art and science of causing change to occur according to Will."

But–my Will, I see now, is that of the Universe–and the NOthing which is the source of the Universe. What change could I ("I") possibly desire to have happen, really? All things change constantly, with the Tao. All things happen according to Universal Law ... and by the innate properties of matter/energy. The informing sprirets of the Kingdom direct natural events—amen.

If there indeed be a plane, or place, wherein the Tao is "defied", it is within the imperfect consciousness of the human self. Were the Mansoul complete, it, too would be Tao.

From individual desire, there are things I'd will to change–the farm

manifesting, for instance—but looking on it from another plane, there's nothing there to will to change–just a rearrangement of Maya... When something calls my attention as "needing Working-on", and a practicable ritual structures itself in my head for doing the job, I generally do it just because it's there—but "heart's desire"? With one exception, what is, is—even if it's unaesthetic, why change anything.

The one exception is the Mansoul. We have the technology for complete Racial suicide. In our nightmare-sleep, we could "push the button." The fact that I have met the Children of Maat assures me that we won't blow ourselves up, but—the reason I've met them, or why they've contacted me, is to insure the Race's continuation so that the Mansoul awakens to the state of consciousness I can only call Maatian. I'm only one agent among many, of course, but that's the only "Magick" worth "doing"... Man's evolution.

Lady Maat! Spirit of the Universal Law!

Teach me all Dances of the Mask, that Man might see his nature. Having truly seen Himself, the Mansoul can do naught but become that which He is.

My Will is my Task, the only reason for assuming flesh—

–To complete the individual process of consciously becoming Tao.

–To function humanly, perfectly, so that all "others" might clearly behold themselves.

–To channel all energies received or generated as an individual to the Tao in its manifestation as the Current of the Aeon.

In other words, there's nothing for "me" to profit from in terms of the energies–none of my petty desires warrant the use of such

power; the only Work that can justify my existence and use of power is the evolution of Man—and even that's Maya.

As a Magickian, I feel like Ferdinand the Bull. Self-castration?

4/27/76 e.v.

Maggie, O mad one–what is Magick for you now?

"The art and science ... etc." as usual, BUT!

BUT?

But from inside-out, or upside-down, or in an interdimensional twist.

Oh?

Magick applies only in an "I-Thou" situation, wherein "I" is Had and "Thou" is NU.

Begin with pure perception (a "perciever" is only an illusion)–then expand with this perception in an outwardly-moving sphere-volume. It encounters an increasingly remote "other-ness" or essence-of-Thou–initially.

But, it were well, when, moving perception outward, one recognizes that-which-is-perceived as the "self" also.

Example–The first perception is the act of perception; then, a sense of "here-and-now". Then the range of non-material activity–mentation, conceptualization, emotional reaction, a "go-ing-ness", visions of light and darkness, sensations of the vast and the miniscule, the feel of a flow, and the whirlpools and eddies that the flow forms, velocity and retardation, heaviness and lightness, being

irradiated and radiating...

Then comes the consciousness of being connected to a material organic complex named the human body. Its senses, and the tools that extend the range of those senses, put the perceiver in touch with the sphere that expands exterior to the body's skin.

One becomes aware of the presence of a multitude of other perceivers, of all levels of refinement—from the slow rock-perceptions of gravity and erosion, through the vegetative tropisms, animal response and human communications.

Here is a quantum-band: by the common human channels of communications, one becomes aware that there is an "objective universe" about which oneself and "others" may reach a vague agreement. The microcosmic aspect of the Cosmic Giggle lies in the ambivalent situation of limited sharing—one knows, in the despair-generating finality of irrefutable fact, that despite the ability of two individuals to perceive a third object, and to agree upon certain aspects of it, there can never be a true unity of viewpoint in the plane of individuality.

Here, then, is Hell.

However, if the process of expansion of the identity matches pace with the process of perception, the "self" transcends the limitations of individuality, and eventually <u>becomes</u> the Cosmos.

Not only is it imperative that one expand along the chthonos axis and incorporate the entire Universe within the self, but it is neeessary to encompass the ychronos axis also.

This means that one accepts one's entire process of becoming—past, present and future. The self-perception of the self for its entire

progress of growth and development is a concomitant requirement for the continuation of On-GOing-ness. The process cannot be stopped,

You, then <u>are</u> the Cosmos—its length, breadth, depth, duration, expansion, origin, growth, and limit. Yes, you are limited by the very essences which you perceive, by which you perceive, and by which you are perceived. You are ancient, and vast, and instantaneous and miniscule.

You are the subatomic particles and the outward-rushing galaxies; you are the compact Ylem and the ever-expanding Universe. You are seed and flower and cycle and spiral—you are the concept which generated yourself and the ultimate reason for your own coming-to-be.

You are consciousness itself, and you are consciousness-aware-of-its-illusory-nature. You are Being, and not-Being also. You are the Nothing from which the totality of you as Being has sprung. You/I are all, and nothing—

Tat Tvam Asi.

And Magick is simply bringing into harmony all of this.

4/29/76 e.v.

THE CHILD AS THE BOOK OF CHANGES

Green-leafed rubies of the snow,
wreath my hair as joy's own crown.
In the shelter-play near snow-flecked trees,
we toy in essence with need of warmth and light.
Woodpile windbreaks, dappled with damp white,
make our huddling-place a holy ground.

Fingers numb and tingling in the cold,
something of great import drives us on,
defying the indifference of wan light
of wintersky and hermit-fields of silence.
The ache, the chill, the wind–
all silently endured;
and to what end?
That children make a shelter in the snow–
It furthers one to have somewhere to go.

Do you remember how important play is?

Do you recall that playing shapes the self, even as the self designs the play––?

"Youmus" and "Imus"–the childhood gods of order and directions.

Youmus be the Daddy and Imus be the Mommy and Mary Ann mus' be the baby.

Why do I always gotta be the baby? That's dumb! I don't get to do anything.

Well, you could be a real mean brat and make all kinds of trouble.

Yeah!

And we're not allowed to get rid of you because you're the Baby, right?

OK!

But we <u>can</u> spank you and maybe even put ground glass in your bottle–

Nah, that's for "Baby and the Witch."

Yeah, we can't really hurt a kid, y'know...

Well, OK...

All roles agreed-upon in advance, the patterns are enacted, each scrap of dialog ad-lib, yet any deviation from character immediately pounced-upon and "called."

Rehearsals for reality, engraving limits on the soul–self-generated, this, in innocence.
And limited by environment!

Imagination feeds on scraps of fantasy, but even fantasy is programmed by the past. Daddies work, Mommies stay home, attention is focussed on the Child. Witches are bad, Fairies are good, Princesses are to be rescued and the persecuted younger son is prime Hero material. Things occur in groups of three, and if one disregards supernatural warnings, disaster inevitably follows... the chivalry of childhood.

Why do I imagine that "stability" (whatever that is) is necessary for successfully discharging my maternal duties?

Maat, lady of Love, let me dance as the feather-flame in all things soever!

Maggie–are you <u>really</u> den-mother to the world?

Yes and no, sometimes, not really, I don't know.

It's good to be home. (As a Mask to Dance.)

Home is where the heart is.

From the Grosset-Webster dictionary:

home, n, 1. One's own dwelling; abode of one's family; the family unit.
2. One's own country; birthplace.
3. Place of origin; source
4. An institution, usually charitable, for the sick, homeless, etc.
5. The after-life; heaven
6. The pith; heart

adj. 1. Connected with one's home or residence
2. Domestic, esp. as opposed to foreign
3. Pointed, close.

adv. 1. To one's home or residence.
2. To one's country.
3. To the point, effectively; thoroughly; closely.

Also, I might add, home = Nuit, Enough.

5/3/76 e.v.

Why is the Maggie-Mask freaking out constantly? (Giggle-voice: for lack of a why-not?)

1) She promised to be "just a human being" instead of a Magickian.

2) This was in the form of a real promise (oath?)

3) This is a double-bind, and a good one, because

 a) Maggie-the-Beaner (upright citizen variety) is the classic, compleat Fuck-Up. (see biography)

 b) Maggie-the-Searcher has found, in Thelemic Magick, an elegant system of life that closely approximates her reality.

 c) Maggie-the-Chela is learning more, fast and furious, from

Magick, in the past three years, than she had learned in her total incarnation before initiation.

d) Maggie-the-Magickian sometimes succeeds in removing Ego enough to act as a Star— and the frequency of these amazing occasions has been increasing.

I will keep silence where silence is demanded. I am what I am, whether that be accepted by any "other individual" or not. I'll be "just a plain human" in the eyes of those who demand such a Mask, consciously or otherwise .... all's fair in love and war.

5/5/76 e.v.

Progress seems to be occurring—and yet—In the three years time since the initial ritual, so much has changed, so many old concepts abandoned and ways of doing things modified—and am 'I', as an individual, any closer to true self-knowledge?

It's realized that one can only "enlighten" others insofar as oneself is—and self-knowledge and realization is the only legitimate "work" afoot.

My center is hollow. I am a fabric of various layers of consciousness (each a succeeding degree subtler as one approaches Centre.) The layer inmost of all surrounds the Universe and NOthing. TAT, NETI, AND TAO.

I manifest in endless variety, each manifestation (theoretically) more subtle and artistic than the last, yet none of which are perfect. My manifestations are far short of what they could be in terms of art, grace, effectiveness.

The astrological revelations have helped, as does the Tarot, the I Ching, the grace of Gary S.'s wisdom, the rituals and interactions.

I have found that works in common unite individuals more than anything else —

It goes.
The moment is supreme and ever-changing.
Cast forward and back,
to rising of the Sun of Time
unto its Setting —
Love, Will, Going, Maat!

Shaped Air, slicing,
feather-blade and black-masked Dancer,
HO! and HA!

O, thou clap of one hand, hail —
Hail to the NONE, the One, and the Many!
Nothing manifest as All,
Purity intangible, now in my hands,
as black loam, stones, roots and beetles.
Ineffable the I, Eye, and Aye,
dancing dazzles, multiform and various —
Snowflakes and flowers, never two the same.
Being most prolific,
Profligate of form and motion,
Showering, outpouring, bounteous, hail!

Webs that gleam and glisten in the moonglow,
gauze-veils thin as air spun in the night —
wrap me roundabout —
hola! we journey!
Rising with the wind, the shadow-born,
aloft on wings of love —
the starswept sky of summer night

summons us to fly —

So dark, so vast, so brilliant-blazing!
NUIT!
We speed to Thee, light-drawn, light-driven —
Breath suspended, awe-struck, worshipful!

NU_MAAT!
Stars, stars, and Space between the Stars!
Sister-lovers, Twins and Opposites,
Self and Shadow-self, one, and All—
Ever onward, fly, we fly to ye—
never reaching
    (for we are surrounded!
      In the midst of Ye,
        we grasp ye Not—
          among, between, and mingled,
    we become!)

Lady lovers, sisters, pierce me through
    with blazing beams of light
        and shadow-shafts.
Spiral nebulae, and galaxies far-strewn,
    vast clouds of dark dust
        and solar winds—
        I am dissolved—
        Nu.
        Maat.
          O

(Typist's note—this one ties in with Don R.'s nature.)

I, the Comet, in my orbit hurled,
not as methane-ice, my dears,
nor in form of asteroid or world,
but as a blazing Sun I course the years,
transcending speed of light, and light of tears.

Beyond all forms and force, I, Comet, go.
The veils before my face dance and depart
and naked Nuit arches me. I know
the ecstasy of fire in my heart,
returning to unite in joy of Art.

Love, love, starbridge to the Night!
In going I become the Path and Goal.
will, strength, victory and might!
From Two to Naught I go, becoming whole.
I shine ongoing Starforce from my soul.

[Cf "... then keep we leashless to the goal,
    Stainless star-rapture of the soul!"
    (AHA!)]

5/10/76 e.v.

Julie U.'s First Communion Sunday—why do I let the kids participate in Osirian rituals? Because they want to; from Death comes Life; a reliving of the history of the Aeons ... But "the old rituals are Black". Even so, even so—its a form of trial, also—for them.

These children are Kings! False humility, guilt, shame, fear, subservience, are not to be found in them.

At this writing, they are Crowned and Conquering Children.

There is much refinement each needs—much learning of the Art and of the Science; and of the fullness of their Star-essences—yet even now they are Kings.

Beyond this, it is not mine to take them. They must venture inward alone.

Have I not therefore completed my Task?

May I now not die?

No, Andahadna, you must live.

To what end?

For the doing of Will, and of Love under Will.

Have I not completed this Will?

One Task is complete, but Will is never completed, at least in the flesh.

Then why may I not now die?

For it is your Will to go on, for a while.

This I know not. What is this Will toward?

Ye shall live among Man, being ANDAHADNA, and dancing all Masks with grace. Finish your accounting of events.

So. Having endured an hour in church (Siebhan terms the ritual <u>heavy</u> sado-masochism; "the joy of submission"), I had my weekend further enlivened by Phyllis phoning to inform me that her father was in surgery after having been struck by a train.

Then, it seems highly likely that John (yes, John U. the ex-husband)

may have syphillis. I'm setting up a doctor's appointment for him.

So much for the jolly adventures of Mad Meg.

Later. Gary S.'s certainly put me into an interesting place—a place where I must contact my Angel—a question of "right action".

Point. Not too long ago, he issued the simple statement that were I to ball anyone, he wouldn't touch me again.

Point. Of late, he's been stressing "individual development", that "he has his own life to lead," and that I'm centered enough to be trusted.

Point. He approves of Lu, Linda G., Gary M. and Ginger M, Don R. and Ben Rowe—in limited amounts.

Point. He's undergoing some ordeal and is not speaking directly about it.

He's said that he can't see group-workings, or even Brotherhoods. His soul is like a dune-mazed desert. (I cannot share his point-of-view, but I may percieve it and act accordingly—if it be my will.)

He says he needs to be alone—fine—but this is hiding his need to be with. He also mentions a test of me in this.

The crux is, however much I love Gary S., I cannot do his will, but only my own. However, since there is no "I" other than Hadit Himself, the term "my will" is meaningless.

In the plane of individuality, separation exists within its own reality, true, and within this plane the will expresses itself through the various "individuals", or Points-of-View. To rephrase: in the Kingdom, what is my will regarding myself, and Gary S., and those whom the Current directs my way? What shall the Quill-Plume write?

Behold, Andahadna, go in unto thy Temple, there to invoke the Lady Maat who is thy Angel, even though she is a goddess and yea, the Shadow-Twin of Nuit.

Invoke in the word of the Beast, and the word of the Aeon, and the word of Her GOing.

5/11/76 e.v.

Did VIII°, invoking Maat, declaring (again) my will to know my will. Very "dead" today; can't consciously remember anything much of the ritual, save drawing upon the 93 and connecting with ShTN.

I think of the farm, of the Journal, of Magick, of the people I know—and there's nothing except a mild aversion to everything. Death keeps returning to "stage center". It would be nice to die now, but that seems highly unlikely.

Strange—no enthusiasm for life or for Death. Not even an expectation, but like a neutral existence, boring. This strikes me as strange–declaring will to know will, forgetting the events of the ritual, and now being in a Limbo of—what? The I Ching #24 to #2.

5/12/76 e.v.

So John U.'s seen the doctor and it's not VD after all—simply "strain" from over-use—or at least that's what John says. Well, as long as it's nothing rampantly contagious, it isn't really my concern. Ah, wretched excess!

5/13/76 e.v.

Foreward drafted and typed for Maat-sendings, as per Randy B.'s request. Not claiming sanction of anyone, it stands or falls on its own. The book is going to happen someday, and the only authority

I'll have is Maat Herself. The roots are the roots and the Current is the Current—let success (or failure) be the proof of the Working.

(My ghod, the trollop is martial tonight! It's probably astrological.)

Aha! Fire, hail, wind, earthquake, destruction! Every time the Tower's built, blast it down! Wham!

We need rain. Badly.

Hail, Typhon! Hare, Varuna! Hola, Jupiter, Dyaus Pitar!

Shake loose that awesome male power, Milords—cleave the heavens with lightning! Cause the Earth to tremble with the thunders! Come rain! come life!

Earth crouches under clouds,
travail brings bemoaning.

Laboring long for life's birthing,
dire drought stays the shoots.
Sky gods! Approach her!
Shower down the saving silver!

She hath yielded to you
her fair waters—
in streams, rivers, oceans—

By the same mouth that drew her vapors forth,
blow Prana-breath so water-laden
over our sweet mother's fevered form!

5/17/76 e.v.

I received a fantastically beautiful letter from Mr. Grant on the 15th. Had it arrived one day earlier, it'd have been incomprehensible.

Friday night's working with Gary S. (and sacrament sub specie THC) effected an opening of vision to a new level.

Gary S. and Mr. Grant are working in tandem from two divergent (but harmonious) view-points. That they should <u>care</u>!

Mr. Grant is perfectly correct—I've been straining (at a gnat and swallowing a camel? If gimel doesn't get me swallowed first, that is.) Ah me, o my—these two stars are more than reason enough to relinquish the flesh-weariness and joyfully dance onward!

5/18/76 e.v.

Completed the letter to Mr. Grant. I really haven't the foggiest what his reply will be to the matter of Gary S. and the Order. I'm getting awfully Solar about it—well, we'll see. I hope I haven't fouled things up.   Not to worry. Tao is Tao.

Sometimes this whole thing seems like "The Autobiography of Alice B. Toklas." Who's kidding whom? Is there any difference? Omnê is Omnê, and K. Grant is definitely Omnê.

Awakened Man! What a delightful human!

One of the nicest things I can imagine would be to achieve a position from whence I could give him (K.Grant) something half so rare and beautiful as that which he's giving me—

SHAITAN, hear me!
Do what thou wilt shall be the whole of the Law!

In the power of the word ABRAHADABRA—
In the power of the word IPSOS—
I claim the right of the Spellmaster!
I claim the right of the Priestess of Maat!

I claim the right of a Hermit of Nuit!
So mote it be.

In the name of Kali-Ma, blest be AOSSIC!
May he ever and always be born and devoured
by the love of Our Lady, Srimati Kali.

In the name of Lord Shiva, blest be AOSSIC!
May he open his Eye upon darkest Confusion,
driving him down to the deep, the Abyss.

In the name of Sri Krsna, blest be AOSSIC!
May he make Beauty the flute of his Being,
drawing the Gopi-souls onward to bliss.

In the name of Lord Brahma, blest be AOSSIC!
May the fair cosmos that he is creating
echo forever the Light of its god.

To his Will, all power given!
To his Word, the sign of Maat!
To his Work, all fruitfulness of harvest!

The Black Flame, the Quill-Plume,
shall gift him with feathers
to aid in his GOing,
to further his flight!

To him is the Swansdown
(and shadowed in scarlet)
to glide on the mirror,
the Ocean of Milk—
Blest be AOSSIC, the Atman, OM.

To him is the feather

of Hadit, the gray Crane,
force in the equipoise,
stalking the shores.
Blest be AOSSIC, his Wisdom and stride.

To him is the Owl's plume,
token of Nuit,
quietly lofting his Form
in the Night.
Blest be AOSSIC, his Sorrow and life.

To him the Akasha-Egg,
enfolding Lord Harpocrat,
Silence in knowledge
and innocence be his—
Blest be AOSSIC, above the Abyss.

To him the twin feathers
of Odin's black ravens,
shimmering blue
in the light of the Throne.
Blest be AOSSIC, the Artist and judge.

To him the bright tokens,
the banners of scarlet—
O Lord of the Morning,
thy cockerel crows!
Blest be AOSSIC, the Warrior-King.

To him the gold wingtips
and Eye of Lord Horus.
Hail, Priest of the Aeon,
Hail Hermit and King!

Blest be AOSSIC, heart of the Ninety-three.

To him is the eye-plume
of the Peacock of Ishtar—
Grace to his workings
and Art to his touch
Blest be AOSSIC, his Love and his Will.

To him is the quill
of the Ibis—Tahuti
hath blessed him
in all of his Work with the Word.
Blest be AOSSIC, in all of his writings.

To him is the feather
of Maut, the great Vulture,
who flies under moonlight
in the Desert of Demons.
Blest be AOSSIC, the Gate of Between.

To him is the crest
of the far-ranging Eagle.
The Keys of the Kingdom
are his to command.
Blest be AOSSIC, the Sign unto Man.

By the power of She-Who-Moves,
By the exaltation of Righteousness,
By the strength of Prana,
Shall all that moves and flows be his!

May all his vows be speedily fulfilled;
may all attainment, yea, the Highest,
be his in this lifetime.

May all who style themselves his enemies
be sealed within mirrors
and folded in Silence forever.

May he forever prosper in peace.

May his Task be completed;
May his Will be fully earthed;
May his Work achieve self-perpetuating Life,
that soon he may GO beyond
all bonds of necessity.

In the name of Shaitan,
In the name of Heru-Ra-Ha,
In the names of Nuit and Hadit,
In the name of Lady Maat—
Through all the Worlds of the World,
So mote it be.

Love is the law, love under will.

5/20/76 e.v.

Randy B. phoned last night requesting my assistance in corresponding with a group of Magickians in Nashville. They'd responded to his flyer about the Journal with a challenge about the line of succession of leadership in the OTO—Randy must've said something about Mr. Grant's support of the Journal__ghods! I'll frame some sort of reply, hopefully enabling them to see how they are wasting their substance on nonsense.

5/22/76 e.v.

Last night at Riddle Crest, Gary S. announced that he wouldn't be over to help prepare for the real estate "open house". Really, it seems

as though Mr. Kammer, the agent, is rushing things a bit.

At any rate, I felt terribly let down and disappointed at Gary S.'s withdrawing his assistance at the most crucial time of need. The Observer was amused (slightly) at my typical reaction. My Mars had been activated all week long by Mr. Harris' erratic expressions of his pressure-to-change, and was instantly "upon" the occasion.

I controlled it (could've done a smoother job, though) and Gary S. and I wound up doing some informal alchemy. He'd been pressured by work, his boss, Dan C., Siebhan, etc., so it was indeed a volatile situation.

At any rate, the kids and I housecleaned—Lili U. and Bill U. were really super, and the babies did their short-attention-spanned best.

Gary S. "checked in" periodically by phone—and the course of the day saw me gradually channelling the Martial energy into work until the work "did itself"—got very Zen.

But somehow Gary S. came a cropper in the meantime—this evening I decided to stay home rather than endure the Tamasic Toad at Riddle Crest. The penultimate phone call revealed that something was amiss with the energies there, and I simply didn't feel that I could've been any benefit there.

Whether or not my absence added to the problem, I couldn't say—Gary S. won't talk, but I can feel his pain.

Really, it 'stanns like someone's been invoking Azrael over there. Phew! It's really an abuse of Death to play with it as a possible escape from difficulties—I should know! But someone's been into considering taking the deep six—either Dan C. or Siebhan or both.

So. Gary S. was most emphatic about not pressing him to talk. Strange. For about twelve hours I was pure Mars—yet when I spoke with him for the last time, I was completely second hexagram. Instant Yin. I let him know that I was available to assist, at his convenience, bade him goodnight, and there it stands.

Perhaps I'm becoming too attached to the joys of (relative) solitide. There isn't anyone (save Gary S. or Don R.) that I'd like to be around. Necessary contacts, such as the children, my boss, John U. and various professionals, are handled with grace and tact—but in a situation of free choice, I'd definitely choose solitude over socializing.

The way the whole nexus feels, I could make a bundle selling Yorick skulls on the streetcorners. I don't have the '76 ephemeris in the house, but I <u>bet</u> the Mars-Saturn conjunction's on again, plus something with Uranus and Pluto. Behold the Kosmik Drag—the Tamasic Toad to the tenth power. Nuts to all that. Hail, Caesar, we who are about to die salute thee! Time for the I Ching. #58. The Joyous, Lake. "True joy, therefore, rests on firmness and strength within, manifesting itself outwardly as yielding and gentle."

Time to go the astral route—to the Plain of the Stars and Babalon Temple—maybe Rosarion and the gang have some wisdom to dispense.

5/25/76 e.v.

Intergroup relations extremely rocky. and it suddenly hit me why <u>I've</u> been so bitchy and hypersensitive lately. The FDA banned my usual contraceptive pill and the new ones work on a different basis. Hence physical discomfort and an inability to handle negative energy. Time for a rebalancing of awareness.

Sister-in-law Mary Sue brought over a yeast culture from the

Phillippines called "virgin Mary" or "Bread of Life". Supposed to be a healing agent.

Some legalities are to be dealt with tomorrow at the realtor's office. John U.'s to sign a quit-claim deed for Dorothy Lane and Riddle Crest, and Riddle Crest is to be listed for sale. Whether or not a farm materializes, change of some sort is due.

5/27/76 e.v.

The legalities were taken care of, and all's ready for events to manifest.

Gary S.'s in a tremendous depression. I spent some time with him last night, being as receptive as possible. He doesn't consider me to be a trustworthy source of positive energy for him, so I quit trying to restore his self-confidence and simply existed with him for a while.

With all the activity in the Kingdom, I haven't done much formal ritual for quite a while. Haven't even been "up the planes" in the usual fashion for a bit. Last night there was an intense transmittal of energy through me to Gary S., and I did intone a blessing on him. This is getting to be an increasingly-frequent happening—just what is this "blessing" business, and who am I to convey it?

It's important to know. I'm going inward for a while, to find out what's been happening while the Outer's been holding my attention so much.

Later. Seems that the office isn't the correct setting. I Ching. #15. Modesty.

5/28/76 e.v.

Gary S. was over for dinner. Seems his Death cycle is heading for a

rebirth (finally!). He plans to move out of Riddle Crest and in with his grandmother for a month.

In discussing the farm, he's stymied as to what arrangements would/will be; he's concerned about pressures. There's a four-cornered possibility of choice.

1) He can leave Cincy altogether, abandoning everything.
2) We can continue as we've been—living apart and seeing each other once or twice a week.
3) He can live with me under some suitable guise, such as tenant landlord.
4) We can marry.

Numbers one and four are both repugnant—three would be ideal—at least from my view. Somehow or other I'm not in the least worried—I continue on, slowly fixing up the house, looking at properties, working, etc.

He said that he couldn't "relate" to Magick anymore, or at least to the systemic concepts of it. Yet later on, alchemy occurred, and he proceeded with the communion of the Elixir as always. Magick is Magick, whether or not it's being named as such. In respect for his sensitivities and rebellion against the status quo, I'll refrain from using the terminology with him—better the act without the word than the word without the act.

Maybe this is being devious, in a very Isian manner, but it works. He asked if I had purified for ritual—when I said that I had, he questioned my "presumption" but—in silence, it was obvious that he also desired it. I should <u>ask</u>? Feh, that would ruin the flow. O! Blessings on the Male, especially on Gary S.!

5/30/76 e.v.

Early a.m. Don R. was over at my house Friday night. Much of the time was spent in silent energy exchanges. He has a lot of power—and patience. I wonder what his game is? Second chakra energies were intense–but there's been no difficulty in keeping them unearthed.It is building up one hell of a charge, though–if he hasn't a specific purpose for it, I do—

Siebhan visited me tonight. We achieved a spectacular high on grass, which state of consciousness acts as sodium pentathol in many cases.

She spoke of Gary S., and his fear of success—this has been emerging as a clear pattern of late—and then she proceeded to echo the sentiments of Myrrh and Gail—that Gary S.'s being an insufferable prick and male chauvinist and how can I possibly <u>stand</u> such treatment?

Now all three of these ladies have received my spontaneous affection—Myrrh's response was to name me as Duruga, as aspecting her own atavar-consciousness as Kalika.

Gail welcomed me as sister—but she was more attached to her sacrificial aspect as Virgo than I was—perpetual innocence.

Siebhan withdrew from my affection in a form of fear; but her point-of-view seems to be sisterly-para-teacher/student.

Each lady cared enough to be concerned and to express her fear of my apparent enslavement to Gary S.

True, he often manifests a stern mask, and he is battling a lot of insecurity about me. He does fear success—such as backing away

from the concept of marriage once such an event was possible—now, backing away from the farm as its possibility moves toward actuality. He's backed away from financial success, Magickal success, interpersonal success…Hell, he could've laid Linda W. and I'd never have even known—but I was a handy excuse for his not having to.

He's backing away from Magick on the brink of the Abyss. This frightens me.

5/31/76 e.v.

IX° last night, in which the flowing, human energies did manifest more completely than ever.

At times I find my vision becomes earthbound. I am aware of the consciousness that is the Magickian, the Priestess, the Hermit-King—and yet the collective influence of each human mind on the planet seems to cloak out myself from myself.

At this point I _am_ alone. I need to venture inward, again. All I have is this lifetime for now. It's my responsibility—and each person, including the kids, is responsible for his own lifetime.

Our social nature (our great DNA unity) as a race permits cooperative human ventures—but unless achieved in unity-consciousness, such a venture has reality only in the Outer. Sunlit melancholy.

Later. Back from Allen H. and Randy B.'s. Randy B. is being very serious and restrictive in his outlining of Beth (whoops—spell that "Bate") Cabal. Allen H.'s being obnoxious but correct in predicting failure for the knowledge-lecture and membership approach.

Damned little to be gained with the Hod-Da'ath approach—<u>do</u> Magick first and check out the explanations afterward.

So Allen H. and I did a kitchen-table ritual with the Tarot. Ace of Disks on a copy of Liber AL, penny atop the card, two halves of an avocado seed, and four random cards which turned out to be Adjustment, Art, Lust and the Tower. We intoned the Law and invoked Maat and the Elder Gods. A rainstorm began at the intonation of the Law—nice touch, I must say.

It all seemed to put Word and Work back into balance.

6/2/76 e.v.

Watched my sister-in-law Robin be baptized as Catholic tonight. Out of courtesy to her I attended the ritual; the priest seemed a bit nervous. Watched the Mass with what might be termed professional criticism. It's been streamlined a bit, but it's still the same old emphasis on sin, redemption, unworthiness, etc.

Gary S. was vocally critical about my writing to the Nashville crew—so tonight Randy B. called me on the phone and read me the gist of his response to them. On his own initiative (one hopes) he's resumed his responsibility of corresponding with prospective Journal subscribers. Great.

The farm thing is moving on its own (Dr. Frankenstein, you have created a monster!) and I find damn little cause of rejoicing. This journal is almost completed. It began by being a record of channellings from the Children of Maat. They've been conspicuous by their silence lately, and this has devolved into a dreary little daybook of mundane events.

Magick is. The Law is. Maat is ... But I feel nothing but desolation. Perhaps it's just another siege of spiritual dryness, coupled with indifference to events on the Outer.

I'm not painting now, and it's been a while since poetry happened. The prospect of living with Dan C. and Gary S. is dreary—what difference between that and being married to John U.—save for the legalities?

Were it possible to live as an Old Æon hermit at this point, I do believe I'd opt for it. But, I offered an environment of freedom to the gentlemen, and I honor my word (if I don't, who will?). I owe Gary S. some form of balance for the three years he invested in my "case"—this is of Maat. It's also love-under-will, with the emphasis on Will at this point.

Perhaps it won't require three years for the balance to be struck— he may choose to live and work elsewhere. Who knows? The farm working continues because there's no alternative visible to me now. This is awfully unenthusiastic—doing something because it's as good as anything else. Is this Will? Is this Art? Is it Magick?

The only saving grace about life in the flesh is the knowledge that death will end it—soon? If I had the energy, I'd be invoking Azrael daily—but he'll come at the appointed hour—I can wait.

What of the Great Work? What of my Task? I'm an instrument who functions at need. My limited intelligence and vision are not required for the completion of my task.

This Dance of Life goes on, like a role performed thousands of times. It continues by dogged persistence, by rote. I feel no freshness, no inspiration, no enthusiasm. I'm tired. I'd like to rest. I'd like to simply lie down and leave the flesh—but it goes on.

6/3/76 e.v.

Yes, I <u>am</u> riding the edge awfully closely. Gary S. called last night

and remarked on the negative energy generated by his criticism of my letter-writing for Randy B.—and then proceeded to institute a positive direction—and now I'm quite disturbed.

Over the past three years I've had near-disastrous experiences with obsessions—Myrrh, Bob, etc.—and now, older but apparently no wiser, I find myself being influenced inordinately in mood (and thus outlook) by Gary S. himself.

This seems dangerous, wrong, attached—I have no strength of character! Either that, or the link between True Will and waking consciousness has become obscured. In any event I'm beginning to feel like the Queen of Cups again.

Yet, on my own, there's no particular course of action that seems more attractive than any others. The farm proceeds on its own, and Maggie's in stasis.

The clarity of vision with which I once percieved my will has become opaque–O Maya! O Lila! You've done it again!

6/4/76 e.v.

Gary S. visited briefly last night. It was impossible to convey the gist of the concern about "undue influence"; he's intensely involved in his own energy-balances, manifesting much nervousness and tension, so I didn't pursue the subject.

After he left, I began ritual in the temple. I'd banished and invoked Maat—and the wand was alive in my hands! After invocation, in asana bafore the altar, I experienced an intense influx of energy—and the phone rang. I answered, still in that half-suspension of ecstasy—and it was Myrrh, calling from Louisville. She'd received word from her upper-plane contacts to call, and so she did.

Incorporating the conversation into the ritual, I was pleased to learn that she's achieved stability in the Kingdom—drew healing energies toward the relationship between her and Gary S. and it ended in a long-distance mutual hymn-chant to Kali.

Again I might mention that she claims to be an avatar of Kalika, and that I am supposed to be an incarnation of the bright form of Duruga.

After hanging up the phone I returned to the temple and completed the rite VIII°.

Myrrh did warn me that I'll have to soon manifest the destructive aspects of the Goddess—but I'm not going to speculate in absence of occasion.

Letter from Mr. Grant—I've written a reply, and Gary S. may or may not reply on his own. He (Mr. Grant) has forced the issue of independent act—this, coupled with the fiasco of Summerfair, gives pause to think about the power of a name—it must first acquire power, then be used judiciously.

What's all this emphasis on individuality, anyhow? To me, it's simply one way of existing, one among many.

6/9/76 e.v.

Sent revised letter and pictures of "Demon Feast" to Mr. Grant today. Do I feel "liberated"? Do I feel "free"? Not particularly.

Adrian was importunate last night. No sooner were we alone than he wanted to lay me. I refused, simply because the idea was distasteful. I like him, he's an artist with a camera, but I simply didn't want sex with him.

In the past, when relying on marital fidelity, it would always be countered with enough resentment for John U. that I'd usually acquiesce.

Now that I don't have any social restrictions on my sexuality, I have no trouble refusing a proposition—if I don't want to, I don't want to, and certain persistant people had better learn that quickly.

I'm beginning to see Magick as the prayer of the Tao . . . a total, joyous plunge into things-as-they-are-becoming. The idea of seeking physical phenomena, like levitation, visible evocation-manifestations etc. repels me. Repulsive also is to influence an individual toward or away from any particular action . . . more, it's in lending power to someone's HGA, so the Angel might direct the specific use.

Hesitation in doing an earthing-ritual—why? Is my will not yet consolidated? Do I harbor doubts about the farm? I was able to say "no" to Adrian last night, with a strength and surety based on will. Can I not say "yes" to the farm with the same surety?

Perhaps the ritual should be lunar rather than solar—a total receptivity-working.

The moon is my mirror
soft and silver
distant, clear, and bright.
In Our Lady's temple, vast and dark,
she shines, the Lamp of Spirit.

La lune, serene—
instruct my soul
in the ways of celestial waters.
Let this fire-sprite become
the Cup of Nuit's star-flow.

Lady Nu! You arch above,
over and around, encompassing.
I go to meet you now,
within the silent centre of the soul.

I invoke Hadit, my Star and Angel!
He, the Atman shining forth
from eyes and hands and heart,
shall become my consciousness
from now and onward.

By the same mouth, O Centre of the Soul, is the invocation sung
and the temple-prayer answered.
By the same mouth, O Shadow of Nuit, is the question asked and
the answer given.
O pearl within the lotus, OM.
O black pearl within the crystal lotus, IPSOS.

Ritual—Declaration of the Law, banishment. Inward-going by neti-neti. e.g. I am not my physical body, nor my astral, etheric, etc., until there was nothing left but the Angel. Becoming It, I looked within—and something intense, devastating and instantaneous happened, along with the sure knowledge that in my present state of consciousness-evolution, I couldn't handle more than a microsecond's worth of this new reality, whatever it is.

VIII° culminating in declaration of will for the farm, because I know that my Task is to synthesize as—Empress?—to create, to fashion—(Tyger was my sentient-life talisman)

Other interesting things I find out while traversing the planes—

Rosarion, Rotat and Navhem are of the same essence as the "Seth"

being in the Jane Roberts books—more evolved than human, and with a love very refined and subtle.

The corker was the appearance of a being named Kriztovov. He(?) is a huge, segmented thing like a worm, of a dark bronze-copper color. He can be a building (a structured shelter), or a life-form. He's mostly hollow for the length of his interior, and has a marvelous laugh. He said he was "spun by the Star-Spider", which might be a punful way of declaring himself a creature of my imagination. (Which he is anyhow, as well as everything else.)

6/13/76 e.v.

Today Gary S. and I went for a hike along the East Fork river. Last night and today were the first chances I've had for a direct, in-person perception of his development since the decision to diverge our courses in re. the O.T.O.

I'd gone prepared to meet a stranger, and found much more of Gary S. And despite his claim of finding the power gone from Magick, he's a much subtler and more powerful Magickian now. As for his Mystic aspect, he seeks the Tao in all things—and it appears that he is of the Tao in most things.

He sees "committment" as expectations of performance imposed by others by custom or habit. A taking-for-granted. It seems a strange definition of the word (for I see a committment as a course of action dictated by Will—either as the main flow or as an accident to the major flow.) But his definition makes sense in his universe.

As I told him, my only expectation is that he do his will. Right action will inevitably follow, if one is being centered, acting as one's own HGA, being the Tao, doing Will.

There are times when I consider the use of pronouns in connection with Will to be a misleading concept-seed.

Do what <u>thou</u> wilt. And who art "thou"? Individuality exists only in the manifestation and expression of Will. Will is. Not "mine", "yours", or "his", save in the unique manifestations.

Will is—God?

Surely, if Tao is God. If OM is God; if Man is God.

What is the Will?

Master Therion! How deceptively simple your words, how artistic the truth.

Do what thou wilt shall be the whole of the Law.

DO This is the command of existence in the Kingdom. Even in a coma, one breathes, one lives, one whirls about through space as the planet moves. Even in non-action, there is the "doing" of deliberate not-doing.

We are be-ings, and go-ers (bodhi svaha) and do-ers. Since the "doing" is unavoidable, our only freedom lies in the choice of <u>what</u>. We are verb-makers, creators of action, the servants of Change. But as Kings, we must choose the "what".

WHAT is the subject of the rest of the statement.

THOU. One is being spoken to, addressed by the Voice of the Law. <u>All</u> are being spolen to, in the singular mode. This "thou" affirms our individuality, while at the same time, subtly effecting its negation.

"Thou" is an entity composed of a unique selection of experiences. The genetic coding of the DNA ensures certain capacities of the

physical body and the mind. This coding is the record of survival-success of our ancestors; as heirs to the treasure of our race's experience, we are combined of such a large number of possibilities that, save for twinning, no two humans are physically identical.

Even more distinct are our personal journeys of the soul. The Akasha records the universal cycles and patterns which guide the course of events—and it holds the most refined minituae of the soul. This "soul" is the unbroken integrity of experience as lived by a named entity. Our mortal names change often; our Angel's name remains ever the same.

Yet, beyond and within the soul is the Thou of the statement, "Thou art That". It is this "Thou" that the Law brings into completion. The Voice of the Law is THAT. The Universe is THAT. Thou art THAT. TAT TVAM ASI.

WILT. Will is a verb here, not a noun. Tao is a verb also. So is Love.

How does one know when one is doing will?

There dwells within, beyond the Vision of Sorrow, and past the Vision of No Difference, a place of joy. When Will is being done, no matter how dire the consequences, this deep and abiding joy is present and perceptible.

When will is being opposed, or evaded, or defied, the joy is NOT present, . . . There is only strife, failure, despair, confusion, confinement, restriction. If one is attuned to that joy, Will is being done.

SHALL BE. This doing, this willing, all takes place within the stream of Time. The force of Ychronos, which is the urge-to-become, Kether, and God-the-Creator, is the power that makes Change possible and

inevitable.

The Law shall be, not "the Law is . . ." The Law is, but forever incomplete. There is the rushing-together of attraction-to-Unity, of the Law and its fulfillment. The Law is ever in the process of becoming—and so are they who "love my law and keep it."

THE WHOLE. There is no need of further instruction, "Do what thou wilt" completely suffices for every initiation and ordeal. As an ethical guide of conduct, nothing is simpler than the receiving of one's own joy. If one's actions are correct, in conformity with Will, then joy abounds. If one acts contrary to one's honest self-knowledge, or the instinctive manifestation of unconscious Will, then restriction and confusion will reign.

Thelema is the quintessence of enlightened self-interest. "If it feels good, do it"? Not exactly—Will may require the experience of pain. Pain is not evil; it is but intense experience . . . and pain doesn't "feel good".

The enlightened self-interest of Thelema rests upon the joy within. One does will because the joy of doing it is sufficient reward.

OF THE LAW. The Law: that which may be opposed, but never conquered; that which establishes Order by nature of Art, from the forces of Chaos, by nature indifferent; that which inevitably rules Karma and stands beyond it—this is the Law of Will.

When the Christians cry, "Not my will, but Thine be done, O Lord," they pay homage to Thelema in an unconscious and distorted manner, but it is a true acknowledgement.

Law is Will is Tao is God is Man.

How can I, as individual, claim anything as being "my" will? Am I

great enough to own, to possess exclusively, the Tao? Can "I" contain God?

Yes.

But only when I <u>am</u> God may I "have" god. Only when I <u>am</u> Tao may I "own" it. When I become God, I cease being "I". I can do will only by becoming will. The "I" that "owns" Will dissolves within the possession of it. If one truly "does his will", he will achieve the NOthing.

Enough.

6/14/76 e.v.

Two more days and the nine months will have been completed. Where do I stand with the O.T.O., with Mr. Grant? How much judgement is exercised in admittance to the Order? I'm sure the minimal concepts I have on it are completely wrong.

Does it matter whether or not I'm admitted to the Order? Ultimately, no, for I am integral and complete in myself. In other ways—I want/will to be of the Order. For the temporal-space in which I find myself, it were well to be of a society of fellow-sojourners—Ah, we are <u>all</u> voyageurs, the entire race! But some are passively drawn on with the tides of the flow, and others bravely ride these tides.

My hand is weary. What more is there to say? That I may have lost my opportunity? True. I shall wait word from Mr. Grant.

And what about Gary S.? The Watcher waits. It can never be the same as it was, surely.

We've learned the ritual forms from our intuition and knowledge-gathering. We've used them and—changed. The forms no longer

apply. There is some new birth happening, and it awaits to be known.

I Ching. #51 the Arousing to #45 Gathering Together.

Vast and lonely.
No light to guide;
nor the smallest star in Nuit's body shines
to lead in trackless night.

Should I be still,
and curl within the silence
to await a dubious dawn?

Or should I wander
naked-handed,
with neither staff nor lantern
in this unknown place?

Even danger would be welcome now,
would be a friend and comrade
to me here.

No sound occurs,
save my shuffling footsteps
in the unseen sands.
I shout, I scream, I cry and laugh aloud—
and no echo comes, nor answer.

There is no breeze to bear the flower-scents,
or salt-spray from a mythic ocean.
Even the charnel smell of burning-ghat
would hearten my resolve;
Nothing but the sterile air
to keep the life-force living—

why?

I go on, whither I know not.
There is that demon driving from within,
that bids me pace along.
I go.

6/15/76 e.v.

Gary S. phoned last night, twice. He was speaking from his Da'ath.

The Wheel turns.
   The Chariot of Destruction rumbles on,
       careening wildly down the hill of Time—
Ride it!

Harnessed four-abreast,
   the dire steeds of the Apocalypse
      trample and crush the souls of men—
Ride them!

Standing, bareback, balanced on the thunder of their force—
Cossack, mad barbarian!
Reins clenched in your left hand,
   right hand bearing poised the lightning-lance.

Storm-rider!
   Mountains shake beneath your passing;
     the cavern-temples of the planet-Mother
       tremble with the echoes of your power.

Hmm—but that's only from <u>my</u> viewpoint.   Perhaps-

The Tree stands desolate.
Bloodstained,

barren,
bereft in desert winds,
it mourns its loss.

Vultures wheeling overhead
must live with hunger now—
there is no corpse-flesh waiting for them.

At the oasis, the polished pool is still.
How is it, stranger, friend and brother,
that your footprints fill with blood?

The Sun is brass.
Merciless, it hammers down,
then drains all life back to the blazing sky.
Neither you nor your robes cast a shadow.

I live in this desert,
brother with no name,
for the sake of the stars at night.
Why do you wander in this place of desolation?

There is no bidding "stay!" or "now, depart!"—
only the meeting glance of eyes,
distant-visioned, light-blinded, bare.

In silence I will wander with you for a while.
There will be a sunset.
We will find, then,
that the sand becomes an ocean-shore.

Is this love? Some hard, arid, rocky thing that looms eternally, implacably as fact? Is love a fate that one is doomed to, a thing of Karma? Broken bones on stones—cliffs, shale, boulders—!

Magnificent, austere, fearsome! Hooves drumming on the mountaintop. So mote it be.

Circumstance seems to have me in a place now with nothing to do but contemplate and meditate and be. Enforced instant mini-retreat.

I can't see a panoramic future spread before me, loaded with great deeds, High Magick and immortal Art. Nothing. Much of my past has mercifully veiled itself from my vision also. What's left? Here-and-now, and infinite eternity. Same thing.

Maggie, me ghirl, you're on your own. No-one can touch you, should even one care to try. What now?

To treat each moment as a jewel, savoring its glow, being enraptured by its beauty—and releasing it for its own pace of passage.

You grow old. You are subject to the laws of time and space. You are immortal—the essence of your Self can never die. What shall you do with your time left in the flesh?

Savor the beauty of Our Lady Earth! Such a fair planet she is, a living opal set in space. Let Nuit draw forth your very soul unto the embrace of her far-flung galaxies! Love the Shadow of Nuit as her priestess, diligently learning all her temple-rites.

Hymn to Pan and haunt his woodland often! Salute Our Lord Heru, as Ra-Hoor-Khuit and Heru-Pa-Kraath. Receive Shaitan and His Angel—unite! unite!

Go within thy soul, Andahadna! Meet therein the All and Nothing. In the midst of crowds or on the mountain of solitude, there is no difference. I Ching #58 Joyous, to #10 Treading.

4:30 p.m. Another bout of tachycardia—can't let Gary S. find out or

he'll know that his death-energies have reached me. I just rode it out until it stopped suddenly... but I'm extremely astral now because of it. Have to earth properly before driving home.

11:55 p.m. Gary S. asked me to take him to the river. We went, then to his place and ritual—Maat-working...
By the same mouth that receives the nectar, is the fire-seed returned unto the hell-flower. (And it did burn, O brother-love!)

6/16/76 e.v.

Today's the last official day of the Record, as kept for the O.T.O. I intend to keep a journal indefinitely, of course—when one has a memory like a sieve, it serves to write things down. Hail, Tahuti.

So it began as a record of events, writings, etc., as sent by the Children of Maat. It sort of evolved into a catch-all—but now, even more than at the beginning—do I affirm the reality and importance of our future children-selves and their/our influence on the present

Hail Nuit!   Hail Hadit!   Hail Ra-Hoor-Khuit!

Dawn greetings to Heru-Ra-Ha.
Noon greetings to Pan.
Sunset greetings unto BABALON.
Midnight greetings to Lord Shaitan and His Angel.
Praise of the Blood-Moon to Mahamata!
Praise of the interstellar Space unto Maat!

Andahadna 124 stands as shadow to the Black Flame. There are masks to be learned, and dances to do—!

It matters not to move mountains or to cleanse the hearts of Men—these things are the business of mountains and Men and Tao. All things needful shall come to pass by Tao.
It is my will to shine forth the Light of the Children—the Crowned and Conquering Children—the Children of Maat.

Ad lux filiorum!

I shall balance. Where there is yin, I shall be yang, and the reverse. Where there is confusion, I shall be clarity; where deadly precise logic prevails, I shall be Madness incarnate!

To the best of my clumsy ability, I shall dance Lila in grace and joy, proclaiming the triumphant Lust of Life to all who labor restrictedly. Be free! be free!

Society crumbles–Shiva wakes! The restrictions are not imposed from without, but from lack of self-awareness.

(Arise, my beloved, and come! the time of pruning is at hand, and the voice of the turtle-dove is heard in the land.)

I haven't any idea of a specific form that my work will take. I invoke the Force of Thelema and Maat, and it will shape its own Form.

I proclaim my love for Being (and non-Being); for the Law of Thelema; for Life itself, on all planes; for the gods of man's worshipping, and man's demons also.

Glory to all that is, and was, and shall be! Praise also to the "roads not taken", for without them, there would be no freedom. Glory also to that which is impossible to become, for such shapes our natures into Form.

My love and gratitude to all who have danced as enemy or friend.

Myrrandha Arkaen, Bob R. the Warlock, all covens in the area—blessed be!

To Hymnot, the Dream Master of Tarion, hail! And to Bear Claw, medicine chief of the Adenas, greetings. To my beloved geometrics Rosarion, Rotat and Navhem, my thanks for their guardianship. To my brothers and sisters of Aleph Cabal and Beth Cabal—hail.

To the Master Vampyr—profound respect and affection. An eternal Dance, sir—for the Blood of Life wells ever from the heart of the Black Flame; drink deep, and often—the blood-kiss is ecstasy!

To Gary S.—Shadow, Warrior, Watcher—be love under will.

One Postscript:

Rolling through the Bardos
to the light of your mother's womb,
did you forget—again?

In the light and the cold and the weight and air
of your first-breath's cry,
you must have lost a key.

Again you tread the path of pain and sorrow,
searching for the soul-ghost,
searching for an answer to the Why.

(The name is Because,
who dwells among damned dogs
of mind's futility.)

Why live? Why strive?
Why love and work and struggle and survive
only to be spat upon by Fate,

and be shunned by Man in cold indifference?

To measure out one's giving—
to calculate the justice of return—
to fear a draining of the life-force—
to turn away from Earth's blind Children—
This is the Abyss!

Maat is veiled in the Kingdom—
justice will not serve
to recompense what has been spent.

To expect return, or even thanks,
will poison any Work;
far better to do nothing
than to do it guardedly.

Be no miser with yourself,
fearful of all promises and pledges;
a King is bound
only by his Will.
None may take from you against your Will;
what you give must all be freely given.

Vampires cannot drain an empty vessel.

Pour yourself out, joyously,
to the blood's last drop—
unto our Lady NU.

Those who would hoard their life,
or strength, or power, or their love
dwell in the Abyss.
They eke out their days

fearing to spend their precious coin of self.

Live! die! And rise up as the Phoenix!

Scatter recklessly all that you are,
all that you possess!

Throw your golden grains of self
unto the blazing stars of night!

Hold back nothing, nor expect return—
Why live?   Why love?

For the mad rapture of Our Nuit's love!
For the ecstacy of the Black Flame's burning!
For the Hawk-flight straight into the Sun!

May the lance of Nu's starfire pierce your soul in sweetest agony!

May the Quill-Plume scribe your name in burning letters on your naked heart!

May Pan take and ravish you within the forest-glade!

By the same mouth, O Son of Sorrows, is the kiss given and the heartsblood drained.

Love is the law, love under will.

Afterword

Thus began Great Adventures of a Leading Occultist.

This journal was for admittance to Kenneth Grant's Magickal Order. How did he take it? Not to detract from the forthcoming letters (to be published –ed.), but in a letter dated 16 October 76 Grant begins:

Your magical record has been read and assessed and found acceptable. You will receive a Certificate of Order Membership some time before the Solstice...

This is followed in the next paragraph:

Now to your Record: IT is so rich in beauty and so full of fire and fervour that to discuss its many facets - as I would certainly like to do - is out of the question at this time. I shall therefore select various portions. To begin with, your statement of p. 17 I take to be the core of your aspiration: "If there is no loving Godhead, I will become It". On p. 7 you have already formulated your incarnational task: "to assist the progress of the Aeon of Horus via the influx of the Maat current". This you elaborate on p. 28, where you declare: "For myself...Maat is the core of yet another Thelemic system of Magic. It's been developing invisibly since Liber PP happened"...

Your work then is clear; it is to formulate, and later possibly to teach, that system of Magick.

She was off and running. Shortly afterward, Grant talked about her position in the Order hierarchy (6 December 76):

And this brings me to your personal relation with the

Order. Your position is exceptional owing to your prominent participation in the Maatian Current and the receipt of Liber PP, which is in direct evolutive line with Liber AL. Your present position as a member of the II° is therefore somewhat anomalous because your immediate function in the Order comports a Task of a far more advanced Grade. It is therefore necessary to advance you at the earliest possible opportunity, but I cannot do this until you have fulfilled several intermediate Tasks. What I am able to do, however, is to recognize your receipt of Liber PP, with all that led up to it, as a fulfillment of the Task of the III°, which involves devotion to a particular deity – in this case, Maat. As you will see from the Synopsis of Grades (which I send to you shortly), this entitles you to the IV°. The task of the IV° is already being achieved by you in that you are the Centre or nucleus of a group that constitutes a Magical Power-Zone in Cincinnati. This paves the way for the V°, which is of vital importance in that it tests your ability to govern that Zone, and it also authorizes you to read and assess the Magical Records of prospective candidates (for order membership).

Of course this is but a very small snapshot of a very long career. Perhaps someone will attempt an actual biography of Nema. (Hmmm...) Until then I can only read the letters and speculate about what happened during this time period ... the buying (and sale) of the farm, the Warrior Lord Workings, the meeting with the Grove of the Star and the Snake, the founding of the Horus Maat Lodge (which continues to this day in electronic form), and the many trials and tribulations that awaited Nema. Alas, I did not come on the scene until 1983. But then, nothing happens until it is Time. Or so a reliable occult source informs me.

Michael Ingalls
July 29, 2015

Liber Pennae Praenumbra

The following is a communication received and scribed by a magickian working in the Cincinnati area. The writing of it was not achieved by individual effort.

In the Akasha-Echo is this inscribed:
By the same mouth, O Mother of the Sun, is the word breathed forth and the nectar received. By the same breath, O Counterweight of the Heart, is the manifest created and destroyed.

There is but one gate, though there appear to be nine, Mime-dancer of the Stars. How beautiful thy weft and web, a-shim-mering in the fire-dark of space!

The two that are nothing salute you, Black Flame that moves Hadit! The less and less One grows, the more and more Pra-NU may manifest. Do thou now speak to use, the children of the time-to-come; declare thy will and grant thy Love to us!

Then Spake She That Moves:

I hurl upon ye, Children of Heru! All ye who love the Law and keep it, keeping Naught unto yourselves, are ye a-blest. Ye have sought the scattered pieces of Our Lord, ceasing never to assemble all that has been. And in the Realm of the Dead have ye begotten from the Dead the Shining One. Ye then gave birth, and nourished Him.

Thy Land of Milk shall have honey also, dropped down as dew by

the Divine Gynander. The pleasure and delight lie in the Working, the Whole surpassing far the Parts together. The Lord of Parts is placed within His kingdom, as done by Beast and Bird. The land of Sun is open but to Children. Heed the Eternal Child – his Way is flowing-free, and suited to the Nature of your being.

A Voice crieth in the Crystal Echo:
What means this showing-forth? Is Time Itself awry? The Hawk has flown but threescore and ten in His allotted course! She smiles, as beauteous as Night:

Behold, He spreads His pinions yet in flight, showering and shaking forth the Golden Light upon the hearts of men. And wherein doth He fly, and by what means? The Feather and the Air are His to ride, to bear him ever in His GO-ing.

The pylons of the ages are unshaken, firmly are they Set. The Day of the Hawk is but seen its dawning, and will see its due measure according to the Laws of Time and Space.

The Voice then spoke:
Then has the Vision failed? Do I behold Thee crookedly, thinking Thee to be Whom Thou art Not?
She danced and whirled, scattering starlight in her silent laughter.

I Am Whom I appear to be, at times, and then again I wear a triple veil. Be not confused! Above all, Truth prevails. I am the Unconfined. Who is there to say me nay, to say, "Thou shalt not pass."? Who indeed may say, "Thy time is yet to come", when Time itself is my chief serving-maid, and Space the Major-domo of my Temple?

Indeed, O Voice of the Akasha, I am the means by which you speak. By the same mouth that breathes the Air, do words of doubt pour

forth.

In silence then, do know Me. For I am come with purpose at this time, to aid the Lovers of the Hawk to fly.

The Word of Flight

Who Falters In the Flight Must Thereby Fall:
The Greatness of the Gods in the GO-ing.
When first ye fledged, Beloved of Heru, the shall which had protected long had broken. Upon the Wings of Will ye ventured forth, gaining strength and power as ye flew. Ye gained all knowledge of the Feathered Kingdom, whereby ye became as perfect as the Sun. The friends and teachers all became as brothers.

The regal Swan, the Heron and the Owl – the Raven and the Cockerel did aid ye. The Beauty of the Hawk Himself was granted, the virtues of the Peacock, the Hummingbird and Loon. The Eagle did reveal her inner nature and the Mysteries thereof – behold, ye witnessed how, with her Lion, she became the Swan. And the Ibis of the Abyss did show the Knowledge.

Ye flew, O Kings and Hermits! And ye fly even now, within the bending loveliness of NU. But there are those among ye, and below ye, who would snare your wings and drag ye from the sky.

Look well within! Judge well your Heart! If ye be pure, it weighs no more than I. It will not bear ye down to the Abyss. For Gold is Light, but Lead is fatal unto flying - plumb your own depths, in Truth and in self-knowledge. If aught would hinder thee, it is thy doing. Behold this teaching now within the Temple.

So saying, She-Who-Moves assumed the form of the great Black

Flame, growing from the central shaft and billowing out into the Void. The Children of Heru beheld in silence, and listened to Her words form in their hearts.

Behold! This lens of Stars now turning in Space before ye · men have named it well Andromeda. Through it I flow unto the holy Moondog, and thence to Ra, and thence to ye, O Priests. Ye must not rest content whilst in the Kingdom, but strive and so exceed in what is done. In Love of the Lady of the North, and in Will of the Prince of the South, do every thing soever. In the power of the Seven-rayed Star do ye comprehend the Beast. And from HAD of the Heart do delight in thy star-arched darling.

Do all this, and then, pass beyond. Abandon aught that might distinguish thee from any other thing, yea, or from nothing. If the fowler would snare thee, leave thy feather-cloak a- dangle in his hand and soar naked and invisible beyond! But now! As priests within the Temple are ye here, as Kings, and Warriors, Magicians all. The Way is in the Work. The Hidden One of the Abyss now gives the two wherein is wrought the higher Alchemy: supporting Earth is Chthonos · learn it well, and all bonds shall be loosed for the Will's Working. Surmounting Spirit, there is Ychronos, whose nature is duration and the passing-away thereof.

The two are one, and form the Kingdom's essence. Who masters them is Master of the World. They are the utter keys of Transmutation, and keys of the power of the other Elements. The Warrior-Priests received the Keys, and placed them within their robes, to hold them hidden well above their hearts. The Black Flame danced and dwindled, becoming small, a quill pen, plumed and pointed. There being naught upon which to write, one among the Priests came forth, and laid his body's skin upon the altar as living parchment. She-Who-Moves wrote thereupon a Word, but shew it not before him. In patience waited all the Kings and Hermits, assured full well

of the final Understanding.

The Feather grew again, and rounded close its edges, becoming to their eyes the Yonilignam. The image came of Ancient Baphomet, the Horned One, who spoke:

Of old ye knew the knew of the Two-in-One conjoined. Ye have lived and loved full measure as NU and HAD, as PAN and BABALON. The Mystery of mine own image do ye also know, for such a Truth was for the ancient Orders of the East and West.

Bipartite has the Race of Man been in its span. The Father and the Mother made a Child. I am the elder of the Children, true - but now the younger rises to His Day.

The nature of true Alchemy is that it changes not alone the substance of the Work, but also changes thence the Alchemist. Ye whose Will it is to Work thereby, behold mine inverse image, and consider well its meaning for thy Task.

The Showing of the Image

From out the Yonilignam drifted forth a Cloud, violet and light-shot. In the misty heart thereof a sound arose, vibrating soft, yet filling everywhere. Jeweled and flashing rainbow-lights from wings, there hovered in the midst an humble BEE. Striped gold and brown, soft-haired and curved in form, it shone its eyes unto the Priests and Kings assembled.

Spoke then She-Who-Moves from out the mist surrounding: This is the symbol of the Work-to-come. The Great Gynander in its Earthly form. The Magician shall grow like unto the BEE as the Aeon unfolds, a leader and sign unto the Race of Man.

What then of its nature doth the BEE show forth?
Behold, it is not male nor female in the singular. It labors forth by day in constant flight, an egoless do-er, whose Will and the Hive Will are but one.

It gathers up the flower-nectar, flies to Hive and there, in pure Comm-Union, doth in its very body Transubstantiate. The Nectar is now Honey. Bee to bee, it is transferred, speaking all Hive Mysteries from and to each mouth. By the same mouth that first ingathered, is the Honey spent, the secret Alchemy within the Centers turning Silver – Gold. The Hive now lives, immortal. With queen and workers, drones and builder-bees, soldiers, foster-mothers · all are one. In constant life-renewal, the Hive breathes as One Being · for so indeed it is. In the Will of the Hive is the Will of the Bee fulfilled. Each in its appointed place, the Bees work out their Will in ordered harmony.

The image fades. Now the poised Plume moves in dancing fash·ion, unfolding from the center shaft long wings, transforming to the shape of the dark Vulture.

But know, O Children of the Hawk, a Man is not a Bee. He may profit from the image thereof, to learn of Wisdom in the Working. Behold in Me another image for thy heart's instruction.

There rose before their eyes the Tower of Silence, wherein the Lovers of Fire lay their dead.

The Vulture form alighted soft therein, and ate the flesh from corpses, to the bone. The wind howled, desolate, in this fearsome place, fluttering the cerements about the ivory bones.

Silently, the Winged One stared, gore smeared about her beak. Into the eyes of each Priest there assembled, her baleful gaze did search.

In perfect peace did they behold her searching., for each, as Warrior, had made of Death a brother. Deliberately then, she unfolded out her wings, and took to the wind, and soared up from that place.

The Giving of the Word

Eternity then reigned, Infinite the veil that hung about them.

Somewhere, sometime, the veil parted for a moment, and She-Who-Moves strode forth. More comely than mortal woman ever was, She glowed in radiance of pearl and amethyst. Fine pleated linen was Her gown, girded in gold and silver, and on Her head, a nemyss of starred blue. Her crown was but a single plume, free-standing, and in her hands the Ankh and Wand of healing.

Unto each Warrior-Priest she moved, embraced and kissed them. Then, seated in the midst, She spoke as comrade equally-ranked.

"All ye who practice well the High Art, hearken. There shall be nothing hidden from thy sight. All formulae and Words shalt thou discover, being initiated by those whose Work it is to aid the Law of Will.

"Ye have worked well in all that has been given; upon the Tree of Life are ye founded. In Tetragrammaton have ye proceeded; in all the Beast hath given have ye practiced well. Ye have become Hadit, and NU, and Ra-Hoor-Khuit also. As Heru-Pa-Kraath did ye abide in silence. Ye know PAN as lover and as god form, and BABALON is bride and Self to you.

"The forces of Shaitan have ye engendered, calling forth the nexus of the ninety-three wherein to work your Will. Separation for the joy of Union have ye known, and Alchemy is Science to your Art.

"For those who know, and will, and dare, and keep in silence, it goes not further.

"In death is Life · for now as ever has it been so. The Willed Death is eternal · keep it so. Self of Ego, selfson born of Maya, must be slain on the moment of birth. The unsleeping Eye must vigil keep, O Warriors, for the illusion is self-generate.

"Constant watchfulness is the first Act – the Abyss is crossed by minutes, every day.

"If ye would dance the Mask, then mask the Dance. Exquisite must be the Art in this wise; and balance in the Center be maintained, or else ye shall give unwonted Life unto thine own creations. Tread carefully this path of Working, Mage. A tool, by Will devised, makes an ill master.

"Now in the Mass, the Eagle must be fed upon what she has shared in making. By the same mouth that roars upon the mountain, is the word-act of No Difference given.

"And when Will declares, therein shall join the BEE to add the gold to red and white. The essence of Shaitan is Nectar here, the Temple is the Hive. The Lion is the Flower, now betimes, the Eagle invokes the nature of the BEE.

"Within the triple-chambered shrine is the first nectar pooled. The summons of the wand of PAN awakens the portal- opening bliss. And from the third and inmost chamber, in joy supreme, the Sothis-gift, quintessential mead, bounds forth to join Eagle-tears and Lion-blood.

"Solve et Coagula. Comm-Union thereby, whereof the Cosmos itself dissolveth, and reforms by Will. And know, if aught can be so ordered in the Kingdom, that three or more is zero, as well as older truths."

Then stirred the Warrior-Priests, and of their number, a nameless one stepped forth.

"We know thee, Lady, unspoken though Thy name has been thus far. But say now - what was written on the manskin? What is the word Thou givest?"

She smiled and drew from out her robe a parchment scroll, shaped even as a Star. Unrolling it, She turned it roundabout, so all might see.

IPSOS

"What is this Word, O Lady – how may it be used?"

"In silent wisdom, King and Warrior-Priest. Let the deed shine forth and the word be hidden; the deed is lamp enough to veil the face.

"It is the word of the twenty-third path, whose number is fifty and six. It is the unspoken Abode, wherein the Dance of the Mask is taught by Me. Tahuti watches without the Ape; I am the Vulture also.

"It is the Chalice of Air and Wand of Water, the Sword of Earth and the Pantacle of Fire. It is the hourglass and tail-biting serpent. It is the Ganges becoming Ocean, the Way of the Eternal Child.

"It names the Source of Mine Own Being – and yours. It is the origin of this sending, that channels through Andromeda and Set. What

race of gods do speak to Man, O Willed Ones? The word of them is both the Name and Fact.

"It is for thee mantram and incantation. To speak it is to being about certain change. Be circumspect in its usage - for if its truth be known abroad, it would perchance drive the slaves to madness and despair.

"Only a true Priest-King may know it fully, and stay in balance through his GO-ing flight. This is all I speak for now. The Book of the Preshadowing of the Feather is complete.

"Do what thou wilt shall be the whole of the Law. Love is the law, love under will."

Donat per Omne'
Scriba – Nema
Sol in Capricornus
Anno Heru LXX

Cincinnati, Ohio USA

INDEX

The reader may have noticed that a Magickal Record, while paying a deep homage to Kronos, does not lend itself to chapter and section headings. It is our hope that this Index, at least in part, makes up for the lack of chapters and sections headings.

Such an Index is an ongoing affair. Readers are invited to send additional words/subjects to *blackmoon@blackmoonpublishing.com* for inclusion in future editions. Those who do so will be credited.

Abyss, 46, 55, 79, 82, 88, 89, 93, 98-100, 111, 119, 137, 154, 207, 267, 268, 276, 295, 301, 302, 306
Achad, Frater, 16, 183
Adenas, 294
Aeon of Maat, see Maat
Aion 131, 20
Akashic record, 79, 285
alchemy, 51, 57, 73, 88, 102, 114, 122-125, 135, 142, 191, 195, 196, 217, 271, 274, 302, 303 - 305
Aleph Cabal, 12, 294
Allen H., 38, 40, 41, 73, 90, 106, 107, 163, 165, 187, 202, 276, 277
Alsace-Lorraine, 37
Anderson's Ferry, 190
Anubis, Fra., 122
Aossic, see Grant, Kenneth
Aquila, 145, 205, 206
Atlantis (ean), 33, 37, 60, 69, 184, 188
attack, 216, 220, 229, 230,
    heart, 235
Austin Osman Spare, Images and Oracles of, 170, 189,

awaken(ing/ed), 18, 66, 71, 89, 91, 195, 207-209, 222, 239, 243, 245, 247, 251, 266, 306
Azrael, 271, 278

Babalon, 38, 40, 53, 68, 73, 110, 114, 115, 125, 143, 175, 195, 229, 237, 272, 292, 303
    united with Maat, 125
Bardo(s), 209, 294
Bate/Beth Cabal, 12, 16, 185, 276, 294
    bate definition, 12
Bear Claw, 73, 145, 217, 294
bee, 49, 85, 141, 205, 303, 304, 306
Belisarius, 64, 65
Ben Rowe, 162, 165, 173, 179, 189, 198, 200, 201-203, 263
    channeling Mahara, 253, 162
Bhakti/Bhakti Yoga, 130, 193, 226
Black Flame(s), 18, 28, 30, 38, 43, 44, 47, 77, 83, 88, 176, 178, 209, 211, 225, 237, 267, 292, 294, 296, 299, 301, 302
Boddhisattva/Boddhisattvic Vow, 55, 75
born from this moving pen, 213
    Godot, Waiting for, 215
Bounds, Joe, 12, 236
Buddha, 10, 29, 33

Casey, 50, 56, 57, 64, 107, 109, 112, 123, 132, 188
chakra(s), 54, 56, 57, 58, 62, 106, 109, 112, 114, 122, 126, 141, 142, 174-176, 178, 188, 202, 211, 216, 275
chaos, 16, 223, 242, 249, 286
Child as the Book of Changes, The, 254
Children of Maat (C. of M.), see Maat
Choronzon, 55, 85, 169, 208, 223, 241, 242
Christian(s), 11, 49, 61, 102, 132, 171, 215, 222, 247, 286

Chi, 59, 88, 165, 211
Cincinnati (vortex), 8, 10, 68, 73, 101, 185, 205, 217, 219, 221, 298, 299, 308
Cincinnati Journal of Ceremonial Magick (CJCM), 12, 16
  Conquering Child Publishing (C.C.P.), 203
  The Journal, 12, 16, 86, 103-107, 117, 237, 270, 277
  Journal Rituals with Lu, 104-106
circle (not cast), 211, 225
comity of stars, 39, 60
compassion, 28, 49, 54, 65, 142, 184, 192
cone of power, 68
Cook, Maggie, see Nema
Cults of the Shadow (cults-abrev.), 170, 171, 173, 183, 186

Da'ath, 120, 141, 166, 217, 241, 244, 276, 289
Dance(s) of the Mask, see Mask
Dawn of Light (D.O.L.), 49, 215
Dan C., 40, 41, 45, 46, 50, 56, 58, 64, 65, 69, 75, 81, 90, 98, 100, 112, 118, 121-123, 125, 126, 136, 141, 143, 144, 164, 188, 189, 197, 200, 202, 203, 206, 219, 221, 222, 230, 232, 234-238, 271, 278
Demon(s/ically), 48, 53, 54, 74, 81, 117, 119, 123, 140, 141, 192, 218, 220, 231, 237, 247, 249, 269, 280, 298, 293
  named envy, 220
die, 13, 46, 55, 62, 126, 128, 131, 132, 136, 156, 195, 198, 208, 234, 238, 240, 250, 262, 264, 272, 291, 296
  Then why may I not now die?, 262
  essence of your Self can never die, 291
  what to do with time left in flesh, 291
  maintain acquired awareness, 55
Dorothy Lane (house), 231, 232, 273
Double Current, 18, 19, 41, 59, 68, 104, 115
Double Tree, 90, 211, 224

Do what thou wilt shall be the whole of the Law (a word by word examination), 284-286

ego, 61, 124, 160, 170, 183, 201, 203, 206, 217, 230, 246-248, 306
   alter, 81
   egoism, 112
   egoless, 304
   egomaniac, 41
   egotistical, 239
   removing, 258
   semi-mortal, 246
Elder Gods, 34, 44, 53, 69, 83, 102, 123, 160, 185, 187, 192, 207- 212, 225, 277
elixir, 46, 73, 122, 124, 175, 176, 179, 212
   in sexual magick, 176, 179, 212, 274
extraterrestrial, 184

Farm (Horus-Maat Abbey), 9, 14, 18, 19, 166, 189, 190, 197, 202, 203, 227, 229, 231, 232, 233, 235, 237, 238, 250, 264, 273, 274, 276, 277, 278, 279, 281, 282, 298
   Abbess, Dance of, 190
   Georgetown, Ohio, 230
   householder, 190, 227
   in Mount Orab, Ohio, 37
   Oz (farm), 37, 42, 43, 136, 166, 188
fear(ful/ing/less/some), 18, 33, 45, 47, 48, 107, 127, 131, 157, 184, 193, 211, 230, 244, 245, 261, 275, 291, 295, 296, 304
feather(ed/s), 28, 29, 33, 34, 36, 38, 50, 51, 54, 69, 71, 77, 83, 105, 114, 123, 141, 143, 145, 186, 197, 199, 211, 212, 224, 237, 256, 259, 267 269, 300-303, 308
   dance of the, see mask, dance of
Forgotten Ones, 45, 53, 69, 101, 102
   Second Book of, 163

future selves, 63, 70, 74, 85, 184

Gary M., 37, 42, 43, 136, 263
Gary S. 10, 11, 38-41, 43, 45-47, 49, 50, 54, 56, 58, 64, 65, 70, 73-75, 81, 86, 89, 90, 98, 101, 102, 106, 107, 112, 113, 118, 120-123, 125, 126, 128, 132, 135-137, 141, 143, 144, 154, 163-167, 169, 170, 173, 174, 180, 182 185, 187-189, 191, 193, 195, 197, 200-203, 205-207, 212, 215, 217 224, 226, 227, 229, 231-239, 247, 248, 258, 263, 266, 270 275, 277-280, 283, 287, 289, 291, 292, 294
   true self, 129, 228
Ginger M, 37, 136
Gorge, the, see Red River Gorge rites
Grant, Kenneth (K.G.), 3, 7, 9, 16, 23, 104, 112, 122, 266, 297
   Aossic, 267-269,
      praise song, 267-269

Had(it), 28, 31, 32, 43, 44, 47, 50, 53, 62, 82, 84, 85, 96, 98, 104, 111, 114, 115, 121, 122, 134, 144, 147, 180, 181, 194, 204, 217, 236, 240, 248, 252, 263, 268, 270, 282, 292, 299, 302, 303, 305
   Dance of the Crane of, see mask, dance of
Herb Z., 56, 126, 237
HGA (Holy Guardian Angel), 45, 47, 52, 129, 192, 247, 281, 283
Horus Maat Lodge (HML), 18, 19, 298
Hunt callers, 67, 68, 69
Hymnot, 294

I Ching, 15, 42, 49, 63, 65, 73, 86, 189, 243, 258, 264, 272, 273, 288, 291
initiation, 45, 59, 67, 68, 118, 124, 140, 142, 143, 166, 170, 180, 188, 200, 218, 239, 258, 286
   of Maat, see Maat
incarnational task, 38, 190, 297
inventory, personal, 118, 139, 235

Ipsos, 17, 19, 20, 39, 40, 44, 46, 68, 87, 121, 133, 146, 175, 176, 266, 282

John (Jack) U., 42, 64, 100, 106, 132, 154, 165, 166, 169, 188, 189, 192, 193, 230, 231, 238, 262, 264, 272, 273, 278, 281

Kaedmon, Adam, 212
Knight, Tom, 103, 117, 136, 167, 170
Kriztovov, 283

Lamp and the Sword, The, (poem), 130
Liber Al, 165, 202, 277, 298
Liber Aleph, 10, 11
Liber Oz, 161
Liber Pennae Prenumbra (Liber P.P.), 17, 37, 38, 75, 76, 83, 103, 105, 122, 143, 166, 170, 175, 183, 185, 239, 297, 298
   to Kenneth Grant, 39
   the document, 299
   writing of, 38
lodge, 185, 218
   in Alsace-Lorraine, 37
Louis Martinié (Frater Lugis Thor/S. M. Ch. H. 353/Lu), 8, 10, 43, 86, 89, 90, 101, 103, 104-106, 111, 117, 118, 133, 165, 170, 186, 187, 203, 226, 236, 263
   Cincinnati Vortex, 185
   First contact with Maat, 37
Love('s/ly/er/ers/be/ed/making/song), 9, 17, 19, 28, 29, 34, 43, 44-46, 50, 51, 53-57, 59, 72, 77, 83-88, 90-92, 94. 97, 98, 100, 101, 103, 114, 118, 119, 123, 124, 127, 129, 130, 133, 136, 137, 140, 142, 146, 148, 156, 158, 159, 161, 162, 165-167, 168, 191, 193-195, 199, 204, 207, 210, 219, 222, 229, 239, 241, 243, 245, 246, 256, 258-263, 267, 269, 270, 278, 283, 285, 286, 290, 291-296, 299, 301-305, 308
Lu, see Louis Martinié

Lunar rite, 69, 179, 281
Lunar-male, female-solar formula, 170

Maat(i/ian/ians), 9, 14, 16-19, 28, 35, 36-38, 40-44, 47, 50, 52, 53. 60, 63,
    65, 73, 75-77, 79, 82-86, 88-90, 105, 107, 125, 141, 145, 160, 162,
    166, 167, 169, 175, 178, 179, 181, 183, 184, 187, 188, 190, 192, 197,
    199, 205-207, 209, 211, 212, 217, 224,225, 234, 237, 239, 251,
    256, 259, 260, 264, 265, 267, 270, 277-279, 292, 293, 295, 297, 298
  Aeon of, 37, 60, 63, 85, 207
  channeling of the Children of, 27, 55, 277, 292
  Children of, 13, 14, 27, 40, 41, 43, 49, 55, 70, 71, 74, 75, 88, 188,
    235, 237, 238, 247, 251, 292, 293, 299
  Children/Rituals to earth Maat current, 38
  Dance of, 92, 94, 95, 99, 210
  first initiation of, 76
  Lady Maat Angel of Andahadadna, 264
  Mass of, 14, 122, 175, 179-181, 187, 211-212, 225
    detailed description 175-179
    DNA, 177
    Kreta, 178
    Kretalo, 179
    (value), 182
  Mask of, 82, 85
  Oz Farm initial contact, 37
  Priestess of, declare right of, 244, 266
  Rite for evolution of Maat consciousness, 44, 45
  Shadow of Nuit, 47, 96
  who is, 145-149, 159
magick(al/ian), 7-20, 25, 27, 41, 45, 55-57, 63, 67, 75, 80, 81, 89, 92, 95, 96,
    99, 101-104, 106, 107, 111-113, 115, 118, 119, 122, 123, 126, 127, 129,
    133, 134, 142, 148, 162, 166, 167, 175, 181, 185-187, 189, 190, 193,
    194, 203, 206, 207, 210, 211, 213, 215, 221, 223, 232, 234, 237, 247,

    248, 250, 252, 254, 257, 258, 264, 270, 274, 276-278, 281, 283, 291, 297, 299
  child, 185
  Childe (shop), 15, 16
  worth doing, 251
Mahara, 252, 162
Mark of the Beast, 39, 46, 50
mask(s/un/proto/ed), 10, 13, 35, 40, 48, 54, 60-62, 85, 86, 88-92, 94, 99, 103, 108, 109, 114, 119-121, 123, 127, 172, 189-191, 194, 200, 201, 204, 206, 211, 218, 224, 234-236, 258, 259, 275, 292, 306
  as instrument, 81
  behind the, 204
  Dance of the, 13, 14, 28, 32, 36, 63, 75-78, 81, 85, 87-90, 94, 97-100, 103, 108-110, 122, 140, 143, 190, 194, 203, 205, 207-212, 223, 251, 256, 262, 306, 307
    as duality, 99
    as a magickal system, 92
    end of, 99
    How is high and low magick done from?, 89
    of the Crane of Hadit, 93-95, 96, 99
    of the Feather, 88, 92, 114
    of Gaia, 78
    of Heru-Pa-Kraath, 98
    of the Hermit, aim, 115
    of Heru-Pa-Kraath, 98-100
    of as joy unto Nuit, 140
    of Maat, 82, 85, 94, 210
    of Maut, 88
    of the Owl of Nuit, 96-97, 99
    of the Ravens, 98
    of the Shadow of Hadit, 114
    of the Swan, 90, 92, 93, 99, 110

      suggested music (diagram), 110
      Tree of, (diagram), 87
dead, 121
dead, eaten by Maut, 120,121
nothing behind (Kenneth Grant), 103
of Maggie, 257, 258
of the Double tree, 211, 224
of Maya, 91
same time, schizophrenic, 100
Mass of the Holy Ghost, 175, 185
Maut, 28, 43, 47, 77, 84, 85, 101, 120, 175, 212, 269,
    Dance of, 88
Maya, 91, 97, 118, 122, 164, 165, 195, 208, 216, 241, 251, 252, 279, 306
M.B., 41
Mike C., 40, 43
Melor, Sir, 151-154
Mount Airy, 46, 49, 50, 70, 154, 230
Mutant(s), 19, 29, 32, 33
Myrrh (Myrrandha Arkaen), 187, 275, 279, 280, 294

Navhem, 55, 282, 294
   geometrical intelligence, 38
necklace, astral, 113
NEMA,
   Andahadna, 17, 203, 241, 247, 262, 264, 291, 292
      as Higher Self, 247
      number of, 194
   Adahan (double of Nahada), 115, 180, 194
   Maggie C., 9-14, 27, 63, 65, 69, 74, 128, 170, 183, 219, 230,233, 234,
      236, 241, 242, 245, 247, 252, 256, 257, 258, 279, 291
   Nahada, 71-74, 86, 104, 115, 145, 160, 164, 180, 182, 190, 194, 206,
      207, 214, 219

    as Maya, 164
    name accepted, 73, 74
    numeration, 71, 164, 194
Nightmare, 208, 210, 251
  sleep, 251
No*, 36, 69, 70
Nothingness, 249
  Nothingness (self), 204, 205
  self as hollow onion, layers, 118
Nuit (Nu), 29 ,32, 36, 40, 43, 44, 47, 49, 53, 60, 77, 83, 84, 86, 94, 96-98,
    111, 122, 134, 140, 144, 147, 149, 162, 168, 180, 181, 204, 230, 234,
    240, 252, 257, 260, 261, 264, 267, 268, 270, 281, 282, 288, 291,
    292, 295, 296, 299, 301, 303, 305
  see White Flame

O.T.O., (the Order, Typhonian Order), 7, 113, 236, 249, 266, 283
  admittance, 8, 9, 39, 63, 75, 129, 287, 292, 297
  Certificate of Membership, 297
  Grade in the, 297, 298
Oz Farm, see farm, Oz
Oz, Liber, 161

Painting(s), 39, 50, 54, 56, 57, 64, 66-68, 119, 136, 140, 154, 162, 166,
    193, 217, 221, 226, 234, 239
  struggle to afford paint, 66
Patrick M., 49, 141, 165, 216, 218,
  Aleph Cabal, 218
  conversion, 215-217, 225, 226
  Kenneth Grant on conversion, 225, 226
Postscript, 19, 294
Priestess Must Remember, The (poem), 155-159

Quantum (band), 107, 179, 253

Randy B., 86, 90, 101, 111, 117, 161, 170, 186, 187, 203, 221, 264, 270, 276, 277, 279
Randy (last name unknown), 198, 201
Magickal Record(s/Record/recorders/MR), 7, 8, 10-15, 18-20, 27, 31, 38, 50, 63, 71, 74-76, 102, 111, 123, 124, 126, 128, 129, 133, 143, 145, 167, 175, 213, 219, 228, 235, 237, 277, 292
    chosen practice, 27
    discipline, 121
    here begins..., 27
    Kenneth Grant, record as mirror, 102
    Kenneth Grant, comments on the record, 297, 298
    last official day of, 292
    OTO, record found acceptable, 297
    recorders, first contact with Maat-force, 37
    Tao is writing this MR, 219
    uttered Her Word, 18

Red River Gorge rites (the Gorge), 45, 46, 56, 220, 224, 237
    Mark of the Beast on chest, 39
    stone phallus, 46
Regardie, Israel, 112
Riddle Crest (house), 56, 89, 101, 123, 137, 141, 164, 200, 221, 222, 231, 270, 271, 273, 274
    Tamasic Toad, 206, 271
roar, power (technique described), 173, 174
Roberts, Jane (Seth), 282, 283
Rosarion, 38, 40, 55, 272, 282, 294
    geometrical intelligence, 38
Rotat, 55, 282, 294
    geometrical intelligence, 38

Rowe, Ben; see Ben Rowe

S., Fra., 122, 123
Salamander (a tale, the secret of the universe), 149-154
scarlet woman, 101, 117
Seth, see Roberts, Jane
sex(ual/bi/a), 14, 46, 54, 85, 91, 104, 105, 107, 109, 117, 127, 163, 167, 168, 176, 177, 245, 280, 281
   Mass of Maat, see Maat, Mass of
Shadow(ing/y/pre/of Thelemic deities/Maat as Shadow of Nuit), 30, 43-45, 47, 50, 71, 96, 104, 114, 115, 122, 147, 149, 157, 170, 180, 183, 184, 194, 205, 210, 243, 260, 264, 267, 282, 290-292, 294, 308
   nightmare, 210
   shadow-born, 259
Shaitan, 36, 52, 53, 266, 270, 291-292, 305, 306
She Who Moves, 28, 43, 83, 184, 269, 301-303, 305
Shiva (puja), 29, 58, 76, 78, 83, 88, 91, 110, 165, 169, 229, 230, 267, 293
subconscious, 50, 53, 55, 95, 96, 113, 209, 218, 247
   oceanic subconscious, 96
   see Elder Gods
   see Forgotten Ones

Tachycardia, 187, 247, 291
Tahuti (Thoth), 44, 53, 79, 86, 121, 133-135, 164, 198, 207, 228, 269, 292, 307
   Thoth-Hermes, 69
   word/sigil, 135
talam, 177, 178, 179
   definition, 176
   sealed in uterus, 177
tamas, 189, 206, 223,

see Toad, Tamasic
Tao, 13, 41, 49, 54, 55, 62, 73, 74, 76, 79, 84, 88, 89, 92, 103, 108, 120, 124, 139, 148, 179, 217, 219, 228, 233, 236, 249, 250, 251, 258, 266, 281, 283, 284, 285, 286, 287, 293
Tarion, 294
Tarot, 15, 41, 63, 68, 73, 161, 188, 199, 206, 258, 277
Thelemite (Thelema), 15-17, 19, 46, 49, 52, 62, 75, 103, 115, 117, 122, 161, 175, 257, 286, 293, 297
tired, 13, 205, 234, 249, 278
Trance of Sorrow, 101
Tree of Life, 41, 198, 241, 305
Tree of Death, 241
TUD'L (dolphin), 222

Unborn, Place of, 207-209, 211, 212, 224, 225
   Spring Equinox, 1976 e.v. ritual (the Task), 211

Vampyr, Master, 294
Verbs not nouns, we are, 191
Vision of No Difference, 91, 285
Vision of Sorrow, 223, 285
Voodoo, 66, 67
Vow(s/ed/ing), 10, 28, 55, 75, 121, 127, 131, 190, 269
Vulture, 47, 51, 84, 85, 110, 241, 269, 290, 304, 307

Wicca(n), 15, 68, 186, 215, 221
Witch(es), 15, 68, 90, 117, 186, 255, 256
White Flame as Nu, 43, 237
Will(s/ed/ing/ingly/non), 30, 34, 37, 39, 45, 50, 52-56, 58, 62, 68, 70, 71, 73, 78, 81-86, 89-93, 95, 96, 98, 99-103, 106, 108, 109, 114, 115, 118, 120-125, 127-130, 132, 134, 136, 137, 140, 142, 146, 148, 160, 162, 163, 166-168, 179, 182, 183, 186-188, 194, 196, 197, 200,

205, 207, 208, 210, 211, 226, 227, 229, 233-235, 238, 242, 244, 246, 247, 250, 251, 259, 261-264, 266, 267, 269, 270, 278, 279, 281-287, 293-296, 299, 301-306, 308

X, Fra., 123

III°, 298
IV°, 298
V°, 298
VIII°, 39, 46, 57, 73, 107, 113, 173, 197, 199, 205, 230, 264, 280, 282
IX°, 39, 54, 65, 135, 166, 167, 222, 231, 276
XI°, 122, 298,
93 (current), 15, 17, 38, 52, 68, 74, 104, 115, 116, 139, 185, 191, 193, 207, 209, 217, 218, 236, 264, 293
93 (page number), 93

Other Publications by
Black Moon Publishing

~ The Faces of Babalon ~
A Compilation of Women's Voices
by Mishlen Linden, Linda Falorio, Soror Chen, Nema
and Raven Greywalker

~ Women of Babalon: A Howling of Women's Voices ~
By Mishlen Linden and several other authors

~ Typhonian Teratomas: The Shadows of the Abyss ~
by Mishlen Linden

~ Waters of Return: The Aeonic Flow of Voudoo ~
by Louis Martinié

~ A Priest's Head, A Drummer's Hands ~
New Orleans Voodoo Order of Service
by Louis Martinié

~ Talking to God With Food: Questioning Animal Sacrifice ~
by Louis Martinié

~ Dr. John Montanee: A Grimoire ~
by Dr. Louie Martinié

~ The Priesthood: Parameters and Responsibilities by Nema ~

~ Maatian Meditations and Considerations ~
A Continuation of Past Writings on "She Who Moves"
by Nema

~ Feather and Firesnake by Nema ~

~ Wings of Rapture by Nema ~

~ Enochian Temples by Benjamin Rowe ~

~ The Book of the Seniors by Benjamin Rowe ~

~ The 91 Parts of the Earth by Benjamin Rowe ~

BLACKMOONPUBLISHING.COM

Nema's chosen practice in keeping this nine month Magickal Record (1975-1976) for admittance to the Typhonian OTO was to "maintain an open channel with the Children of Maat, so they may speak through me. This to my own instruction and for the evolution of the Race... ." The Magical Record chronicles this instruction, guidance, and the rituals she used to gain and maintain this contact.

Carl R. Rogers observed, "What is most personal is the most universal." Maggie's attainment and her humanity shines through this record. The MR flows between the emotional heights evident in the praise of Aossic Aiwass to the angst that washes over her, "I am so tired...I wish I could die now." in a dark night of the soul.

The full range of both human and magical experience are richly expressed. The trials and triumphs that swim in the oceans of experience common to all of us all surface in Maggie's words.

Meticulous self-examination and self-appraisal are a significant part of the record demonstrating a profound level of introspection in which the Tao is frequently invoked.

Nema's optimism shines like a Grail for the rest of us. Its brightness beckons us to think and act likewise. I believe we will all be the better for it.

Horus-Maat Lodge ‹HorusMaatLodge.com› is a working occult Lodge acting as a focal point for the Maatian Current.

The publication includes:
· An in depth description of the Mass of Maat as a sexual rite.
· Dances of the Tree of Life
· Masks of the Tree of Life.
· A word by word analysis of, "Do what thou wilt shall be the whole of the Law."
· The complete text of Liber Pennae Praenumbra
· An extensive index.

"Now to your Record: IT is so rich in beauty and so full of fire and fervour ..."
　　–Letter to Nema dated 16 October 1976, from Kenneth Grant.

www.ingramcontent.com/pod-product-compliance
Lightning Source LLC
Chambersburg PA
CBHW030851170426
43193CB00009BA/562